LOVE ONE ANOTHER

The Boston College Church in the 21st Century Series

Patricia De Leeuw and James F. Keenan, S.J.,
General Editors

Titles in this series include:

Church Ethics and Its Organizational Context
Edited by Jean M. Bartunek, Mary Ann Hinsdale,
and James F. Keenan, S.J.

Handing on the Faith: The Church's Mission and Challenge
Edited by Robert P. Imbelli

Inculturation and the Church in North America
Edited by T. Frank Kennedy, S.J.

Priests for the 21st Century
Edited by Donald Dietrich

Prophetic Witness: Catholic Women's Strategies for Reform
Edited by Colleen Griffith

Sexuality and the U.S. Catholic Church
Edited by Lisa Sowle Cahill, John Garvey, and T. Frank Kennedy, S.J.

Take Heart: Catholic Writers on Hope in Our Time
Edited by Ben Birnbaum

*Two Centuries of Faith:
The Influence of Catholicism on Boston: 1808–2008*
Edited by Thomas O'Connor

Voices of the Faithful: Loyal Catholics Striving for Change
By William D'Antonio and Anthony Pogorelc

The Church in the 21st Century Center at Boston College seeks to be a catalyst and resource for the renewal of the Catholic Church in the United States by engaging critical issues facing the Catholic community. Drawing from both the Boston College community and others, its activities currently are focused on four challenges: handing on and sharing the Catholic faith, especially with younger Catholics; fostering relationships built on mutual trust and support among lay men and women, vowed religious, deacons, priests, and bishops; developing an approach to sexuality mindful of human experience and reflective of Catholic tradition; and advancing contemporary reflection on the Catholic intellectual tradition.

LOVE ONE ANOTHER

Catholic Reflections on How to Sustain Marriages Today

TIM MULDOON AND
CYNTHIA S. DOBRZYNSKI,
EDITORS

A *Herder & Herder* Book
The Crossroad Publishing Company
New York

The Crossroad Publishing Company
www.crossroadpublishing.com

© 2010 by the Trustees of Boston College, acting by and through
The Church in the 21st Century Center

All rights reserved. No part of this book may be reproduced, stored in a retrieval system, or transmitted, in any form or by any means, electronic, mechanical, photocopying, recording, or otherwise, without the written permission of The Crossroad Publishing Company.

In continuation of our 200-year tradition of independent publishing, The Crossroad Publishing Company proudly offers a variety of books with strong, original voices and diverse perspectives. The viewpoints expressed in our books are not necessarily those of The Crossroad Publishing Company, any of its imprints, or of its employees. No claims are made or responsibility assumed for any health or other benefit.

Printed in the United States of America

The text of this book is set in 10/14 Sabon.

Library of Congress Cataloging-in-Publication Data

National Marriage Symposium (2007 : Boston College)
    Love one another : Catholic reflections on how to sustain marriages today / edited by Tim Muldoon and Cynthia Dobrzynski.
      p. cm.
    "A Herder & Herder book."
    Includes bibliographical references and index.
    ISBN 978-0-8245-2589-7 (alk. paper)
    1. Marriage – Religious aspects – Catholic Church – Congresses. I. Muldoon, Tim. II. Dobrzynski, Cynthia. III. Title.
BX2250.N38 2007
234′.165 – dc22   2010007342

This printing: October 2018

Contents

Acknowledgments	vii
Introduction	1

Part One
FOUNDATIONS

1. Signs of Hope in Marriage Today DAVID THOMAS	6
2. A Spirituality for the Vocation to Marriage WILLIAM P. ROBERTS	10
3. A Theology for Married People TIM MULDOON	20

Part Two
CHALLENGES AND RESOURCES

4. The Marriage-Friendly Parish JULIE HANLON RUBIO	34
5. Living the Dream DAVID MATZKO MCCARTHY	46
6. Spirituality and the Family Life Cycle FLORENCE CAFFREY BOURG	57
7. Marriage among the Spiritual but Not Religious JAMES HEALY	76
8. Layers of Marriage Preparation and the Family Life Cycle JOANN HEANEY-HUNTER	89
9. Learning from the Liturgy PAUL COVINO	106

Part Three
COMMUNITIES

10. Marriage and Family Ministry among Hispanic/Latino Catholics — 122
    ALEJANDRO AGUILERA-TITUS

11. Marriage and Family Ministry among African American Catholics — 136
    ANDREW LYKE

12. Marriage and Family Ministry among Asian American Catholics — 152
    JONATHAN Y. TAN

13. Interchurch Marriages: Challenges and Blessings — 169
    BONNIE P. MACK

14. Interchurch Couples: Potential Challenges and Blessings — 184
    LEE WILLIAMS

Conclusions — 199
    CYNTHIA DOBRZYNSKI

Contributors — 203

Notes — 207

Index — 229

Acknowledgments

Thanks are due to the steering committee and staff of the Church in the 21st Century Center at Boston College, for their support of the September 2007 National Marriage Symposium, which gave rise to this volume. In particular, we thank Nayla Raffol and Susan Burton for their work to make the symposium a reality.

We thank Rick McCord and the leadership of the Secretariat for Family, Women, Laity, and Youth of the U.S. Bishops' Conference for initiating conversations that led to the symposium. We thank the leadership of the National Association of Catholic Family Life Ministers, especially Steve Beirne and William Urbine, and Leif Kehrwald of the Center for Ministry Development for their ideas and support of the initiative.

We thank John Eagleson and Bob Land for their careful copyediting and proofreading of the text, and John Jones for his stewardship of this and all the volumes in the Church in the 21st Century series.

Finally, we thank all the participants in the symposium for their contributions, energy, and work to enhance the married lives of those to whom they minister regularly.

Tim Muldoon's essay "A Theology for Married People" first appeared in *Origins,* October 11, 2007, 279–85.

Paul Covino's essay "Learning from the Liturgy" first appeared in *Origins,* November 1, 2007, 333–39, under the title "Marriage Ministry and the Rite of Marriage."

Alejandro Aguilera-Titus's essay "Marriage and Family Ministry among Hispanic/Latino Catholics" first appeared in *Origins,* January 10, 2008, 481–86.

Introduction

IT HAS LONG BEEN OBSERVED that the state of marriage in the United States is fragmented, with high divorce rates and significant numbers of children born outside of families held together by a married couple. Within this cultural situation, the Catholic Church has sought to celebrate and sustain marriage as a pastoral imperative flowing from Jesus' observation that what God has joined, no one must separate (cf. Mark 10:9, Matt. 19:6). The church's ministry toward marriage is not only a function of its sacramental life; it is also part of its social justice ministry, since the way that the community helps people to sustain good marriages will have repercussions both for the church and the wider U.S. culture. Catholic reflection on marriage strives to be "good news" — the proclamation (*euangelion*) of the way that God invites people into intimate relationships of life-giving love.

In September 2007, twenty-two experts in theology and pastoral ministry came together to explore the way that the Catholic Church speaks to those who are married, and to those who minister to them. The impetus was the National Pastoral Initiative on Marriage of the U.S. Bishops' Conference, to which the symposium sought to contribute observations and suggestions. The goal, however, was broader: to articulate a Catholic approach to marriage, one that invites reflection on the biblical foundations; the lessons from our cultural situation and history; and the spiritual and moral dimensions of married life. Taken together, the papers presented at the symposium address many dimensions of married life and the ways that the church in the United States might foster it and contribute to its flourishing.

There are two primary audiences for the volume: one general, one more specific. The general audience is married Catholics, and perhaps especially those who are considering marriage. One presupposition that guided the symposium was that with more and more educated Catholics, there is increasing need for thoughtful reflection on church life. This volume fills a need for such reflection: it is neither pedantic — of the sort one often finds given to those in marriage preparation — nor abstract, designed only for professionals in the field. It pioneers a middle ground, articulating key themes from Catholic tradition, but also raising questions for how Catholics will respond to challenges facing couples, parishes, and the church as a whole.

The more specific audience includes pastoral ministers, pastors, and leaders in the Catholic community who deal with questions about how to structure programs and initiatives that address married life in the church. Our belief is that Jesus' command about what God has joined ought to be read in light of the more general exhortation that his followers love one another as Jesus loved the disciples (John 13:34; cf. Rom. 13:8, 1 Pet. 1:22). As a consequence, then, the task of the community of faith is to cultivate authentic love in the "domestic church," as the Fathers of the Second Vatican Council described it.[1]

We believe that the interest in this volume will come from those who want to consider new ways of reflecting upon Catholic tradition as a resource for married people today: an invitation to a model of marriage as a spirituality, a vocation, a practice rooted in the most fundamental posture of radical openness to God's grace — but also a summons to think clearly about what people are actually facing as married people in the world today.

There are three parts in the book. In the first part, entitled "Foundations," we present three essays that explore the distinctively Catholic approach to marriage — that is, as rooted in a particular way of thinking about God, human love, and the community. David Thomas's introductory essay sets the table, as it were, by pointing to some signs of hope among those who enter married life with realistic expectations. William P. Roberts then explores the resources of the Christian spiritual tradition, a history of people trying to live out their Christian faith in the context of married life. Tim Muldoon's essay explores a theology for married people: a way to invite ordinary people to consider marriage as the place where husbands and wives can discover God in ordinary life.

The second part, entitled "Challenges and Resources," includes six essays that explore how married people negotiate life in the twenty-first-century United States. Julie Hanlon Rubio sketches contemporary Catholic family life and the ways that parishes have responded to the challenges of Catholics' move from the margins to the center of U.S. life. David Matzko McCarthy's essay critiques the isolation of the romanticized, atomic family, seeking to highlight the broader social role of the family within a richer understanding of the church as a community. Florence Caffrey-Bourg explores the moral challenges of living an authentic life amid the vagaries of raising children.

James Healy then takes a look at the way young people today — the "spiritual but not religious" generation — enter marriage and offers reflections on how the church might respond to their often unacknowledged pastoral needs. Joann Heaney-Hunter offers reflections on how Catholics might prepare young people for marriage, for a particular lifestyle rooted in faith and Christian vocation. Finally, Paul Covino explores the richness of Catholic liturgy as a resource for understanding how marriage has emerged as a significant public sacramental celebration in the church.

The third part, entitled "Communities," takes a close look at specific populations within the U.S. church that merit particular attention in marriage ministry. Alejandro Aguilera-Titus offers a bird's-eye view of the influential and growing Hispanic/Latino community and places consideration of the pastoral ministry toward marriage in that community within a larger framework of how Hispanics/Latinos are reshaping the church. Andrew Lyke recounts his experience as an African American Catholic in a marriage enrichment program and his developing understanding of how racial and cultural considerations impact the way Catholics talk about marriage today. Similarly, Jonathan Y. Tan explores the cultural assumptions about marriage that influence different generations of Asian American Catholics, assumptions that call for careful reflection on the presuppositions of any who would talk about marriage today. The final two essays, by Bonnie P. Mack and Lee Williams, explore how interchurch marriages — those between Catholics and non-Catholics — offer both challenges and blessings to the Catholic community in the United States.

Taken together, the essays in this volume offer readers a long look at the challenges facing married Catholics today, but also at the resources from Christian tradition that can help couples and families forge a long and satisfying relationship with one another, with children, and with the communities of the church and society. It is worth noting that all of the contributors to this volume are themselves married people, and so their collected wisdom represents not only an appropriation of the theological and spiritual traditions of the church, but also a practical understanding of what it really means to sustain a marriage in our time. There is a clear consensus that Catholic marriage today is often difficult, but immensely rewarding. Our hope, therefore, is that these essays might serve as a catalyst for further conversation about Catholics' understanding of the hopefulness that emerges from the face-to-face work of marriage.

Part One

FOUNDATIONS

Chapter One

Signs of Hope in Marriage Today

David Thomas

Despite the often-quoted statistics about the high rate of divorce, a decline in the number of weddings celebrated in church settings, and the later age for first marriages, there remain some positive indicators that marriage may be enjoying some of its finest moments. This is because marriage today has moved into the territory of free, conscious, deliberate, and more mature choice for those entering its challenges. In other words, while we may have fewer marriages, many of them may be better than those in the past.

Increased freedom, of course, carries the added burden of a new set of responsibilities. Society, extended family, and the church as institution have receded as influential factors in determining both the decision to marry and the ongoing intent to remain married. As effective supports of marriage, they are mostly in the past. More than ever, the couple are now on their own and its life is largely under their own control. If they survive, or even prosper, the couple can take center stage and be acknowledged as their own primary reason for success. Further, many couples know this. There seems to be increased deliberateness about marriage that is worth noting, perhaps causing delay entering marital waters. They are consciously serious about their relationship and know that they are mostly in charge of their marriage, for better or worse.

In these days, their love for each other is less likely to be under narrow notions of romanticism, which social commentators have noted is often like a firecracker in the night, a bright explosion, but soon dims into darkness. Such illusions are no longer the mainstay of movies, television, and novels, all of which have generally taken a more realistic approach to relational life. Most married couples have also witnessed marital breakdown, perhaps in the marriages of their own parents. Recognized more clearly is the vulnerability of marriage along with its highs and the lows, the inevitable times of ease and times of difficulty. Responsible couples recognize and accept these weather patterns and at least have a greater possibility of weathering hard times because they are not surprised or defeated by their arrival. Some seek assistance from professionals, which can be used without the stigma that might have once prevented such an "intervention."

In general, the church continues to present a positive hopefulness about marital success. Even its occasional bemoaning of failure can be viewed as a sign of support. There is an ongoing church effort to prepare couples for marriage that includes a good dose of the realism about marital life. While preparation can always be better, there seems a genuine will to improve these programs. The most obvious gap in marital support and education covers the time after the marriage. Some programs like Marriage Encounter have clearly helped some couples.

But such assistance is definitely an uphill climb. First, there's little precedence for church assistance in marriage enrichment, and the church does best when it can offer that which it always has. Second, church leadership rightfully moves slowly in determining exactly what the church can effectively offer in support of existing marriages. We know that if we're unsure about what to do, it's best not to rush ahead, but rather to live with the open question. We must continue to research possibilities, ask professional family ministers, and above all seek guidance from the married. Finally, the church now suffers from people's impression that as a result of the sexual abuse crisis it may not be the best place for someone to go for assistance in matters dealing with intimacy and sexuality.

Our society as a whole also wants marriages to succeed; and while it may seem that there exists indifference to this, it may result more from a sense of impotence to do very much about either marital success or failure. Why complain about bad weather when there's little one can do to prevent its occasional occurrence? On the other hand, we are seeing a decided growth in various secular marriage enrichment opportunities for couples in terms of helpful therapy and educational programs, including an initiative by the U.S. Department of Health and Human Services.[1] Plus, as this volume will show, there is a growing consensus, founded on good research, about what's needed especially in troubled marriages, and there is a growing body of literature to support marital survival.

In summary, while we can point to significant will on the part of both church and society to affirm marriage, there remains the undeniable fact that most of what it takes to create a good marriage resides fully with the couple themselves. They are out in the open sea in a rowboat: they enjoy the privacy in which they bob up and down in the waves, but should a storm arise, they will have to depend on their own resources to survive. That many don't make it should be of no surprise to those who recognize the difficult situations couples face.

Marital life is very much filled with uncertainty about its unknown future. The same can be said for marital love. Genuine marital love is based on knowing the other, especially that knowing that's derived from experience of the one loved. But such knowledge is only gradually revealed. The mysterious depth of each person always contains surprises. And there's really no map to mystery.

Recent theological approaches to marriage emphasize that marriage is more a covenantal relationship than a contractual one. Covenants concern promises made between persons before God supporting an ongoing and open-ended pledge to "have and to hold" one's spouse throughout their shared lifetime as a couple. Focusing on interpersonal love has been central to our current understanding of marriage. And the love called for is comprehensive, embracing the erotic, sensual, philial, and agapaic dimensions of their life.

The challenges inherent in contemporary marriage, steeped in this interpersonal focus, make this form of life perhaps the most complex, confusing, demanding, and arduous of all human endeavors. It may also be the most satisfying one as well. And to add that its claims are lifelong, we are not surprised that when Jesus spoke of this, his disciples wondered whether this is really possible. Jesus quipped that it was, but only with God's help. Today, a deep respect for the difficulties involved in a successful marriage may be an important part of its enactment. For those thinking that the winds will always be favorable may be setting themselves up for eventual failure.

Focusing on the interpersonal love within marriage answers one question (what's most important?), but this emphasis also brings in many other questions. What are the "ways of love"? How does it deepen or grow? What helps love and what doesn't? Are there universal truths about love or is it so personal that comparisons and generalizations are often inadequate to the reality? What *must* be done to support the essentially fragile nature of interpersonal love? And what can "outsiders" do to support or help marital love in its precarious dimensions? And finally, what happens if love exits the marriage? Is it so existentially damaged that it can't be revived? And if we add a Christian dimension to all this, what's the role of God's grace and the possibility of reconciliation? Does hope for the couple bloom eternal?

Because love is at the heart of Christian marriage, we are alerted to the fact that its presence brings God right into the middle of the marriage. The deep interrelationship between love of God and love of neighbor is played out in full force in a loving marriage. Years back, a bishop who was somewhat of a TV star wrote a book on marriage affirming the fact that it takes three to get married. He was right on. God is involved, whether acknowledged or not. God, it would seem, has a decided interest in marital success, because it is the holy ground where many people learn what it means to love.

Further, it would be helpful to examine the unique nature of marital love, including an inquiry about whether it really *is* unique. Like research into the dynamics of the human body, the more we can learn about this "love reality," especially in marriage, the more those who love and those who seek to help them can do what's necessary to keep love healthy and alive. This is not only a question about the human reality of marriage; it is also, in the words of Edward Schillebeeckx, a matter of entering more deeply into what about it is a "saving mystery."

Chapter Two

A Spirituality for the Vocation to Marriage

WILLIAM P. ROBERTS

THE WORD "SPIRITUALITY" has a triple meaning. First, it signifies the holistic growth of an individual to become all he or she is called to be, physically, intellectually, emotionally, and religiously. It is being fully alive as a human being, an embodied spirit, an inspirited body, present to oneself, present to others and to one's world, and present to the Transcendent One who beckons us beyond ourselves.

Second, it is being open to the Spirit of God. It is allowing the Spirit to penetrate our being, to fill us with her wisdom and her love, and to lead us where She will.

Third, it is to live in the spirit of Christ's Gospel, allowing him to reign in our lives, to influence our thoughts and our attitudes, our words and our actions.

This basic spirituality, common to all Christian life, is cultivated in diverse ways according to the different states of life. The focus of this essay is to probe what growth in spirituality means in practical terms in the ordinariness of everyday married life.

A God-given Vocation[1]

It is no secret that the church has had significant difficulty over the centuries in acknowledging marriage as an authentic divine vocation on a par with religious life and the celibate state. While the past half century has seen a much more positive shift in the hierarchy's attitude toward marriage, the official bias in favor of the celibate state of life is still quite evident as reflected, for example, in the church's far greater preoccupation with Mary's virginity than with her faith and her openness to the Word of God,[2] and with the Latin rite's view of marriage as a disqualification for ordained priestly ministry.³ This bias, I maintain, presents an obstacle to convincing younger and older couples that their marriage is a true calling from God and on an equal plane with the celibate and single states.

A real appreciation of marriage as a response to God's call in one's life serves as a significant basis for a spirituality of marriage. We here probe some of the elements of marriage as a vocation. But it is not a vocation that stands alone. It is rooted in two more basic callings: the one written into creation, and the one we receive through baptism.

In God's creation the will of God for humans is manifested in God's creating them female and male in the image and likeness of God (Gen. 1:27). Human gender and sexuality, therefore, are not only gifts of God, but in a finite way reflect something that is part of who God is. To grow as mature sexual beings who integrate their sexuality in personal commitment and love, whether single, celibate, or married, is to grow in the image of our Maker.

God's will for us is also expressed in the creation account in Genesis 2 where woman and man are created equal as humans, bone of the same bone, flesh of the same flesh (v. 23), and in such a way that the two may become one (v. 24).

In the call to be married, one looks into oneself and in light of one's unique gifts, virtues, temperament, and the physical and psychological structure of one's being, and in light of the possibilities available one chooses marriage as the way in which one believes he or she can best become all he or she is called to be as the unique giving and loving human being the creating God wishes.

In baptism we are empowered by the Spirit to live in Christ, and through him to be daughters and sons of the God whom Jesus calls Abba, Father. All the baptized are called to holiness, to the fullness of Christian life, and to the perfection of charity.⁴ "The forms and tasks of life are many but there is one holiness, which is cultivated by all who are led by God's Spirit and, obeying the Father's voice and adoring God the Father in spirit and in truth, follow Christ, poor and humble in carrying his cross, that they may deserve to be sharers in his glory."⁵

In the sacrament of marriage the couple are called to live out their baptismal commitment to the fullness of Christian life and love by growing in unique intimacy with one another and by being visible, effective signs to each other and to the wider community of the redeeming presence and love of the crucified and risen Christ. By ever entering into deeper authentic communion with each other and sharing the fruits of this union in terms of concern and service to others, they contribute as a leaven in the dough to the fulfillment of Christ's wish for all his followers, "May they all be one, just as, Father, you are in me and I am in you, so that they may also be in us, so that the world may believe that it was you who sent me" (John 17:21).[6]

From their earliest years through adulthood young people should learn through teaching and preaching about the baptismal vocation to grow into the fullness of holiness and to participate in Christ's ongoing mission of service. In that context married life, religious life, and celibate life need to be seen as diverse ways in which Christians are called to live out to the fullest their baptismal vocation. In the abstract there is no superiority or inferiority among diverse lifestyles. Each individual must discern the way of life to which he or she is called on the basis of which one is most conducive for growth in holiness and for serving the human community. Pertinent here is Paul's vision of the church as the Body of Christ with many diverse gifts and parts (1 Cor. 12). One member cannot say to another, "I have no need of you" (v. 21). All the parts are needed for the integrity of the body. The challenge is to become the best one can be in the unique context of one's life.

Since liturgy is an important form of catechesis, the renewal of baptismal promises made at Easter and on other occasions ought to be revised to include not just the negative elements that are now present, but also a commitment to some of the positive meanings of being a baptized person, such as openness to the Spirit, following the Gospel of Jesus, and promoting the reign of God's truth, love, justice, and peace. Marriage ceremonies could include such a renewal of baptismal promises and a resolve to live these out in the marriage. The marriage vows themselves are also in serious need of revision. They should include an explicit commitment on the part of the couple to be faithful to the ongoing creation of their marriage as an intimate partnership of life and love[7] and to live the sacrament of marriage by treating and loving each other as Christ does.[8] The present official formulas contain no reference to the Christian and sacramental dimensions of baptism or of marriage. This is a serious loss of catechetical opportunity.

A Trinitarian Spirituality

We are baptized "in the name of the Father and of the Son and of the Holy Spirit." We affirm our baptism into the Trinity each time we make the sign of the cross, especially when we do so with the Easter water[9] provided at the entrance of the church. It is significant that when we do so we add to the formula the word "Amen," "so be it." "So be it," not only that we pray in the name of our Trinitarian God, but also that we strive to live our baptismal lives in that name. We reflect here on some of the ways in which a couple can live their marriage in the name and presence of the Divine Trinity.[10]

In the name of the Father

We believe, our Nicene Creed states, "in one God, the Father, the Almighty, maker of heaven and earth, of all that is seen and unseen." The God we believe in is the ultimate giver of all that is, that has been, and that will be. He is the absolute source of all life, the one who will never abandon us and who will always be for us.[11] "Can a woman forget her baby at her breast, feel no pity for the child she has borne? Even if these were to forget, I shall not forget you. Look, I have engraved you on the palms of my hands" (Isa. 49:15, 16).

There are three ways in particular in which a couple can live their marriage in the Father's name. First, a couple through prayer and reflection can grow in their awareness that all they are and all they have, as individuals, as sexual beings, as spouses comes from the hands of God, who is ever present with them, bestowing upon them countless blessings. This is the root of a humble attitude enabling them to realize that all the gifts of their being and of their marital relationship are due not to them but to God.

This awareness can also foster in them a trust that God will be with them in the unseen and unforeseen aspects of their marital journey. Fear of the unknown future in a world marked by widespread divorce, infidelity, spousal abuse, and marital unhappiness is for many young people today a major deterrent to making a lifelong, exclusive commitment to this one particular person. It is also a fear that can hover over even the best of marriages as the journey takes many turns, brings us to various crossroads, and demands decisions with unknown consequences. Belief that God, our Father, our Mother, our Creator is at our side, even if we "walk in a ravine as dark as death" (Ps. 23:4) can be a strong antidote to such fears. A saying attributed to Ralph Waldo Emerson is apropos here: "For all I have seen I trust the Creator for all I have not seen."

Second, couples live their marriage in the name of the Father by participating in unique ways in the creative life-giving love of God for humanity. By God's power they create the intimate bond of their marital relationship, and in giving of themselves in body, mind, heart, and soul they affirm and bring new life to each other's being. In their self-giving they truly become sacraments to one another of God's very Self-giving.

They share also in God's creative life-giving when they bring children into this world and rear them to adulthood to become all they can be. The couple participates further in the Father's life-giving by extending the gift of their love and their talents for the benefit of those beyond the walls of their family, especially the poor, the disadvantaged, and the lonely.

Third, the name "Father" that Jesus addressed to God brings out a very special kind of personally intimate relationship and bond between God and Jesus, and through Jesus between God and us. This is brought out even further in Mark 14:36 when Jesus calls God his Abba, "a familiar address used by children."[12] A couple live out their marriage in this intimate name and reflect God's intimate communion with Christ and with us as they grow in true personal intimacy with each other.

In the name of the Son

In the Nicene Creed we profess that we "believe in one Lord, Jesus Christ, the only Son of God, eternally begotten of the Father." We further proclaim that he came down from heaven for us humans and "for our salvation."

One of the ways we live our married lives in the name of the Son is to accept Jesus as our Savior. This implies some understanding of how Jesus' coming was for our salvation, and how we can allow Christ's saving power to touch and heal us in the context of our marriage.

For our sake God, Paul tells us, made Christ "the sinless one a victim for sin,[13] so that in him we might become the uprightness of God" (2 Cor. 5:21). The First Letter of Peter reflects a similar theme: "He was bearing our sins in his own body on the cross, so that we might die to our sins and live for uprightness; through his bruises you have been healed. You had gone astray like sheep but now have returned to the shepherd and guardian of your souls" (2:24–25).

Benedict XVI mirrors this insight in conjunction with his reflection on Jesus' baptism in the Jordan. "Jesus loaded the burden of all mankind's guilt upon his shoulders; he bore it down into the depths of the Jordan. He inaugurated his public activity by stepping into the place of sinners. His inaugural gesture is in anticipation of the Cross."[14]

Becoming one with us in all things except sin (Heb. 4:15), Jesus in his ministry became a sign of God's forgiveness. He associated with sinners (Matt. 9:10–13, Luke 19:5–7), and forgave the sins of the paralytic, of the woman caught in adultery, and of Peter. He is, as our eucharistic liturgy proclaims, the "Lamb of God who takes away the sins of the world."

There are two aspects of living our marriage in the name of Christ our Savior. First, we acknowledge our need of Christ's saving grace. We admit that we are limited human beings, that each of us has a dark side within, and that our relationship itself is not without flaws. We own the fact that in such an intimate relationship as marriage even small omissions, words, or actions can deeply hurt the other and have a negative impact on the relationship itself. We are aware that even with the best intentions we can unconsciously offend.

Second, we admit and apologize to each other when we are wrong. We both ask for forgiveness and grant it. We work together to heal any rifts that have come between us and proceed to deepen the bond that holds us together. In doing so we share in Jesus' ministry of forgiveness and become sacraments of his saving power. We allow Christ to effect his reconciling forgiveness in us through our reconciling forgiveness of each other. We thus bring to realization Jesus' own prayer, "forgive us our trespasses as we forgive those who trespass against us."

In the name of the Holy Spirit

We proclaim in the Nicene Creed that we believe "in the Holy Spirit, the Lord, the giver of life, who proceeds from the Father and the Son." It is this Sanctifying Spirit, dwelling within us,[15] who empowers us now to possess eternal life, which Jesus tells us is "to know you, the only true God, and Jesus Christ whom you have sent" (John 17:3).

We live our married lives in the name of this life-giving Spirit by allowing the Spirit to bring us to closer personal intimacy with Christ and the Father through our own grace-filled intimacy with each other. We open ourselves to the Spirit to sanctify us through each other. We also live in the name of the Spirit by respecting one another's bodies as temples of this Spirit. Negatively, we do this by avoiding every kind of verbal, emotional, and physical abuse. Positively, we do it by beholding and treating each other with love, kindness, goodness, gentleness, self-control, peace, and joy, to name some of the qualities that Paul identifies as "fruit of the Spirit" (Gal. 5:22).

Many preachers and catechists avoid talking about the Trinity because, in the words of some, "it is such a great mystery," and in the view of others, "What can you say about it that makes sense to the people in the pews?" I think this attitude is often rooted in the belief that one has to try to explain what the Trinity is in itself, how there can be three "Persons" in one God. It is far better to begin by pointing out how Christians experience in their faith lives and in the liturgy God as their Father, Son, and Holy Spirit, as the source of their grace and holiness. In this way people can be shown how their married lives can be prayerful responses to the Trinitarian God who created them, redeems them, and dwells within them to bring them to ever closer intimacy with God, with one another, and with humankind. Trinity Sunday affords the greatest — but not the only — opportunity in which this can be done.

The Paschal Mystery and the Lifelong Marital Cycle

One of the most fundamental beliefs that we hold in common with Christians of all denominations is that Jesus, who was crucified and died on Good Friday, rose from the dead on Easter Sunday. We also believe that we are called to share in Christ's death and resurrection. While this sharing culminates at the final moment of our earthly life, it begins with our baptism. As Paul tells us, we were baptized into Christ's death and buried with him, so that as he "was raised from the dead by the Father's glorious power, we too should begin living a new life" (Rom. 6:4). And further he states, "we believe that, if we died with Christ, then we shall live with him too.... For by dying he is dead to sin once and for all, and now the life he lives is life with God. In the same way, you must see yourselves as being dead to sin but alive for God in Christ Jesus" (Rom. 6:8, 10–11).

All baptismal life, then, is meant to be an ongoing process in which we daily die further to that which is sin and darkness in us in order to live more fully in the grace-filled life and light of Christ. Since, as we have seen earlier in this essay, the call to sacramental marriage is rooted in our baptism, we probe here some of the unique ways in which we are challenged to participate in the dying and rising of Christ precisely in terms of the commitment to create together an intimate partnership of life and love that sacramentalizes Christ's self-giving presence and love of us.

The decision a couple makes to get married involves dying to living as a single, independent individual, dying to all other possible marriages, and placing the spousal relationship before all others. This frees them to give of themselves to each other without reservation and to make their marriage their highest priority.

In the immediate preparation for marriage the couple must face themselves and their relationship and dispel any misconceptions they might have about marriage and what they are each bringing to the wedding ceremony. This process can be painful but serves as an essential foundation for a truthful lasting relationship. In her book *Lies at the Altar,* Robin Smith describes at length what she considers "ten top lies" that couples often bring into a marriage, and "ten top truths" that give the death to those lies.[16]

As those early months of marriage are experienced, we are challenged to put aside any illusions we may still have that we can be the "perfect couple," and that all should be "marital bliss," free of any hurts and flaws. We must grow up to accept what is good in each other, improve in one another what we can, and accommodate to the imperfections that can never completely go away. We also need to correct the misconception that one person's efforts can make up for the other's lack of resolve. It takes two, putting their best foot forward, to make this dance go.

Another step in the process of dying to self in order to live for others takes place when children, by birth or adoption, enter the family scene. The two must grow from being just a married couple to also becoming co-parents. Patterns of living that they had gotten accustomed to when it was just the two of them must give way to a significant loss of privacy, free time, and control over one's schedule. Chores must be realigned to make for a fair distribution of responsibilities.

In these early years of marriage and in the many years of parenting, one of the major inclinations we need to die to is trying to make our spouse and our children into our own image and likeness and into what we think they ought to become. Rather, we ought to help them discover who it is God is calling them to be and affirm and support that vision and dream.[17] It's a death, in other words, to a possessive, controlling kind of "love," and a conversion to an authentic life-giving love. This dying and rising is illustrated quite poignantly in a story told by the late Indian Jesuit Anthony De Mello. After the birth of his first child the Master was asked, "What do you want him to be when he grows up?" "Outrageously happy," the Master replied.[18] This attitude involves a real "letting go" but underscores what true love really desires for others, namely, that, in the words of Jesus, their "joy be complete" (John 15:11; see also 16:24).

As the years of marriage continue to pass by, the couple must resist falling into the temptation of settling into a monotonous routine that takes each other for granted and that puts their relationship on hold while they become increasingly involved with making a living and providing for their children. They must die to such inertia, and continue to become more personally, emotionally, and romantically present to each other. Marital intimacy either grows or fades!

The paschal mystery is embraced further as the couple face the empty nest and confront the adjustments required in the postretirement stage and in the ongoing process of aging. If their marital union has deepened throughout the years, they will be able to discover new ways of expressing their love for one another and their service to the broader community.

Paradoxical though it be, life grows through dying. The life of the marital journey is no exception. It is by embracing the many dyings along the way that our marriage becomes more filled with life and more life-giving to others. And the seeming end of the earthly marital journey finally gives way to that toward which it was ever intended to lead, the eternal wedding feast of the Lamb where all love in this life is brought to new fulfillment forever (see Rev. 19:7–9; also Matt. 22:1ff.).

Three of the personal virtues needed for a marriage to participate in the paschal mystery along the lines suggested above are unselfishness, adaptability, and faithfulness. These need to be inculcated in our children from the earliest years. Such formation provides important remote preparation for a later marriage. In a serious dating relationship and in proximate marriage preparation the presence or absence of these qualities should serve as important criteria for the couple's judgment regarding the future possibilities of their relationship.

Unselfishness allows us to love one's spouse as one's self (see Luke 10:27, Eph. 5:28) and to go beyond the narrow limits of one's self-interest to embrace the needs and desires of the other. Adaptability is important in order to move away from patterns of lifestyle that were suitable to early stages of the marriage in order to accommodate meaningfully to new changing circumstances. Faithfulness is far more than avoiding adultery and divorce. It is being fully committed to growing together in the kind of personal presence, conversation, and companionship unique to the marital union.

Living the paschal dimension of marriage presupposes a solidly grounded relationship. Unfortunately the contemporary culture militates against establishing such a relational foundation. It clearly gives the impression that it is normal and fine for a couple to become sexually involved early in the dating process, often before they hardly know each other. The problem with this is the couple can be led to mistake "good sex" for true love and to confuse sexual compatibility with marital compatibility. Reversing this mind-set and advocating the discipline needed to postpone sexual involvement present a gigantic pastoral challenge, but one that is essential to meet if we are to do justice to any marriage preparation program.

John Van Epp presents an insightful approach that can serve as a significant antidote to the modern media culture. He offers what he calls a Relationship Attachment Model (RAM).[19] There are "five universal human dynamics," he says, that work together in a romantic relationship. These "five fundamental dynamics are the depth to which you *know*,[20] *trust, rely on, have a commitment to,* and *have sexual involvement with* another person."[21] "The *balance* of all five bonding dynamics determines the healthiness of your relationship and the clarity of your perspective on your partner."[22] One keeps a balance among these five relationship dynamics by "not moving further ahead in one area than in any of the others."[23] "One of the most common ways you become set up to get involved with a jerk is by accelerating the pace of your relationship."[24] Including these insights in any catechetical program will most probably prove to be a hard sell, but is certainly worth the effort.

Conclusion

This essay has addressed the question of how to cultivate a spirituality for the marital journey. Doing justice to this topic could take at least another book. I have selected brief reflections on only three aspects of a Christian marital spirituality: its vocational, Trinitarian, and paschal dimensions. Hopefully, these can contribute to the reader's perception of the potential holiness of a sacramental marriage and how marital catechesis can be more effectively implemented to support couples in achieving this ideal.

Chapter Three

A Theology for Married People
Tim Muldoon

It is the peculiar habit of theologians to see everything under the sun as manifesting some theological truth, even when such truth is not as patently self-evident to the rest of the world. Hence there is the tendency to preface nearly any term with the phrase "A Theology of..." and work from God through revelation to the specific topic at hand, whether it be work, the family, or the body. The implication is that through the eyes of Christian faith, it is possible to see everything as a manifestation of who God is and what God is doing, and thereby to develop a systematic account of all truth, both eternal and temporal.

A thumbnail sketch, therefore, of a "theology of marriage" would look very much like what we find, for example, in the *Catechism of the Catholic Church* and, for that matter, in the *Code of Canon Law* — both being attempts to foreground the Catholic understanding of marriage against the background of the story of salvation history, from God to Israel to Christ to church to doctrine to liturgy to spirituality to ethics. Consider the logic of the treatment of marriage (or rather "the sacrament of matrimony") in the *Catechism* — article 7 of Section Two ("The Seven Sacraments of the Church") in Part Two ("The Celebration of the Christian Mystery"):

1. marriage is created by God (1602–5)

2. marriage as created by God is marred by sin (1606–8)

3. God has given the law in order to teach us what God intended in marriage (1609–11)

4. marriage in the light of Christ is transformed into a model of salvation (1612–17)

5. forsaking the good of marriage altogether for the sake of Christ is a great good (1618–20)

This theology of marriage is an attempt to show how this practice is caught up in the narrative of God's creation and redemption of the world. And it is important; this theology represents the culmination of a millennium of Christian reflection on what is fundamentally a secular practice — a practice which, according to canon law, Christ has "raised to the dignity of a sacrament."

Theologians are unusual people, though. In truth, most people marry because they see something good coming from being with the other in a publicly recognized, formalized relationship, and few would point to anything resembling theological reasoning as a motivating or sustaining factor. Theology, in other words, is more often useful for those who are interested in the church than for those who are interested in getting married.

I make this initial observation in order to highlight what is a key challenge in the pastoral care of Catholics and by extension a challenge in the way that Catholic leaders can speak broadly to people either getting married or working at staying married. The challenge is to bridge the vast, systematic, historically and legally nuanced, theologically and philosophically precise, carefully reasoned and debated superstructure of Catholic reflection on marriage, on the one hand, and the ordinary, quotidian concerns of domestic life from childhood through adulthood, mating, marrying, working, bearing and raising children, growing old, and dying, on the other.

I believe that there are really two issues, one significantly more important than the other. The first issue is inviting Catholics (and their spouses, and others) to consider daily life through the lens of Christian faith; and the second issue is to do that specifically in their married lives. If we get the first issue right, the second will naturally follow. What I am interested in, then, is not so much "a theology of marriage" that is appropriate for catechisms, canon law, and documents and texts that professionals use when debating ways that marriage ought to be understood as an element in the systematic understanding of God and the cosmos. Rather I'm interested in a "theology for married people" — an invitation to married people to look at their daily lives as wives and husbands, as sisters and brothers, as daughters and sons, as friends, colleagues, neighbors, associates, and acquaintances, as fellow Catholics, fellow Christians, fellow human beings — which helps them to understand what roles they play in the divine order. Such a theology would have a heavy dose of themes like relationship, friendship, love, freedom and responsibility, self-donation, sexuality, creativity and fruitfulness — all relational terms that invite people to think of themselves always and everywhere not as isolated monads with isolated personal desires that have little or no impact on the social order, but rather as necessarily relational persons, whose desires are already manifestations of God's imprint on all human living, even amid a world tarnished by sin. And the relevance of this theology would be in the ways that it invites people to think of their married lives as the privileged places of encounter with God, the holy ground upon which God invites them to work out their salvation and the salvation of their spouses, children, extended families, and communities.

Marriage in the United States Today

What we know from census data is that many people are living together outside of marriage, marrying later in life, having fewer children, and frequently getting divorced. These broad brushstrokes, while inadequate to the task of helping us formulate clear pastoral imperatives among various populations, ought to help us see something of the background against which our finer conclusions must be drawn. Many people in the United States — especially young people — approach marriage with a good deal of trepidation. Moreover, significant numbers of people live much of their adult lives without children.[1] Broadly speaking, the social institution of marriage has weakened over the last several decades. No longer is it possible to speak of marriage as a natural stage of adult development, with shared cultural understanding, expectations, and structures. Instead, marriage has become one option — albeit a still comparatively popular one — in U.S. society, alongside other social arrangements we broadly describe with terms like "single life," "cohabitation," "serial monogamy," and others. Further, it is difficult to make the case that Catholics are markedly different in their practices with regard to marriage than other members of U.S. society. On the whole, the story of U.S. Catholics is a story of becoming assimilated to the mores of the wider culture,[2] suggesting that they are not likely as a community to hold attitudes toward marriage very different from other U.S. Americans.[3]

It is not the task of this essay to parse what we know about the attitudes of U.S. Americans toward marriage, or how attitudes of Catholics compare to those of others. Rather, my point is to suggest with these brief indicators that U.S. Catholic pastoral leaders are ill advised to assume that there is a consistent, systematic belief among their congregants that marriage is the natural course for many young lay people, or that those who are married will stay that way, or that children will be raised in Catholic households with two parents. There is a lingering assumption that the social structures that Catholics built so remarkably during the twentieth century will remain in perpetuity — an effect, I assume, of the tendency to treat living memory (perhaps eighty years, give or take) as representative of how things have always been. In short, Catholic leaders are faced with a much more fundamental challenge, one that likely bears more resemblance to the challenges faced by bishops of the early medieval period than by bishops of the recent past. The challenge is this: to articulate a theology for married people that invites them to see marriage as a particular kind of invitation to a life that is holy — and by this I mean a life that is fully free precisely because it is lived in faithfulness to the will of God. And they must do this amid a dearth of clear cultural supports for the institution.

A Church Learning from Its Past

I draw the parallel to the early medieval period, because it was in the centuries following the fall of the Roman Empire that church leaders, motivated by pastoral necessity, gradually assumed a more precise juridical posture toward marriages among the baptized. The dissolution of the empire led to competing social orders (or in some places, it seems, complete lack of any social order), and within this pluralistic context church leaders found themselves responding to the challenges left in the wake of unstable contexts for marrying and child raising. Some men married multiple women surreptitiously, begat children out of wedlock, or abandoned spouses and children. Moreover, as the church engaged cultures with differing practices with regard to marriage, there arose pressing questions about how and when legal marriage contracts (especially between noble families or even kingdoms) were ratified.[4] The church's involvement in marriage can be described as a desire to establish rules or laws that ensured the fair exchange of terms to the marriage contract, while at the same time bringing certain already established social mores concerning virginity, sexuality, and marrying into the life of the Christian community. The development took centuries, to be sure, but the end result is that the church developed a rather precise legal structure with regard to marriage, which led to an increasingly expansive theology that recognized marriage as a basic human reality, transformed by life in Christ.

The early medieval period makes for an interesting case study for those considering the church's pastoral work in marriage in the contemporary U.S. context. Today, our situation is similar in key ways. First, in some ways what we are seeing in contemporary debates about globalization is the waning of an "empire," if it is possible to speak of the predominance of Europe as such. Just as the church eventually had to consider marriage practices not only from Roman law, but also from such distinctive cultures as those of the Franks, Goths, and others, so too must Catholics today consider marriage practices that look very different from those that have been predominant in living memory.[5] What makes the contemporary context distinct is that many of these practices are really not in any precise sense "cultural" practices, i.e., practices that have been developed and nurtured within generations of ethnic, religious, or linguistic kinship networks. Rather, they are more properly described as personal attitudes that have arisen amid the milieu of American democratic liberalism, as personal commitments untethered by the boundary-setting tendencies of large communities of shared purpose. Cohabitation, to take one broad example, encompasses a cluster of practices that are very often motivated not by recognizable cultural convictions, but by individual economic necessity. The important point of convergence between the medieval and the contemporary U.S. challenges is that both have arisen because of the dual movements of breakdown and expansion — breakdown of older cultural practices and expansion of a community's cultural lens through encounter with other cultures.

Second, there is a similar dynamic in the relationship between church and state in the twilight of the Roman Empire and in the postmodern church. "Christian" marriage as such did not exist in the early centuries of the church's life under the Roman Empire, nor did it immediately take shape after Constantine. What we see is a gradual development of the church's response to Roman marriage law, suggesting that in the early church marriage was regarded as a secular matter.[6] Over time, Christians had their marriages blessed by clerics, but it was not until the end of the first millennium that we find anything resembling a commonly used marriage liturgy. For its first thousand years, the church saw marriage as a concern primarily of the state. The church's concern was not the state's laws regarding marriages, but rather the exhortation to the baptized to bring their marriage practices into conformity with the faith, and to avoid those pagan celebrations (such as those involving sacrifices) that conflicted with the faith. Today, interestingly, the church confronts a similar challenge: to weigh its own practices against those of the state and exhort its members to fidelity to the divine law. With the developing debates over state legislation concerning gay marriage, it is interesting to ask whether it is the task of the church to impact what states decide marriage is, or rather to provide pastoral guidance for the baptized such that their practices and beliefs comport with a broader commitment to the Gospel. For clearly in the first millennium of the church's life, the latter task was the more prominent thrust of its ministry toward marriage.

Third, the implication of this breakdown and expansion is that it is impossible to speak about a univocal understanding of marriage among either the communities of the faithful or the wider societies of which they are a part. For the majority of U.S. history, Catholics could rely on a more-or-less shared understanding of marriage, due to the influence of the various European Protestant communities that shaped the landscape of early life in the colonies and United States. Because of extensive shared sexual and marital mores among Protestants and Catholics (even in spite of doctrinal and liturgical differences), Catholic practices met little resistance in U.S. society until the twentieth century.[7] Today, however, the Catholic understanding of marriage is one among many, and young people in particular are unlikely to embrace this understanding freely unless they are guided deliberately by those who are themselves committed to it. The response of the church during the early medieval period to the challenges of breakdown and expansion are illustrative here, for they show a community struggling to develop not only a catechesis for marriage as a mode of Christian living (hence St. Augustine's *On the Good of Marriage*), but also a liturgy and a theology that situate Christian marriage practices firmly (albeit grudgingly) in the context of the apostolic tradition.

There was a profound development from the earliest writings on marriage, from figures like Tertullian, Augustine, Jerome, and John Chrysostom, to the high medieval writings on marriage by the likes of Peter Lombard, Gratian, and Thomas Aquinas — a development that amounted to a near turnaround on the question of whether sexuality could be seen as an integral dimension of a sacramental marriage. Further, with the growing influence of personalist philosophy in the twentieth century — a philosophy that had an important impact on the writings of Pope John Paul II — we see still more development, moving Catholics to consider marriage not as a grudging permission by God to avoid sexual immorality (with St. Paul), nor as a legal contract that the church might for good cause extend a blessing upon (with the bishops of the first few centuries CE), nor even as a solemn liturgical act in which the church saw a type of Christ (with the scholastics). Instead, Catholics have been invited to see marriage as a religious vocation in which partners pledge to live out their salvation and to help each other achieve Christian perfection. Today, the church has indeed developed a "theology for married people" which is more personal and pastoral than simply the application of a more patristic or scholastic "theology of marriage." And yet what is perplexing is how seldom we find this theology informing the way Catholics in the United States actually enter into marriage or live it out in the context of parish life. The remainder of this essay, therefore, will explore first the elements of this theology, and second its pastoral implications.

Inviting People to View Marriage through a Theological Lens

The starting point for a contemporary pastoral theology for married people is a reflection on God's observation in Genesis: it is not good to be alone (Gen. 2:18). Existential solitude does not suit the human being, and one might surmise that the Yahwist author did not consider even the contemplative relationship between the human being and God as being sufficient for God's purposes for the human being. God's creation of woman is first an answer to the need not for offspring, but rather companionship.[8] Jesus affirms this fundamental meaning of marriage by citing the Yahwist text in his comment on marriage in both Mark's and Matthew's Gospels (Mark 10:6–9 and Matt. 19:4–6).

This observation from scripture reflects what people know through experience: a happy life depends upon friendships.[9] And from this general observation it is possible to move to a more specific one: human beings desire not only friendships, but also a deep, intimate relationship with another person. For only in such relationships are people capable of exploring that which is most intimate to one's own experience, and therefore most precious, most holy. Marriage is not fundamentally about sex, or childbearing, or social status, though it may include all of these things and may, in fact, be motivated by one or more of these things. It is fundamentally about seeking out a person whose solitude complements my own, because it is not good to be alone. In a word: marriage is a sacrament of communion.

My thesis is that the weight of Catholic tradition must be oriented toward the fundamental commitment to invite human beings to grow in love, and that our teaching and preaching on marriage will flow logically from this most basic commitment. Following Augustine, our invitation must be simple: love, and do what you will.

There are two corollaries to this basic thesis. The first is that solitude can be an authentic means toward the greater end of communion. Hence what we posit about chastity and celibacy ought therefore to open us up in love toward God, God's creatures, and the rest of God's creation. The second corollary is that we must consider single life carefully, because sometimes it is chosen and other times it is not. In both cases, the pastoral challenge is to help the person understand single life as no less an invitation from God into communion.

From this thesis it is possible to build a more developed theology for married people that can serve as an invitation to the shared practice of the spiritual life. For if we begin by asking people to consider that God is inviting them into the Trinitarian communion by means of communion with the beloved, then by extension everything in married life — from paying bills to shopping to nights out to struggles at work to raising children to coping with sickness and even death — becomes part of the shared pilgrimage toward ever greater communion. I find the metaphor of pilgrimage particularly compelling, as it suggests the importance not only of the destination, but also the path. In the Christian life, both the destination and the path are graced — and in the context of marriage this is especially true. Marital difficulties are fundamentally life difficulties, and it is therefore possible to invite couples to a deeper understanding of those difficulties as part of the very nature of pilgrimage. The act of faith on any pilgrimage is to give energy to the work of overcoming the difficulties, when it may seem easier to give up. The promise, however, is that there is a great good to be achieved not only through the perseverance on the pilgrimage when the road is difficult, but also by deepening one's communion with God by means of the deepening of communion with the beloved. In more pedestrian language, the fundamental act of faith in marriage is to face life's problems with someone you love rather than alone.

Of course no one can enter into marriage — or any friendship, for that matter — without prior experience of other kinds of relationships. The life of the church must be oriented around enabling people to grow in these relationships: with parents, sisters and brothers, peers, teachers and mentors, strangers and even enemies. Jesus' exhortations to love the enemy can be read as challenges to overcome the most difficult barriers to communion so that we might grow in the love of God. Indeed, the very theme that Jesus preached, especially prominent in the Synoptic Gospels, of "the kingdom of God" is one in which the relationships between human beings mirror the relations within the Trinity, of self-giving agapic love. When Pope John Paul II wrote about the need for remote, proximate, and immediate formation for marriage,[10] I believe he had this same sense in mind: namely, that the life of the church ought to involve an integrated commitment to helping people grow in their ability to love as Jesus loved, in the context of the religious vow of marriage. What we seek as Catholics is to live a life that takes as its starting point what Jesus has taught us about God, inviting others to do the same.

Implications of This Theology

Because I am a theologian and therefore share the tendency to think systematically, I will pause from the line of this argument to make a few parenthetical observations, implications of this theology that centers the sacramental life on friendship and, therefore, moves marriage close to the center of the sacramental economy. First, if the fundamental invitation by God is to communion, then marriage is a particular kind of religious vow. Of course the history of the church's reflection on sexuality betrays a slightly different approach — the church recognized a sacramental vow to holy orders long before it recognized a sacramental vow to marriage. In my view, which for the sake of brevity I shall not develop here, the development of patristic theologies of discipleship and vocation within the context of Neoplatonic and ascetic trajectories encouraged the more rapid development of appreciation for religious (especially monastic) life. I am not challenging the development of these theologies; I am rather seeking to reorient them within the broader context of discipleship. For while the sacramental theology of marriage developed in the church much later, its import is such that it is necessary to reconsider the nature of the whole sacramental economy. To clarify: from the early centuries of the church, one draws the observation that Christian perfection was seen primarily as willingness to withdraw from the sinful world in prayer, to assume a life of poverty, chastity, and obedience in radical faithfulness to God. I am suggesting, however, that this understanding of Christian perfection rests upon a more fundamental, implicit theology of grace: that God invites people to love God unconditionally, as God loves us. And I am suggesting that today it is possible to reorient the patristic view by inserting the further claim that God draws us into communion through the love of others, and that the fullest expression of that love means either that God calls us into marriage or God calls us into some form of single life in community with others.

The implications of this understanding of vowed life are both theological and practical. Theologically, it means that all Christians are called to perfection through whatever vocation God calls them to live. Practically, it means that most Christians will marry; many will stay single; and some will take other kinds of religious vows. The minority — those who take nonmarital religious vows — are the *ministerium,* the ministers, those who serve the body of the faithful.[11] And some will perform this service through leadership, while others will serve in other ways. But all are called to nurture and promote the shared life of communion.

Second, we must observe that through fear, limitation, and sin, people will fail in their vocations. The development of the sacramental theology of reconciliation in the first millennium of the Christian era demonstrates how the community of faith sought to address the reality of failure in communion, from the public confessions of those who defected from the church in the Roman era to the development of private confession among the Irish monks. Of course the development took time and arose out of pastoral need. Today, and perhaps for the next several hundred years, our challenge as a church will be to develop the implications of our sacramental theology of reconciliation as it applies to marriage — i.e., those who experience divorce or whose sexual and/or marital practices are not in accord with present doctrine and canon law. One might flippantly observe that since our sacramental theology concerning marriage is only a millennium old, it's still too early to strike the right note between marriage and reconciliation. As others have observed, however, we might with great profit learn from our brothers and sisters of the Orthodox churches.

Third, this theology, while rooted in the biblical and magisterial traditions of the church, foregrounds the practical meaning of marriage for married people in such a way as to move some elements of other doctrinal treatments of marriage into the background. This point becomes clear by looking briefly at how marriage is treated, for example, in the *Code of Canon Law:*

> The matrimonial covenant, by which a man and a woman establish between themselves a partnership of the whole of life and which is ordered by its nature to the good of the spouses and the procreation

and education of offspring, has been raised by Christ the Lord to the dignity of a sacrament between the baptized. (Canon 1055, section 1)

What this theology involves is a focus on the "partnership of the whole of life" (*consortium omnis vitae*) — an ancient phrase from the Roman jurists that only hints at the kind of pilgrimage that God invites spouses to undertake together. If, as I am suggesting, the primary fruit of marriage is communion, this means that the invitation to married life is an invitation to the hard work of seeing the world, the other, and the self in the fullness of reality; of admitting sin, undertaking reconciliation, and discovering that our most authentic desires are often buried underneath more fleeting ones.

Fourth, by foregrounding the life of communion in marriage, it becomes clear that the related fruits of the marriage vocation have to do with relationship to the rest of the church and the rest of the world. What this means in practice is that biological children are very often (but not always) the fruit of that vocation. In every sacramental marriage, the fruit is communion; in some, the fruit is biological children; in others, the fruit is children by adoption; or fostering; or the invitation to singles or parents or others in the community. As a theologian, I understand the development of the doctrine on marriage and recognize the social and ecclesial import of its definition of marriage as being ordered toward procreation. Yet as an adoptive parent, I also want to claim that the more expansive notion of the "partnership of the whole of life" can (and indeed ought to) include the complementary notions of biological and adoptive parenthood. This complementarity becomes especially clear when we consider that the vast number of orphans in the world — a number exacerbated by the AIDS crisis — represents a moral summons especially to married people of faith.[12]

Implications for Pastoral Practice

For the sake of brevity, I shall use this last section to make observations and suggestions about how our church can foster greater understanding about how to invite men and women into sustained reflection on married life as a pilgrimage of communion.

1. *Marriage formation.* A broad pastoral challenge facing all Catholics is developing communities of faith in light of changing demographics. The subcultures that nurtured generations of European American

Catholics have changed dramatically, meaning that sharing and handing on faith among different generations within families takes intentional decision making regarding such challenges as education and regular religious practices and celebrations. Even among more recent immigrants, there are significant challenges in sharing family and religious mores in the midst of contemporary U.S. culture. If our role as a church is the formation of boys and girls and men and women for lives of covenantal love, then we must give serious thought to how we foster a "mystagogy of communion,"[13] i.e., a kind of mentoring of young people in forming and sustaining agapic relationships as children, adolescents, and young adults. How might we teach them how to love? How might we form structures that encourage loving relationships? How might their play dates, socials, dating, courtship reflect their deepening commitment to life as followers of Christ?

2. *Marriage celebration.* Today, the wedding liturgy itself is an opportunity for evangelization, in the sense that it can manifest what the church does in inviting people to respond to God in marriage. Fundamentally, the liturgy is a celebration of communion. It celebrates a prophetic vision of marriage, in stark contrast to the consumerist, individualist models of weddings that prevail as a massive industry in U.S. culture. Our challenge is to ask how in our parishes we send the message that marriages affect the whole community, inviting couples to challenge the assumption that the wedding is little more than an expensive private party. Moreover, our opportunity is to invite couples to use the liturgy as an opportunity for spiritual growth. Let us invite them to think of the liturgy as that for which they will spend weeks and months preparing—a kind of process of "rehearsal" that amounts to a process of formation.

3. *Sustaining marriage.* How does our church foster a spirituality of communion in the face of all the vagaries of life today — a "domestic church"? Rules of life developed in religious communities as early as the fifth century CE, but there really has never developed a parallel "rule" for married people or families. To be sure, one might argue that all families are different, and that a rule is more appropriate for extended communities. But the more basic question is this: What resources do we offer married people who seek to deepen their spiritual lives precisely as married people (and perhaps too as parents)?

4. *Promoting marriage.* The church's missionary role is to be leaven in society calling people to love, and inviting them into the sacramental celebration. Fundamentally, this role is one of *diakonia* and *martyrion*, service and witness. Today, this missionary role calls for humility: the community of the church might not be able to influence legislation on marriage, but it can manifest to the rest of the world the joy of living out the pilgrimage of marriage in light of the Gospel.

5. *Balancing marriage and single life.* A key pastoral challenge today is that of single adults. At present, there are some structures in the church that address the ministry to singles, though they tend to be tied to youth. There are very few resources for older adults who are single, whether through choice or lack of choice, through death or divorce of spouse. We must recognize that single life, while common for many Catholics today, is the state of life — perhaps even vocation — for which there is no corresponding sacramental celebration, as with marriage and holy orders. Accordingly, our challenge is to inquire about how to draw single adults into community while at the same time retaining a commitment to marriage and family life in parishes.

It is important for Catholics and their leaders to recall that our reflection on marriage is both ancient and yet developing. The way that we approach marriage — both as individuals and as a church — has changed much in recent decades. Yet at the root of the Catholic vision of marriage is a fundamental theological truth, about God's presence to human beings through sacramental signs. What we are doing in celebrating the sacrament of marriage is what we are doing every time we celebrate a sacrament: from the Sunday Eucharist to the practice of Reconciliation to the more life-changing moments of baptism and confirmation, holy orders, and anointing of the sick. We are celebrating the grace that God suffuses throughout all human living. As a community of faith, it is our task to do everything we can to invite young people to appropriate this most basic truth. Moreover, it is our constant challenge to help married people at every stage of life to recall and live out this basic truth, to make it present and operative in the midst of their busy lives.

Part Two

CHALLENGES AND RESOURCES

Chapter Four

The Marriage-Friendly Parish

Julie Hanlon Rubio

I AM AWARE of very few Catholic married folks who are slackers; everyone I know is busy. When they meet each other, it is on the sidelines of soccer games, dance classes, and baseball diamonds; when working booths at parish festivals; bringing yet another side dish for a school party; on our way in or out of grocery stores late at night as we run in to buy birthday treats for a child's class; borrowing chairs for an extended family gathering in our home; volunteering at the book fair; chaperoning the field trip; running to parent-teacher conferences; slipping into Home Depot to pick up a forgotten item for another home repair project; gratefully sinking down in the pews at mass, hoping this time we will not have to struggle with restless children who would rather be elsewhere. Their conversations center on the details of our busy lives and concerns about teachers, activities, and the well-being of our children. These are not frivolous people whose energy is consumed with fashion, self-promotion, or entertainment. Like most middle- and upper-middle-class American Catholics, they are hardworking, family-centered, and devoted to the common good of their communities.

It would be difficult to say of them, using John Kavanaugh's well-known categories, that they are living in the material mode rather than the personal mode,[1] or that they, in John Paul II's terms, have lives consumed with having rather than being.[2] And yet most people I encounter acknowledge a yearning for a slower pace, deeper friendships, and more down time to simply be with their spouses and their children. There is a certain emptiness that is evident amid the fullness of middle-class American suburban life, a suspicion that busyness does not allow us to live below the surface, a sense that this life is less than it ought to be. It is not that people are not generally satisfied with their families and communities, but they know at some level that there is something amiss.

The longer I am married, the more I have come to believe that this emptiness in busyness is paradoxically connected to low expectations for marriage. The modern Catholic vision for marriage and family developed by John Paul II asks for much more than what most families would dare to hope for. In the 1981 document *Familiaris Consortio*,[3] the late pope speaks of relationships between husbands and wives using the term "communion," suggesting a certain depth in both physical and emotional connection. He asks families to serve life, by welcoming children, honoring life in all its forms, and creating an environment where the countercultural values of the Christian tradition can flourish. He gives families a mission to serve society, working to transform its unjust structures and soften its hard edges with works of charity, mercy, and hospitality. Finally, he calls families to own their identity as domestic churches in prayer, witness, and service.

This, John Paul II writes, is the fourfold mission of the family: to love, serve life, serve society, and be the church in their home. It is lofty and inspiring vision. However, given the heavy load most married people are carrying, it seems all but impossible. Yet I want to suggest that the work of this mission, the very work that seems as if it would burden families, is the work of communion that will actually fulfill families. It is the work of communion when husbands and wives take time to nurture their intimate relationships, when parents and children support each other and challenge each other to value all life, when families open themselves to being in communion with the needy and growing in faith together. This is not a way to emptiness but to fullness.

Why are most middle- and upper-middle-class Catholic families unaware of what is asked of them and/or unready to embrace this life of communion? An obvious place to turn is the parish, for if American middle-class culture is at odds with the Catholic vision for families, parishes should be places of refuge where an alternative way of life is nurtured. Two-thirds of all Catholics are registered parishioners, and most attend their local parish.[4] Another 16 percent attend one parish more than any other but are not registered, while only 16 percent are not affiliated at all.[5] Parishes are the communities that most Catholics call home. They are ideally placed to form families in Christian family values. However, as much as I want to believe that if the culture is working against marriage, the church is building it up, I am concerned that this is only rarely the case. In fact, my research on Catholic parishes leads me to believe that most are not supportive of marriage, at least not supportive of the kind of marriages Catholics have been called to live in the post–Vatican II context.

This essay will address the problem in three parts. Part 1 describes how American parishes functioned to sustain marriage and families in the early twentieth century. Part 2 discusses changes in the late twentieth century and their impact on families. Part 3 offers suggestions for change. I want to argue that if parishes are to sustain marriages that are distinctively Catholic in their striving for communion and help families overcome the problem of emptiness, they will have to question much that they have taken on as they have traveled from the margins to the center of middle-class American life.

Before moving to the meat of the essay, I want to point out that I will be using the terms "marriage" and "family" interchangeably. Theologians have traditionally separated discussions of marriage from analyses of family. However, when I am asked to discuss marriage, I find it impossible not to talk about family. In my life, marriage and family subsist together. For me, and for most theologians of my generation, it makes little sense to speak of marriage outside of the context of family, because families are where married folks live. And it is in families that marriages take shape, for better or worse. My hope is that paying attention to how Catholic parishes form families will contribute to the ability of more Catholic married couples to live out the vision to which they are called.

Pre–Vatican II American Parishes

Most American Catholic families lived in cities from the 1880s well until the 1950s and were deeply loyal to the ethnic parish neighborhoods that were the center of their existence.[6] The number of the Catholics in America expanded as immigrants from southern and eastern Europe flooded into American cities. From the late 1800s until the mid-1960s, Catholics were underrepresented in the upper class, somewhat overrepresented in the middle class, and very overrepresented in the lower classes.[7] Marginalized by ethnicity, class, and religion, they remained to a large extent outside the mainstream of American society. Parishes functioned as indispensable subcultures for these immigrant Catholics, providing social services, education, social life, and moral boundaries. Historians of this period speak in a common voice of a "unified family-based parish as the source of internalized Catholic identity."[8] Even today, the generation of pre–Vatican II Catholics is more strongly identified with the church than younger generations. Ninety percent say being Roman Catholic is an important part of who they are, 85 percent say it is important that the younger generation in their family grow up Catholic, 66 percent say the church is the most important of important parts of their lives, and 57 percent attend mass weekly.[9]

Parishes during this period provided a wide variety of activities and services to respond to the needs of their congregations. Social services such as food pantries, orphanages, soup kitchens, building and loan associations, and dues-paying societies that paid out benefits when family members got sick or died were necessary to meet the needs of those struggling to make a living.[10] Social life was rich and varied, including sports clubs, social clubs, dances, picnics, carnivals, and variety shows.[11] Small parishes could support a wide range of activities because they served as the central gathering place for parishioners who were united not only by faith but by ethnicity, class, proximity, and family ties. There were also a range of opportunities to deepen one's spiritual life in the company of friends and neighbors, such as Legion of Mary, St. Vincent de Paul, Young Catholic Students, Young Catholic Workers, the Altar Society, the Holy Name Society, Christian Life Community, etc.[12]

Parish-based groups such as these inculturated people into their faith, but so did the whole of parish life. As one theologian puts it, "The living tradition must be passed on at least in part...through festivity, that is, through the live interaction of the community engaged in celebrating its own life."[13] Ethnic urban parishes that drew people not only for mass, spiritual associations, and parties but for novenas, Saturday confession, holy days, parish missions, festivals honoring saints, ethnic traditions, Lenten suppers, and other spiritual-social celebrations formed Catholics in a life centered around the church.

I do not want to suggest that pre–Vatican II ethnic Catholic parishes necessarily would have prepared families to live out the sort of mission given them by John Paul II. Marriages in this era were longer lasting, but it is hard to determine if they were also rooted in self-giving and directed to communion. Families were larger and family life necessarily welcomed more of the marginalized because Catholics themselves were on the margins of American culture, but did they "serve life" as fully as John Paul II suggests they should? The directive to serve society may be better directed to a secure people with the resources to take on the struggles of the poor, rather than to those who are still struggling themselves. The ideal of family as domestic church may have been actualized in ritual practices but not necessarily in depth of faith or service. In sum, identity can be more cultural than religious and does not guarantee radical commitment. Nonetheless, the parishes of an earlier era could count on things that few contemporary parishes can because they were at the center of families' lives. Family, extended family, neighborhood, parish, school, and social network were one, and that integration produced Catholic community and Catholic identity that are uncommon today. American Catholics cannot go back in time and should not discount the good things about contemporary parish life. In fact, one Catholic historian suggests that because we now have to ask what it means to be Catholic, we have a new "opportunity for building a Catholic community based not on ethnicity or on defense, but on religion."[14] Still, we would do well to consider how parishes have changed in order to better understand where we are and what reforms might be necessary to get where we want to be.

The Changing Shape of Parish Life

I want to highlight several aspects of contemporary parish life that impede the realization of Catholic hopes for marriage and family life: upward mobility, a disconnected approach to social justice, and overinvestment in the wrong sorts of activities. I hope to show that aspects of parish life generally understood as positive and progressive — even those that may contribute in some way to the happiness of Catholic lay people — must be questioned if the vision of marriage as a community of disciples working toward communion at home and in the world is to have a fighting chance of capturing the hearts and minds, let alone the lives, of ordinary families.

First, the upward mobility of American Catholics in the last fifty years has been extraordinary, and it has loosened their identification with their parishes. As James Davidson shows using a number of key indicators, "Catholics are now firmly planted in the nation's upper middle class."[15] After World War II, Catholics, like many Americans, left factory jobs to become employees in white-collar companies, moved from urban neighborhoods to suburbs, sent more of their own to college, and saw their family incomes rise.[16] However, they rose faster than Protestants, in part because they had further to go. No longer segregated in Catholic-only neighborhoods, Catholics now live next to, go to school with, work with, befriend, and marry more people of other faiths than ever before.[17] With upward mobility came integration into American middle-class society and a loss of a certain kind of distinctive Catholic identity. Says Catholic historian James

Fisher, "By the 1990s it appeared that Catholics truly were 'like everyone else' in the U.S., but it was not entirely clear just what made them Catholic."[18] If Dorothy Day was once attracted to the Catholic Church because she saw in it working-class and poor believers devoted to their church, today she would see a very different reality.[19]

Parishes have also become upwardly mobile. Many parishes have new buildings to accommodate a growing range of activities, new gyms for extensive sports programs, and paid, professional staff to do what used to be done by priests or volunteers.[20] Parishes are bigger, too, to accommodate larger suburban populations. Though about one-quarter of parishes are small, having fewer than five hundred members, the average parish today has twenty-five hundred members, and one-quarter count more than three thousand.[21] Parishes have to respond to the demands of parishioners, and those parishioners are increasingly middle- and upper-middle-class suburbanites for whom the parish is one of many loyalties. Most families do not see their parish as their primary source of community, but they are not disturbed by this.[22] They are more invested elsewhere, and parishes are not providing a compelling alternative.

Social mobility has transformed many aspects of parish life, including parish efforts for social justice. In the early twentieth century, Catholics often were poor, and their parishes both met their needs and brought together a network of families who could share resources and responsibilities. Modest lifestyles were common because most people could not afford anything else. People in parishes needed each other for social and spiritual support. They suffered no illusions about their independence. They knew firsthand the struggle of poverty, and they could have identified with the poor masses identified in Catholic social documents of the time, though they were much more likely to work on those struggles in the labor movement or various incarnations of Catholic Action than read or learn about them in theory.

When Catholics moved into the middle classes, social justice became something removed from everyday existence. Most no longer came to a parish seeking social support. Although most stay in their neighborhood parish, they do not feel compelled to either by tradition, ethnicity, class, or need. Financially comfortable younger Catholics today choose the parish they like, one that will help in their quest for greater spiritual growth and their desire to do something for others, others who probably do not live in their neighborhood.[23] Half of all parishes do engage in at least some direct social ministry and one-third engage in some advocacy,[24] and Catholics generally support this. But few parishioners are involved in these efforts in a significant way, and half believe one can be a good Catholic without doing anything for the poor.[25] Most are sympathetic to the social teachings of the universal church: 82 percent say charity is important (in theory), 71 percent agree that God is present in the poor in a special way.[26] They are proud that their church takes prophetic stands on social issues. Yet working for social justice seems to be an option for some, one possible way to live out one's faith rather than part of life in an interdependent community with needs of its own.

Troubling as it may be for church leaders to acknowledge, most Catholics make decisions about how to spend their time and money without guidance from their parishes. In fact, contemporary Catholics are largely satisfied with their parishes and rate them high on friendliness, average on meeting their spiritual needs, but lowest on helping them with ethical questions related to their daily lives at home and work.[27] Parishes provide spiritual nourishment and social interaction, but do not play a central role in their lives, and most are comfortable with this arrangement.

In truth, the structure of middle-class American life does not allow for very much direct involvement in parishes. More families are balancing two careers (or one career and one parent), multiple schools more likely to be farther from home than the neighborhood parish,[28] more children's activities that require more driving, and more hectic hours at home when chores, homework, family time, and extra work from professional jobs have to be squeezed into a very small number of hours each day. Schools may require service hours for children and work may involve service for parents, but most of this service benefits the middle-class communities in which already privileged families live. All of this leaves very little time for living out the vision of communion that John Paul II calls families to accept.

Due to this time-crunched situation, parishes made up of middle- and upper-middle-class families have a difficult task. Parishioners are sympathetic but unable to commit. They are willing to be members of the church, but not willing to place the church at the center of their lives. Although 81 percent of Catholics still say that being Catholic is an important part of who they are, only 44 percent say the church is most important, and only 37 percent attend mass weekly.[29] Among the youngest generation, the millennial Catholics, only 40 percent say religion is important in their daily lives.[30] For most, the parish experience is something that fits into middle-class culture rather than challenging its terms. That is why they are satisfied with it, even though it has little effect on how they live.

Parishes themselves tend to add to the problem by overinvesting in activities that do not directly pertain to the mission of the families. Parishes offer plenty for families to do,[31] but little of it would be of help to married couples trying to actualize the Christian vision of marriage. It is not that these ministries are bad. CYO sports programs provide a values-centered recreation experience for kids. Men's and women's groups socialize and serve the parish. Religious education programs for children rely on the generosity of committed parent teachers who try their best to pass on the faith they love. Service opportunities to bring food, clothes, or money for the needy are valuable. However, in nearly all cases, spouses are separate from each other, parents are separated from children, siblings are drawn apart. While separate activities are no doubt sometimes necessary and even beneficial, it is disturbing that few programs exist to bring spouses or families together to discuss how to live out their lives as disciples of Christ. Outside of mass, where can married couples or families learn, pray, or serve together?

Parish activities in the middle-class American parish are also more likely to contradict the church's call to families to live more simply out of solidarity with the oppressed. Social events require large investments of parishioners' time and, increasingly, their money.[32] Fundraisers like auctions, dances, and golf tournaments raise money for good causes but are costly to put on and attend. It is not clear how central they are to forming Christian community and Christian families. They seem to mimic the culture rather than building an alternative. John Paul II claims that a commitment to live simply is part of a family's mission to serve life. How is his countercultural plea to be heard when parishes themselves ask for more money from their parishioners and seem to encourage high-end entertainment? In addition, time spent on social activities takes away from time that could be spent in service. Listen to the lists of what most parish families do on the weekends: almost all include public participation in the pursuits of middle-class communities, but very few include service to those who are truly needy. Do middle-class parishes truly build up Christian marriages and families?

Some claim that they do. Andrew and Mary Greeley write with great appreciation of contemporary parish life, with affection for sports teams, open gyms, dances, youth clubs, shows, golf and bowling leagues, card groups, tennis, and socials offered by parishes. They assert that "people will better appreciate the sacramentality of all their experiences when they learn to appreciate the sacramental possibilities of playing."[33] Surely the Greeleys are right to remind us that "discover[ing] the supernatural in the midst of the natural" is a central part of being Catholic. Yet it seems to me that this is not all Christian families are called to do. The task of being Christian in a secular, postmodern world is difficult, and if parishes offer more of what the culture provides and fail to challenge parishioners to shape their lives differently than their neighbors', few Christian families will be able to tackle this on their own.

There are, of course, parish activities that do push adult Catholics. They are groups that help people see the connection between their faith and their work, such as Christian Life Communities, Opus Dei, and Legatus.[34] There are Bible study groups, prayer groups, and small faith communities. But the best estimates indicate that only about 5 percent of Catholics are involved in this kind of group.[35] Some shy away from this kind of high-level commitment, while others do not find it offered in their parishes, but I wonder how many might be drawn to it if their lives were not so consumed by other activities far less essential to living out their faith. Something in parish culture allows most Catholics to assume that they need not take up this challenge, that their efforts in sports, religious education, and social events are central to being Catholic but discerning how to live with others in community is not. Even as they ask too much of Catholic families in some ways, Catholic parishes may be asking far too little of families in others, creating a culture in which deep wrestling with how to live simply does not happen.

All of this creates a particularly difficult situation for married couples and for families. The relationships of communion the church wants them to sustain are threatened by social mobility in parishes, by an increasingly distant approach to social justice, and by overinvestment in activities not directed to their ultimate good.

Suggestions for Reshaping Parish Life

Sustaining marriage in the church has to be about much more than keeping couples who are Christian together and happy. It must also be about sustaining marriages that are Christ-centered. Michael Warren writes with frustration about middle- and upper-class parishes that ignore the Jesus who stood with the poor and emphasize a Jesus who offers self-affirmation and self-aggrandizement. "We end up with a Jesus who affirms our culturally conditioned aspirations, not the Jesus who embraced the lepers and who was condemned and eventually criminalized for healing the blind on the Sabbath. All of us...need to embrace, not just any Jesus but Him who calls us to the hard choices of discipleship in our day."[36] Warren may be overly conscious of the social-political significance of Christ's message, but his remarks about the lukewarm faith of most middle-class parishes merit consideration. One of the most important things parishes can do for married couples is to call them to live out their married lives as a Christian calling. This will not mean downplaying the significance of marriage and family, but striving to transform them in light of contemporary Catholic theology of communion.

First, parishes should encourage upwardly mobile Catholic spouses to critically reflect on the pace of their lives. All who work at home or outside it need space to think about the place of work in their lives. Parents in particular need to be in conversation with other parents about how much activity is too much. If marriages and families are to be sustained, time to be together without hurry is crucial. The communion between the spouses that John Paul II seeks cannot come about when spouses are too busy, both outside the home and in it, to pay attention to the other. Parents and children need to be encouraged to spend time in conversation and play. When children are routinely playing on multiple sports teams each season, when so many suburban streets are empty in the afternoons because activities and homework consume all available free time, it is the churches' responsibility to help their members let go of certain middle-class assumptions about what makes a good life and remember the virtues of home.

Second, parishes and pastors should be encouraged to develop ties that bond parishioners more closely in community, whether it is local or not. Without strong community, Catholics lack a place to be nourished and challenged in ways that will help them stand apart from the excesses of American middle-class life. Instead of offering activities that focus on entertainment, parishes might encourage parishioners to share skills, start babysitting co-ops, visit the sick or elderly in their own community, mentor young married couples, or start a community garden. My colleague David McCarthy writes that a wedding binds a couple closer together and binds the two more closely together in the church.[37] How much more should the parish bind couples together and bind them to their friends in Christ. This is not going to happen if parishioners see each other only at St. Patrick's Day dances and parish carnivals. They need ways to serve each other and they need ways to come together around common interests more significant than their own good. Then their sense of communion will grow.

Third, when parishes do ask a lot of parishioners, it should be for worthwhile endeavors. Central to parish life should be the development of small faith-sharing groups where married couples and single parents can reflect on the struggles of marriage, divorce, intermarriage, and parenting. Without such explicit reflection in community, it is unlikely that Christian marriages will look much different from others. Perhaps during the subculture era such groups were unnecessary because the whole of parish life communicated a distinctive message. Today, when commitments are most diffuse and the culture is in many ways more at odds with Christian life, intentional community building and reflection is more important than ever for sustaining Christian marriages.

Fourth, place opportunities for prayer and service at the center of parish life for families. Parish life before Vatican II included more shared prayer at weekly masses, daily mass, holy days, and ethnic celebrations. Groups such as the Holy Name Society, Sodality, the Christian Family Movement, Marriage Encounter, and Christian Life Communities, which combined spiritual and social fellowship, were much more widely supported. Outside of the liturgy, the contemporary context might call for different forms for shared spiritual experience, but it is crucial that they receive more attention than other sorts of activities. Service should share the center of parish life. If parishioners' energies are not tapped out from social activities and sports, they may be more available for service, not just a once or twice a year delivery of food baskets or presents, but ongoing commitments to people in need. The connection between the spiritual life and social justice cannot be overestimated. True worship is impossible without a context of care for others, especially the poor, and without consciousness of a community's own poverty. It "emerges out of the conviction of one's own poverty and connectedness to that of others."[38] It is precisely the recognition of human vulnerability that comes to us in service to the marginalized that makes possible spiritual growth of true discipleship. This connection must be taught in parishes and, hopefully, brought back into the home.

Finally, the intentional approach to Christian family life that is implicit in my other suggestions only makes sense in a culture in which Christian discipleship is imbued and absorbed. Michael Warren insightfully points out that Catholic parishes count on religious education programs to pass on the faith. However, one hour a week of religious education is far from sufficient when "not integral to the lived life of actual communities.... The main formative agent is the believing community, and, its verbal declarations notwithstanding, its communal or corporate commitments and way of viewing reality are, for better or worse, the key formative factors." What a community does with its time, people, and money says who it is. When much of a community's life is lost, catechists bear the burden of passing on the faith without the life. The tradition must be embodied and practiced in a rich variety of ways if it is to shape the marriages of contemporary believers.

This is the most profound challenge parishes face: finding new ways to embody a tradition in which many if not most of its families have not been inculturated. If parishes strive to become places of serious transformation, families that spring from Christian marriages will have a fighting chance of becoming what they are called to be.

Chapter Five

Living the Dream

David Matzko McCarthy

The challenge that I will identify in this essay has to do with the contrast between how we and our contemporaries celebrate marriage and what is entailed in sustaining its practice. Marriage, in the dominant view of our culture, marks the success of a private relationship, but the practical character of married life appears too weighty for many of these isolated relationships to be sustained. In the face of challenges to marriage, we are quick to turn to shoring up and emphasizing the sexual and interpersonal ideals of nuptial union. I suggest that we decenter these interpersonal goods, not for the sake of some other foundation, but to set marriage within a network of social and interpersonal practices. In our pastoral approach to sustaining marriage, we may benefit from highlighting connections between marriage and the Catholic social tradition and to thinking about marriage and family as dependent on subsidiary associations of households and neighborhoods.

One Challenge (Among Many)

There are many challenges for Catholics in celebrating and sustaining marriage in our time. As I stated in the introduction, I would like to focus on one: the widening gap between celebrating marriage and sustaining it, or in less positive terms, between idealizing and practicing it. Marriage continues to be celebrated as an ideal in American culture, but it is not sustained as a practical necessity for attaining the goods of life that are traditionally connected to marriage. Sexual relations, interpersonal intimacy, sharing and maintaining a household (interpersonally and financially), and having children are now not only independent of marriage, but also independent of each other. Marriage has shifted, from a context through which these goods develop as a whole way of life, to an ideal — a sign of achievement —

when these independent goods of sex, personal intimacy, household maintenance, and parenting are attained separately and then brought together as a whole. According to the predominant view in our culture, marriage is an ideal that marks an endpoint of personal achievement rather than a social form through which a couple begins a course of life.

This contrast between "endpoint of achievement" and "starting point for a course of life" is not controversial (as far as I can tell) among sociologists of marriage and family, and it fits with various contemporary phenomena like the fact that the majority of couples that decide to be married are already living together, that cohabiting couples — when they marry — are more likely to divorce, and that marriage is less likely the lower one's income and job security.[1] For example, a team of sociologists studied the decline of marriage among poor unmarried parents, and it found that marriage continues to be an ideal.[2] In fact, the researchers claim that the ideal of marriage and the standards for *thinking* about getting married are higher than decades ago, precisely because marriage is disconnected from having children and living together.[3] A higher quality of relationship and more stable financial assets (including a modest home and the ability to pay for a "decent" wedding) are seen not as things that are attained during the course of a marriage, but rather as prerequisites for marriage.[4]

A recent study of the relationship between cohabitation and marriage puts this practical shift in terms of how a relationship is supposed to change once a couple is married.[5] Not long ago, conventional wisdom held that cohabitating couples were likely to marry because they thought marriage would "change their lives." Through vows and a public ceremony, it was assumed that the couple would hope to move the relationship to a "higher level" of trust and commitment. The latest studies, in contrast, "suggest that cohabitors believe marriage should occur once something has already changed" in terms of financial assets and relationship quality.[6] Andrew Cherlin (a sociologist at Johns Hopkins) argues that this decline of the practical necessity of marriage can be called its "deinstitutionalization."[7] Marriage is no longer a social context that defines one's social contributions and personal life course; instead, in broad cultural terms, it is a symbolic marker of prestige. "Marriage is a status one builds up to, often by living with a partner beforehand, by attaining steady employment or starting a career, by putting away some savings, and even by having children."[8]

The Deinstitutionalization of Marriage

Cherlin argues that the deinstitutionalization of marriage contributes to its elevation as a symbolic goal for individuals. Marriage, he claims, "has been transformed from a familial and communal institution to an individualized, choice-based achievement."[9] This transformation has occurred amid various social, historical, and economic factors. It is tempting to dwell on these developments at length (as there is a great deal of material to draw from) and to attempt to identify a key reason for the decline of marriage (and find a simple way to restore marriage as the norm). I must admit, for example, that I am drawn to the work of Stephanie Coontz in *Marriage, a History,* where she argues that the sentimentalized and sexualized "love-based" marriage of the modern era has eroded marriage from within.[10] She shows that marriage becomes an ideal of passion and intimacy that seldom can be sustained over time. In a sense, Coontz reverses Cherlin's point of emphasis, and the two sets of arguments complement one another. While Cherlin holds that the deinstitutionalization of marriage heightens its role as an individual's personal ideal, Coontz argues that romantic conceptions of love that emerged in the nineteenth and twentieth centuries in order to buttress and elevate the institution of marriage actually contribute to its displacement by the free-floating love match.[11] The "pure relationship" is prior to and defines marriage.[12]

This connection between the idealization of the pure relationship and the deinstitutionalization of marriage is complex. Marriage cannot be simply "reinstitutionalized." Nor can we discount the goods of companionate marriage. In order to avoid oversimplification, I will quickly review various trends that form a web of challenges to marriage — specifically in terms of divorce and cohabitation. With the rise in cohabitation, fewer couples are getting married, and still the current divorce rate is just about 40 percent.[13] The reasons for divorce are typically divided into three areas: a spouse's profile or relational resumé (matters as divergent as issues of alcoholism or whether a spouse's parents are divorced), interpersonal skills (which tend to correlate with education and class), and socioeconomic factors, including the independence of women and financial stress and insecurity (among the poor).[14] These three sets of factors make the problem of deinstitutionalization complex.

Consider the socioeconomic factors. Stephanie Coontz seems to make too little of the fact that the development of high standards of passion and companionship corresponds to the increase and eventual dominance of the industrial economy. The institution of marriage is challenged not only by the idealization of the love match, but also by the gradual disappearance of the household economy. In this context, the financial independence of women from marriage (in the 1960s and 1970s) simply follows several decades of the social and economic independence of men from the household.[15] The social role of the household becomes, in the early twentieth century, the role of women.[16] Once the household is gendered in a private sphere, the social role of the household, as well as traditional divisions of labor within the family, will be difficult to sustain. In this way, the industrial economy and contractual politics contributes to the deinstitutionalization of the family. The public man is defined outside of the home, and decades later the public woman is freed from the domestic sphere as well.

With no inherited roles, family relations must be created anew for every marriage, and a greater burden is set upon interpersonal skills and (what I have called) one's relational resumé. It is fair to say that the failure of companionate marriages might be due to a foolish romanticism. Many couples preparing for marriage will have a casual attitude toward questions of practical compatibility because only love should matter. Or they will avoid practical questions altogether because they are worried about what might matter other than love. But this romantic standard is hardly the whole story. Two additional (perhaps more fundamental) points should be made.

First, we live in a culture where, according to Robert Bellah, individualism is our primary language of social interaction.[17] The primacy of individualism does not mean that we avoid social roles and service to the common good, but that we have a great deal of difficulty explaining or justifying why we do contribute to common life. We tend to reduce our social participation to individualist categories. As private family relations are quickly reduced to therapeutic and market individualism, major decisions in parenting — like finding a preschool, for example — are sometimes reduced to résumé building and competing with the child's peers. The same holds for companionship in marriage. Romantic relationships are usually understood in terms of what Bellah calls expressive and utilitarian individualism, so that it is often difficult to conceptualize marriage in terms of a common good. Spouses can easily slip into a competition for time and resources. Marriage becomes a burden to the individual's good.

A second point follows: companionate marriage has an uneasy relationship to the practical demands of the home.[18] Whether or not a lovestruck couple avoids practical issues, the "institutional" features of a marriage are likely to be hard to manage. If marriage has been deinstitutionalized, then the division of labor and the home economy has to be worked out by each couple from the preferences that emerge from within their companionship. Amid this negotiation, it is not likely to be clear how our relational résumés and relationship skills translate to the household maintenance and parenting. And it is not likely to be clear until a couple has shared a household for a number of years. Often a couple will settle into a disjunction between the stated equality of companionship and an inequality of roles in the gendered domestic sphere.[19] Women frequently carry the burden of both relationship quality and housework.[20] The high rate of domestic violence, especially among cohabitors, seems to be evidence of a wide disjunction between "the love-match" and roles within the relationship.[21]

Cohabitation, at one time, seemed to be a promising avenue for working out the transitions from romantic love to the home and from traditional household roles to new ones. While many unmarried couples live together with these purposes in the background, cohabitation, by and large, has not improved the transition from companionship to marriage. It seems that living together for any given couple is two things at once. It is typical to divide practices of living together according to whether a couple sees cohabitation as a step toward or an alternative to marriage. However, in both cases, cohabitation provides opportunity for "marriage-like" intimacy and support *and* for freedom from commitment and the binding, enforceable trust of marriage.[22] Even among those thinking about marriage, living together often presents a confusing combination of "the low commitment norms governing dating relationships and the high commitment norms attached to marriage."[23] What seems like a contradiction might not be understood as one from the point of view of the cohabitors. If the trust and steadfast love of marriage are deinstitutionalized, then true commitment will have to emerge out of low commitment norms. True commitment, according to this view, cannot have its foundation in the institution of marriage. Marriage should only confirm steadfast love. The result is that "in the United States, roughly half [of cohabitating unions] end within the first year, and only 1 out of 10 lasts 5 or more years."[24]

Meeting the Challenge

Given the failure of the modern "relationship" to sustain marriage, meeting the challenge requires that we find a way to draw back from idealizing the interpersonal union and to enhance the institutional and social roles of the household. The task will be difficult if, indeed, modern marriage is being eroded from within. An image used by Willard Quine (on a different matter) comes to mind: "if we are to rebuild it, we must rebuild plank by plank while staying afloat in it."[25] The Catholic tradition is well suited to attending to the social nature of the home, insofar as family plays a fundamental role in Catholic social teaching. Drawing back from the interpersonal ideal may be a bit more difficult to imagine. This difficulty can be attributed, in large part, to the deinstitutionalization of home (following the analysis above). However, the idealization of the interpersonal relationship is connected also, ironically, to the social role of family.

Family, today, has become central to understanding social relations in Catholic social thought. Mass production, the industrial economy, our current electronic age, mass politics (which translates to rule by a new aristocracy[26]), and contractual individualism conspire to undermine what we Catholics call subsidiary institutions, not only by taking over the function of local associations but also by reducing these institutions, when they still exist, to economic, utilitarian, and contractual relations.[27] Family has been and continues to be a (the?) key subsidiary institution because it has resisted being defined in utilitarian and economic terms. It represents what Catholic thought proposes for other institutions and the whole of society: it embodies an organic sense of social relations. Within the modern social and economic environment, however, family has resisted utilitarian and contractual relations by an appeal to companionate love and the interpersonal wholeness and integrity of the nuptial union.

The appeal to companionate love is to be expected. *Gaudium et Spes*, for example, repeatedly appeals to love to counterbalance materialist and individualist trends.[28] In the face of modern technology and social change, proper "socialization" is defined as "personalization" (no. 6). Love is a central idea. The human intellect is marked by "a quest and love for what is true and good" (no. 15); conscience is a "summoning...to love good and avoid evil" (no. 16), and the social order, when directed to the common good, is "animated by love" (no. 26). This first part of the document begins with an assertion that the human being is social by nature, and the basis for this claim is Genesis 1:27. "But God did not create man as a solitary. For from the beginning 'male and female he created them' " (no. 12).

In a context where contractual and utilitarian relationships are dominant, the nuptial union has become a social body in itself. Based on interpersonal love, marriage in popular parlance has become the basis for family rather than its extension. When we marry, we "start" a family. At the end of the nineteenth century, however, Leo XIII's appeal to family is indispensable but less expansive. He holds that family is a basic social unit among others with reciprocal responsibilities, and, by doing so, counters individualist (Locke's) and socialist conceptions of property and a laissez faire capitalist (Smith's) conception of wage. A century later, the family's social role expands; it has become *the* socializing agent of society.

For John Paul II, it is the "civilization of love" and site for the "genealogy of persons."[29] But at the same time, nuptial union, as the foundation of family, has become idealized; the ideal of total self-giving counters the meaningless sex of our dominant culture with sex as an ultimate experience of authentic interpersonal union.[30] Sexual intercourse has become sacramental, and nuptial union has become a seamless conceptual framework.[31] It has become a theoretical answer as much as it's a practical problem.[32] The popularity of the theology of the body trades on a vision of purity and total self-giving that stands apart from messiness, not only of the meaningless sex, but also of "mutual self-giving love over a lifetime."[33] While nuptial personalism counters meaningless sex, it heightens the popular idealization of marriage that corresponds to its deinstitutionalization, marriage as "the pure relationship" or as "an exalted and spiritual union of souls."[34]

Could it be that we will do our best work to restore marriage by drawing back from a focus of companionate love and its role in "socializing" society? I do not mean that we should minimize either the goods of nuptial union or family as a "social body." Rather, these goods may have to be decentered, removed from the center point of marriage, not for the sake of some other center point, but for the sake of a web of social institutions and reciprocal relationships of which marriage and family can be a vital part.[35] In short, the best way to reinstitutionalize marriage may be to focus on other subsidiary institutions and social networks that provide a rich environment for families to flourish. When networks of families flourish, marriage may follow. We have to find a way to free marriage from the burden of starting "family" from scratch. To return to the plank-and-boat analogy from the beginning of this section, the problem may be that we are conceiving of marriage as its own interpersonal boat. Once moored to rich social networks, we may be able to rebuild it plank by plank while keeping it afloat.

Marriage and Social Networks

Most of our pastoral approaches to marriage include attention to community and social networks but such considerations are usually tangential, attached to a focus on the relationship between partners. For instance, we recommend volunteer work for couples in their later years that are experiencing an "empty nest" and are trying "[to let] go of the old patterns and roles of their life together."[36] This approach seems to be typical. As "volunteer" activity, social participation is an instrumental relationship to marriage (even though it does have an essential relationship to being an individual citizen). There is no suggestion that a couple's social role could actually sustain the marriage, which seems, instead, to require social autonomy. More consideration needs to be given to the kind of neighborhoods, wider friendships, and social endeavors that create an environment where marriage and family might flourish. Even this way of putting the matter falls short. We should attend to how social cooperation and neighborhood networks are part of marriage and how enlivening of common life in neighborhood, town, and parish is an important route to marriage enrichment.[37]

What do I mean by "social cooperation and neighborhood networks" as part of marriage? The first thing to say is that they are local and intermediate — that is, household networks are subsidiary forms of association. The U.S. bishops' website *For Your Marriage* includes an inventory: "Are you walking with the same moral compass?"[38] The quiz includes household matters like raising and educating children, along with tough issues like tithing, living simply (resisting consumerism), paying taxes (signaling attitudes toward the common good), and our responsibility to help others. The tenor of the social questions is certainly good, but it seems to be weighted toward national and global issues (e.g., broad environmental concerns and working on political campaigns). The survey along with contemporary accounts of marriage tends to reflect the general thinning out of social life (noted in 1931 by Pius XI) to relationships between individual and state. Like the worker in the modern economy, marriage has become a matter for individuals, and individual marriages are left isolated and vulnerable. In *Quadragesimo anno*, Pius XI counters individualism and the division of society into (self-)interest groups with what he calls "functional" associations. Likewise the functions of marriage and family give rise to functional, intermediate organizations.

Too often, we think about the household as simply a unit of consumption. But even in our postindustrial age, the household has a natural economy. Food acquisition, storage, and preparation, cleaning clothes, house and yard cleaning and maintenance, childcare and education, the basics of health care (well care), leisure pursuits (as forms of culture), and the need for social embeddedness and common endeavors are all basic practices of family.[39] On the one hand, these practices are often considered the purview of isolated, autonomous families; on the other hand, every one of these activities can be purchased on the market and not developed within family. Apart from these two poles, we might begin to think of the practical matters of marriage and family in terms of neighborhood and parish economies. When all is said and done, we should think of local economies, not in terms of volunteer work and charity, but as common activities directed to common goods. However, Catholic Charities at the diocesan level, with its array of social networks and attention to the needs of households, might be the place to start. With meal services to the elderly, food banks, and assistance and development programs for at-risk children families, we are not far from food and childcare cooperatives. We just need to get around the idea that healthy families do not need social and economic cooperation. In any case, the point is to think about marriage in terms of intermediate institutions that enrich marriage and family life — in a social and economic setting that leaves marriages "isolated and defenseless."[40]

The proposal is hardly imaginable. Already families tend to cooperate in leisure activities (particularly sports), and although "cooperation" often does overcome social segregation and class divisions, it too often mimics market competition. Schools, both public and Catholic, are subsidiary institutions insofar as they are operated at the county or diocesan level. However, our schools too often reflect social and economic divisions of our cities and suburbs. It is part of American upward mobility to have the freedom to disengage from common life.[41] Our best efforts at social participation have difficulty overcoming the privatization of suburbs and the isolation of urban neighborhoods. Further, subsidiary institutions along with marriage and family have difficulty surviving the contemporary rationing of time. Work- and market-based activities (for both the working and middle class) are dominating the hours of our weeks and days.[42] Marriage and family, in order to flourish, may require a "downsizing" of their dependence upon the market and their lifestyle ambitions.

In short, the divisions of space and time in contemporary life are working against marriage and family, and to sustain and enrich the household, we are undertaking the work, in general, of creating social time and space. The "reinstitutionalization" of marriage corresponds to developing a greater sense of social participation in our lives as a whole.

Conclusion: Telling the Story

I should conclude with the positive trajectory of how we Catholics tell the story of marriage. I began the essay with a contemporary challenge to marriage, that marriage continues to be an ideal, but it has lost its practical significance. In our culture, speaking broadly, marriage no longer is seen as the setting where the traditional goods of marriage are achieved. Rather, it is considered an end point, subsequent to developing a passionate and intimate relationship, maintaining a home, and, often enough, raising children. The idealization of marriage as a version of the "pure relationship" seems to parallel its deinstitutionalization, and typically, the pure relationship cannot sustain the steadfast love and mutual care that we associate with marriage.

As I have noted frequently, we Catholics think about marriage as a social institution, and perhaps we need to be more attentive to how we allow what Stephanie Coontz calls the "sentimentalization" and "sexualization" of marriage to take the place of what I have called the subsidiary economy of household, neighborhood, and parish. The U.S. Conference of Catholic Bishops and dioceses throughout the country are active in promoting the institution of family through issues such as the just wage, health care reform, housing, food and nutrition programs, immigration, family farming, and the needs of farm workers. All of these issues bear on the household and need to be integrated with how we think about marriage and family. We might want to think about shifting the "face to face" orientation of theories about marriage to a "side by side" work of household and community life. We might shift our language of companionship to our (Augustinian and Thomist) traditions of friendship, where friends share a vision of the good, see the (transcendent) good in the other, engage the good in a network of friends, and journey together in order to share this common good.

As we tell the story of marriage, we are fully aware that sex and sentimental companionship will not sustain a marriage. We tell the story of the movement from romance to disillusionment to mature love, and from practical negotiations of the newly married, to the middle years of active parenting, to the later years of the empty nest.[43] We know that the challenges of every stage of marriage are practical. Note this description of the disillusionment stage from the U.S. bishops' website *For Your Marriage*:

> Disillusionment can arise out of silly little things such as fixating on the personality quirks or annoying habits of your spouse. Does she chatter on about insignificant details while you are trying to read the sports page? Does he fuss that your cleaning efforts aren't up to his standards?
>
> The most common (and perhaps troubling) disillusionment, however, often is phrased as "I just don't know if I love him (her) anymore." It's usually accompanied by a general feeling of loss of excitement and passion for your spouse. You wonder where the romantic feelings of earlier days went. Life might be OK. Nothing tragic or earth shattering has happened, but it all just seems dull or boring. Is this all that marriage is supposed to be?[44]

To meet this challenge (as well as challenges of other stages) the couple is advised (in ways appropriate to the severity of the problem) to join together in common work on their interpersonal relationship. Unquestionably, the advice is sound. However, it is not the whole story. The most life-giving marriages may be among couples who are able to live outside of themselves, who shift the enormous interpersonal weight of marriage on to the social side of their shared life. They might even shift interpersonal burdens on to other friends. In doing so, they may be able to see the relative insignificance of annoying habits or require less of their very ordinary sexual relationship. By investing in neighborhood and parish, they may not only enrich the common good and other families, but their own marriages as well. In short, we might close the gap between the ideal of marriage and its practical insignificance by understanding marriage, not as a "pure relationship," but as a social space for working out a practical ideal.

Chapter Six

Spirituality and the Family Life Cycle

FLORENCE CAFFREY BOURG

MANY COUPLES, much as they might like to, will not find much time to attend a marriage encounter retreat, read books on marriage and spirituality, attend lectures, and such — especially if these extra events don't provide childcare. *The church needs to make better use of outlets people already participate in.* We need to instigate occasions for families and couples to begin these reflections, and we need to hear their questions, concerns, and testimonials — even within the liturgy. This may entail rethinking the way we use the pulpit and our sense of proper decorum during liturgy.

Most Catholics don't experience much deliberate support for marriage in parish life. Participants in focus groups gathered to inform the U.S. bishops' pastoral letter on marriage noted that virtually any parish activity, if well-designed, could support marriage, even if that is not the primary purpose of the event.[1] Thus far, it seems many opportunities aren't recognized. Besides marriage preparation and the wedding liturgy itself, as Paul Covino has explained,[2] teachable moments are available during liturgy (especially on Sundays), Catholic school religious formation, required service experiences for high school students and confirmands, parish religious education, parent meetings at Catholic schools, young adult groups like CYO or Theology on Tap, parental preparation for children's sacraments, funerals, or anointing of the sick in a parish context. Opportunities exist even at events such as parish festivals or Catholic school football games.

Before recommending some ways to capitalize on these opportunities, I will explore two fundamental concerns that, in my opinion, sabotage our efforts to cultivate a rich Christian spirituality encompassing marriage and family life. One has a long history in Catholicism; the other is relatively new.

Ranking of Vocations /
Division of Sacred and Secular Life

We need to scrutinize deeply ingrained habits of idealizing "sacredness," "holiness," "religious life," etc. in ways that don't encompass daily activities of married life and family relationships. For many Catholics, these expressions bring to mind clergy, religious sisters, institutional worship, and quasi-institutional devotional practices — modeled upon the celibate lifestyle.[3] When my students study marriage, one of the tools I employ is a photocopy of the 1962 illustrated *Baltimore Catechism*, specifically the lesson on vocations. The text and the visual images are startling. Three pairs of pictures, meant to contrast "secular" life with "religious" life based on the evangelical counsels, are grouped under headings: on the left, "This is Good"; on the right, "This is Better." The pictures on the right show priests and vowed religious sisters and brothers; those on the left show the "secular life." For the pair of pictures depicting chastity, a sister dressed in a habit kneels before a glowing crucifix and says, "I choose Christ as my spouse." The accompanying picture on the left shows a couple at their wedding: "I want to marry the person of my choice." On the right, illustrating the vow of obedience, two men in cassocks read a list of assignments on a bulletin board, commenting, "I want to spend the day the way God prefers." On the left, a picture of a family at the breakfast table (with Mother pouring the milk for Father) is captioned, "I want to spend the day the way I think best." For poverty: on the left, a group of children look in a store window: "I want an air rifle. I want a car. I want jewels. I want pretty clothes." On the right, St. Francis kneels before an appearance of Jesus floating in a cloud: "You can have all that: I want Christ." The lesson never fails to provoke an uproar from my students, who insist marriage is no less holy than other lifestyles. But, truth be told, in their usual "default mode" of thinking, my students adopt essentially the same approach as this catechism lesson.

A disheartening, but revealing incident shows what I have in mind. While covering monasticism in a Catholic high school church history course in 2006, I asked my sophomores to tell me whom they considered to be "holy" people. They named the few religious sisters who worked at the school. I asked, "Do we have any other holy people at this school — any other faculty? Are there any holy students — even one?" There followed an awkward silence. The students were unable to name any other holy people at our school. We had plenty of good people at our school, perhaps, but not holy people. Eventually, someone nominated a girl who was considered holy (by association) because she was the daughter of a Baptist minister. (Others disagreed and said she wasn't holy because she got too many detentions.) I repeated the exercise this past week with two more classes and got similar results. Asked to name holy people, my sophomores immediately named saints, priests, popes, bishops, nuns, brothers, apostles, Mary, Joseph, and Jesus. The juniors began with virtually the same list, until one of them inquired, with a tone of uncertainty, "Wait! Can't people like your grandmother be holy too?" I asked the sophomores to name holy people at our school, and they first named the religious sisters, then added a nursery school teacher. When I asked if we had any holy students, three girls were named, who, it was reported, regularly to go to church. When asked to name holy activities or behaviors, the sophomores cited (in this order): praying, going to church, communion, praying the rosary, going to confession, singing hymns, helping the poor, not sinning — being careful — not going wild, kneeling, and lastly, making good choices. The juniors cited, in order: Bible reading, praying, going to church, doing nice things without being asked, and doing good deeds. I asked the students, Is marriage holy? If so, why? The sophomores said marriage was holy because it happens in a church, you get your kids baptized, and you can go to church together. The juniors (some of whom covered marriage with me last year as sophomores) were initially divided on this point. "Isn't a wedding just a party?" one objected. "Marriage is a sacrament, right?" another inquired. After some discussion, they concluded marriage can be holy for some people, but it isn't holy for everyone. When asked to elaborate about why marriage could be holy, the juniors' first responses were: marriage is "through God"; the couple is connected with God; the wedding is a special ceremony — but that's not exactly the same as the marriage; and if you have a kid, you should be married. In another session, while covering Manicheism, I asked sophomores if activities like eating, having sex, raising children, or working were equally holy as activities like silent contemplation, prayer, and discussion of scripture. The students were somewhat conflicted. Many seemed to think the behaviors in the first group weren't evil, but they weren't holy either. One student described them as "neutral." However, several said the first group of activities was just as holy as the second, because God designed us to eat, have children, work, and so forth. One girl said, "I consider the first group just as holy as the second, but I'm sure the church [by this she seemed to mean Catholic clergy] would disagree."

What can we conclude from these little "focus groups"? For many of my high school students, a lifestyle associated with "holiness" is hardly attainable, or even desirable. Meanwhile, lifestyles considered "normal" and "good," lifestyles they intend to imitate, aren't associated with "holiness." As one student put it, they're "neutral." My students' instinct is to associate "holiness" not with the activities that occupy most of their time, or the time of most married couples and families they know, but with expressions of institutional religion. The idea that "holiness" encompasses one's entire lifestyle, or one's entire marriage, appears mostly as an afterthought (particularly among the sophomores). It isn't what I call their default mode of thinking. I suspect there are adults who think the same way. My students associate "holiness" foremost with priests, religious sisters, and well-known saints — who seem quite different from most people my students know, particularly because they're unmarried and presumably have no desire to be married.

One might think my students have been reading John Paul II's *Familiaris Consortio* (no. 16), which says of consecrated virginity or celibacy, "the Church, throughout her history, has always defended the superiority of this charism to that of marriage, by reason of the wholly singular link which it has with the kingdom of God." Or perhaps my students have been reading the Council of Trent's decree on marriage, which stated, "If anyone says the married state is to be preferred to that of virginity or celibacy, and that it is no better or more blessed to persevere in virginity or celibacy than to be joined in marriage, let him be anathema."[4] I'm quite sure my students haven't actually read these texts. Their default mode of thinking about holiness has become ingrained, through many years of institutional Catholic worship and catechesis, through adopting habits of their elder family members, and perhaps through depictions of "religious" people in popular media.

Is sacramental marriage, as a "sign of Christ's love for the church," objectively inferior to consecrated celibacy "for the sake of the kingdom"? I, for one, would be eager to take part in that theological consultation. Some contemporary Catholics find the ranking of Christian lifestyles a remnant of ancient and medieval cultural preoccupation with social status, one that runs contrary to some key Gospel values (see Mark 9:33–35, Mark 10:35–45, Luke 14:7–11).[5] Because of a narrow image of "holiness" perpetuated by ranking the consecrated celibate lifestyle as superior, people often fail to recognize exemplary Christian role models who don't fit the same paradigm. Moreover, ranking of Christian lifestyles can be counterproductive, for it provides the majority of Christians (who don't feel called to celibacy) a convenient excuse to rationalize a two-tiered interpretation of morality. How easy it is to relieve oneself of the obligation to strive for perfection as a disciple of Jesus when there are full-time professionals assigned to that role! Isn't it the job of priests or nuns to be countercultural, prophetic imitators of Jesus? Isn't common moral decency sufficient for the rest of us? Over my career of high school, undergraduate, and even graduate theological education, I've found such self-excusing is pervasive. Inadvertently, the ranking of Christian lifestyles has contributed to moral minimalism among many Catholics. The dichotomy between sacred and secular life, which Vatican II called "one of the greatest errors of our age,"[6] is still with us more than forty years after the Council.

In a press release from June 2006, Bishop Joseph Kurtz, chairman of the U.S. Catholic Bishops' Marriage and Family Committee, commented on the bishops' marriage initiative by saying: "We pastors need to find *fresh, bold ways* to promote the rich teachings of the Church" (emphasis added).[7] If all options for strengthening Christian marriage, even rather bold ones, are on the table for consideration, the U.S. bishops might lead the way in proposing a reexamination of optional celibacy for Latin-rite Catholic priests. In the 2005 Synod of Bishops on the Eucharist, this proposal was discussed (and eventually tabled),[8] mainly in connection with making the Eucharist more available in places where priests are in short supply. In the future, married priests could be invaluable aides for fostering a rich spirituality of marriage and family among the laity. Perhaps someday, married priests and their spouses could help debunk the misconception that married people aren't expected to pursue holiness on a full-time basis.

In the meantime, the assumption that consecrated celibacy is inherently superior to Christian marriage, and the related premise that "holy" activities are overtly religious ones (ideally taking place in an institutional church setting), make it a challenge to cultivate Christian spirituality encompassing all of marriage and family life. We do indeed need "fresh, bold ways" to convey the church's rich teachings. All the contributors to this volume have presented brilliant articles, books, or lectures on spirituality of marriage and family; the bishops have written some good things too, but much of the richness gets lost somewhere in translation to our fellow believers. *I'm becoming more and more convinced that actions speak louder than words.* Catholics who end up with a "default model" of holiness like that of my students may not be *completely deprived* of exposure to a more holistic model of holiness in their Catholic catechesis, but the problem is that verbal catechesis isn't always reinforced by their observations and concrete practices. When the two don't mesh, people trust their eyes and their lived experience. And their observations and experiences convey the message that what people do in church buildings and devotions, led by "professional, full-time" religious people, is holier than other things they do at home. Even when people find explicit ranking of Christian lifestyles distasteful, they're unpracticed in imagining "religious life" or "holiness" any other way. If we sought more concrete ways for married Catholics and of vowed Catholic celibates to share a *common lifestyle,* perhaps married parishioners and their children would more readily associate their everyday weighing of priorities, their good works and sacrifices, taken up in a spirit of charity, with a lifestyle of holiness. What if the pastor came to the Catholic school parent meeting or the Cub Scout barbecue not just to offer the invocation, but stayed till the end to pick up trash and put away chairs with the moms and dads? What if Catholic parishioners were accustomed to seeing their priests doing yard work for their own residence rather than hiring a lawn care service, or comparing costs and redeeming coupons at the neighborhood grocery store? What if priests made it a point not to take vacations and retreat days beyond the reach of the average family whom they serve? Or what if Catholics were meaningfully invited to determine parish and diocesan budget priorities, just as they do in their households? As I see it, and as people like Julie Rubio have also written, the way we decide how to allocate our time and money speaks volumes about our spiritual and moral priorities. Over time this discernment and decision making form character, more than just about anything else we do. But I'm not sure most Catholics are consciously aware of this connection. This brings me to my next topic: commercialization of marriage.

Romanticizing and Commercializing of Marriage

Marriage preparation ministers encounter couples so preoccupied with wedding day arrangements that they barely attend to spiritual and communal dimensions of the lifelong commitment they're undertaking. David McCarthy and others have spoken of the pitfalls of commercialized weddings and naïvely romanticized marriages. Surely, our surrounding culture contributes to these problems, but have we considered how the institutional church does so as well? As the church demoted the pre-Tridentine custom of betrothal by consolidating the process of establishing marriage to a single high-stakes ritual, weddings became more vulnerable to commercial exploitation, which has reached outrageous proportions in recent decades. The wedding industry capitalizes on the idea that a couple's wedding day is the *most important day of their lives, unlike any other*. Every detail must be perfectly orchestrated; no expense is beyond reason.

The fees some parishes charge for weddings, and wedding-related advertisements that may be found in Catholic newspapers, may unwittingly contribute to this distortion of priorities. The July 1, 2006, issue of the *Clarion Herald*, the newspaper for the Archdiocese of New Orleans, included a twenty-four-page supplementary "Catholic Wedding Guide." Included on every page are advertisements for wedding products and services. These include diamonds ranging in price from $2,295 to $18,900 and catering services starting at $32 per guest, plus tax and gratuity. A list of parish fees reveals rates as high as $2,500 for nonparishioners, $1,200 for parishioners, and $1,400 for a child or grandchild of parishioners. Musicians, wedding coordinators, or popular Friday and Saturday evening times may add additional fees. (I was grateful to learn that my own parish charges just $100 for parishioners and $300 for nonparishioners.) In addition to the list of parish fees compiled by the newspaper, some parishes purchase advertisements in the marriage supplement. One parish took out a quarter-page color advertisement promoting its sanctuary as a site for "Beautiful Beginnings." The advertisement cites fees of $350 for parishioners and $1,000 for nonparishioners (of which $500 is a nonrefundable deposit), and boasts, "Landscaped gardens available for photos!" In the July 2007 issue of the same marriage supplement (but now with a more expensive glossy cover), the "Beautiful Beginnings" ad reappears, but now it must compete with advertisements from other parishes. St. John the Baptist Church advertises itself as "The Pathway to a Loving Catholic Commitment" facilitated by wedding coordinator Mary Ann Ciravolo. A competing solicitation says, "Begin your new life together...from this day forward...at Our Lady of Good Counsel. Wedding coordinator available." Should we be surprised if readers get the impression that the Catholic Church accepts commercialization of marriage and indeed hopes to profit from it? In the 2007 wedding guide, the reader is greeted on the inside front cover with a full-page color glossy photo of a sultry-eyed woman (presumably a bride) dressed in a low-cut dress. In advertisements on other pages of the guide, more brides pose with similar faces and dresses.

Although most articles in the pamphlet do focus on marital spirituality, at times they seem to have been co-opted by the wedding industry. An article that seems oddly out of place, for a church that promotes voluntary simplicity and a preferential option for the poor, is Elizabeth Rackover's article (circulated by Catholic News Service), titled "Exciting Honeymoon Destinations Vary." The point of the article is to alert couples that they don't have to choose the most expensive honeymoon destinations; for instance, rather than spend over $900 apiece on plane tickets to Hawaii, couples could fly instead to Acapulco for $500 per passenger, or choose from a variety of vacation packages, or "escapes," offered by Walt Disney Resorts. In another article, the Archdiocese provides a checklist for planning "the perfect wedding." As a church, do we really do couples a service by emphasizing that brides should be airbrushed models and weddings should be perfect? Even if a perfect wedding day could be attained (which in my experience, is uncommon), would that be the best way to launch the couple into marriage, which is inevitably *imperfect?* The U.S. bishops' *For Your Marriage* website header advertises "Resources for living happily ever after." Does this "fairy tale" slogan adequately convey Catholicism's sense of marriage as a sacramental sign of Christ's love for the church and the paschal mystery of death and new life?

Teachable Moments

What alternative practices could better convey the theology and spirituality of marriage and family that so many of us have devoted our lives to cultivating? Let's think "outside the box." Imagine if engaged couples who contacted a Catholic parish to plan a wedding weren't presented with a list of mandatory fees, but instead invited to view a scrapbook, comprised of pages contributed by couples who'd married at the church previously. On each page, the couples enclosed a picture of themselves and a memento of a service experience they chose to undertake together. One couple committed to bringing the bride's great-grandmother to Sunday mass each week, since she was recently widowed and doesn't drive. Another couple provided free babysitting for a friend, a single mother who was struggling to finish a college degree in the evenings so she could get a better-paying job to support her child. A third couple worked with their employer to establish an on-site recycling program for office waste. The next couple took a week's vacation to travel to the Gulf Coast and build houses for Hurricane Katrina victims with Habitat for Humanity. In a brief letter, each couple described why they chose their particular service experience, the people they met, and what they learned from the experience — about people in need, about each other, about belonging to a Christian community, about their faith. Imagine that the pastor or wedding coordinator explained to the newest engaged couple,

> We're trying to do our part as a parish to encourage couples to make service to community a priority in their marriage. When we say Christian marriage is a sacrament, we mean it's a visible sign of God's love, both for the couple themselves and for others who know them. Our experience, and the testimonials in this scrapbook, convince us that when we show love to people who can use our particular gifts — even when they cannot repay us — we not only help people who need us, but we build habits of attentiveness and generosity needed for a strong marriage. We'd like to invite you to choose a service experience that's valuable to you as a couple and contribute a page to our scrapbook so that future couples can learn from your experience. Our parish ministries are always looking for new volunteers, and we'll be happy to provide contact information to help you get involved. But we want you to find a service experience that's meaningful and do-able for you, even if it's not through our parish. If you're willing to give this a try, we'll forego any fees for use of our church building for your wedding. We still ask that you contract with our musicians to pay them for their work; that's how they support their families. To confirm that you're definitely planning to use the church building, we ask for a $100 reservation fee, which will be fully refunded after the wedding, or if you decide to cancel the wedding or get married elsewhere. We're trying to let couples know that we're not trying to profit from weddings. Our goal is to help couples further their faith journey and strengthen their commitment to each other.

Of course, if a couple wished to make a donation to the parish for use of the church building, that would be welcomed, just as it is for funerals. But the goal would be to show unambiguously that the parish's priority is spiritual formation and service, not making money.

Let's continue to imagine. What if, instead of a monthly second collection for building maintenance, we had a monthly second collection for marriage maintenance? With the proceeds, depending on how much was collected, one or more lucky couples from the parish could be treated to a date (perhaps a dinner gift certificate and childcare funds, if needed); their names could be announced in the bulletin or from the pulpit, and everyone would be asked to keep that couple's marriage in their prayers for the month and to wish them well in person. An inspirational marriage quote could be added for mini-catechesis. Any engaged or married couple registered with the parish could check a box on their donation envelope to be entered in the drawing, no matter how large or small their donation was. Engaged couples who approached the parish to plan a wedding would be invited to register with the parish, attend weekly mass, and take part in the "marriage maintenance" pool. The point would be for the parish to take pleasure in supporting strong marriages within their community, knowing that everyone is enriched by them.

Let's think ahead to other teachable moments in the marital/family life cycle. Most every couple experiences parenthood as a turning point in their marriage, and not uncommonly, it's an experience that prompts them to reexamine their faith. What beliefs, lifestyle priorities, and commitments are so important that I want my child to experience them too? At St. Ignatius parish adjacent to Boston College, the priests we worked with allowed us to take charge of planning the service. They knew me and my husband well and trusted that we were capable. We opted for the baptisms to take place during the mass we normally attended. Prior to the mass, our guests gathered in the sanctuary, where we welcomed them, and, at the suggestion of the pastor, I offered a "mini-sermon" on a scripture text I'd chosen and described what the baptism meant for my husband and me. Not every new parent will be ready to take charge as we did, but all parents should be invited to contribute personally to the baptism of their children. One possibility is for pastors to suggest that new parents compose a letter to their new baby, explaining why they decided to baptize him or her. The letter could be read at the baptism and then kept as a remembrance in the baby's scrapbook. If a parent hasn't yet given the decision much thought, composing that letter and reading it in public should be a potent learning experience. For the guests, too, hearing the testimony from the new parent will be a valuable chance to reflect upon what baptism means.

For the baptism of our fourth child, Elise, we tried something new, an idea borrowed from a book on Christian parenting — one that could also be suggested by the parish minister during baptism preparation. The invitation we sent our guests explained that our fourth child had everything she could possibly need in terms of material gifts. Rather than material gifts, we asked each of our guests to choose a service or charitable donation that was meaningful for them, offer it in Elise's honor, and write her a note explaining what their gift was, and why they chose it. This would be kept as a memento for Elise. Our guests came up with some wonderful ideas. Our neighbors across the street went as a family to visit a friend in a nursing home. Another family bought school supplies and delivered them to an inner-city school to distribute to children whose families would otherwise have to struggle to pay for them. A woman who team-taught with me made a donation to a favorite charity in Malawi, where she'd worked for over ten years, and wrote to her congressional representatives and senators to offer her input about foreign policy that affected Africa. Our older children were given the thrill of opening each letter and reading it for everyone.

Our children's First Communion experiences at two different parishes have been a mixture of "best practices" and practices that, in my opinion, should not be repeated. At our parish in Cincinnati, everything was family-oriented, and parents were treated by parish professionals as trusted collaborators. The religious education director planned two events for participating families. The first was an informational meeting for parents. The director assured us that we were capable of preparing our children for their First Communion, and that the church affirmed parents' responsibility as primary religious educators of our children. She provided us with some adult-oriented literature on the Eucharist, which we could draw upon as needed, and a variety of age-appropriate preparation materials for us to try with our children. She encouraged us to share our memories of our own First Communion and invite older siblings to do the same. Everything was proposed as an invitation, not as a mandate.

The second event was a Saturday morning retreat for all the families. Parents, first communicants, and siblings took part. On-site babysitting was available for the youngest siblings, if parents desired. Traditionally, the childcare service was provided by parents of third graders, whose children had attended the retreat the previous year. First Communions took place at regular Sunday mass; the children were assigned in groups of about eight to all the parish masses over a two-week period. Children were told to wear their Sunday best or a "bride-style" First Communion outfit, whichever they desired. Again, there were no mandates. I enjoyed seeing a girl, whose family was from India (I think), in a distinctive dress reflecting her cultural heritage. She reminded me that "catholic" means "universal." Parents and siblings escorted first communicants into mass. After all the children had their First Communion, there was a party for all the families, and children took a group picture.

For my daughter Cecilia this past year, the experience was very different, from a parent's perspective. At the parents' meeting, it became apparent very quickly that the religious education director and the pastor, both of whom were new to the parish, had already planned everything. Many parents' questions and suggestions were treated dismissively. For instance, the director said she would instruct the children to take communion on their tongues, rather than in their hands, because that was more reverent and appropriate for the special event. When I raised my hand, explained my professional credentials, and insisted there was no reason why receiving communion in the hand was less reverent (surely at the Last Supper, the disciples ate with their hands!), the director said she'd talk to me about it after the meeting. When a second parent raised her hand and said her daughter might be nervous about receiving communion on her tongue, the director changed the subject and didn't respond to her concern.

We learned that, without any consultation with parents, our pastor had decided all girls should wear veils and all boys should wear white ties with an imprint of the Eucharist. These had already been ordered by the religious education director (who isn't a parent) and we were strongly "encouraged" to purchase them so all the children's outfits would match. (I suppose the idea of "catholicity" as diversity/universality/"Here comes everybody" didn't occur to them.) The director also conveyed the pastor's desire that boys wear white suits if at all possible. The authorities didn't seem to consider that many children might be wearing hand-me-down outfits, or that parents who chose to purchase a new outfit for a second-grade boy would be reluctant to buy anything so impractical as a white suit. (Parents simply used their common sense: on First Communion day, all the boys showed up in navy or tan pants and blazers.) Parents learned that children who attended the parish school would attend a retreat during school on the Friday prior to the First Communion. By this point, many parents didn't trust the director's judgment, and, not surprisingly, they asked who would be leading the retreat and why parents weren't invited to help with it. The director said the retreat would be led by unidentified "volunteers" she'd asked to help; parent volunteers were not needed. This decision epitomizes the way that lay Catholics are frequently not consulted or trusted about matters for which they have real expertise — thus exacerbating the exaggerated ranking of clerical and lay vocations described earlier. Such lack of consultation is doubly unfortunate when "experts" rather than building communion make decisions that alienate people at a teachable moment in a family's faith journey. In this case, parents who wished to fulfill their responsibility as primary religious educators of their children felt shut out of the planning process; every parent I spoke to left the meeting angry.

The most disturbing part of the whole experience came when parents were told we couldn't escort our children into mass, sit with them, or even attempt to make eye contact with them while we passed them in the communion line, because this would "distract them from the Lord." The theology behind that statement conflicts deeply with my sense of spirituality in marriage and family life, wherein we learn to love the God we don't see by loving the family we do see. We were forbidden to speak with guests in our pew as we gathered before mass began. We were told, "Jesus gave his life for us. The least we can do is maintain a respectful reverence and silence before mass." To equate reverence with silence is to adopt a narrowly "celibate" model of spirituality. What sort of family celebration or meal has that sort of policy? Anyone who attends mass with small children on a regular basis knows that silence cannot be a fair way of measuring people's devotion to the Lord.[9] At a family gathering, including a First Communion celebration, people naturally want to talk to loved ones they haven't seen in awhile. Why not turn that impulse into a catechetical opportunity? As families gather, why not invite a few parents (and perhaps even siblings, grandparents, godparents) to share a brief testimony for the congregation about the meaning of their child's First Communion and their efforts to share their faith with their child? Then the congregation could be invited to spend the time before mass discussing the significance of the event with those seated around them. For the last few minutes before the mass begins, the congregation could be asked to quiet themselves to allow a chance for silent prayer — but it's unrealistic to expect families waiting in a pew forty-five minutes in advance to sit in silence. In this case, we were led by a stranger (chosen by the religious education director) in reciting the rosary. Harried parents who had important family responsibilities to attend to in connection with the event (such as fielding cell phone calls from godparents who'd gotten lost on the way to the church, or flagging down grandparents as they entered church so that they could sit with their family, or placing a last-minute phone call to Uncle Walter, who was inadvertently left off the guest list, to invite him to the house party afterward) probably felt guilty for disturbing the reverence of the event. By why should this be so? Isn't the very gathering of families part of the communion celebration?

Besides the First Communion testimonial proposed above, there are countless other occasions where lay people, including married people, might contribute to each others' faith formation within the Sunday liturgy. I once attended a Thanksgiving Day mass in which the pastor gave a brief sermon suited to the day's readings and then ventured down the aisle with his microphone. He asked the congregation to come forward and share stories of blessings that they wished to thank God for. It's been many years since that mass, but I still remember two of the testimonials — one from a religious sister who thanked God for her religious community, and the other from a mother who thanked God for her adult children, who'd grown up to be the sort of people she would choose as her best friends. I've witnessed similar testimonials at a parish Lenten reconciliation service. After the priest's homily, a few parishioners were invited to describe occasions of forgiveness in their lives, and then all were given an opportunity to confess their sins to a priest, as usual. It's not hard to envision how such testimonials from lay people could also be appropriate for occasions such as Father's Day, Mother's Day, parish commemorations of silver and golden wedding anniversaries, Vocations Sunday, etc. At St. Ignatius parish at Boston College, I recall how the "family mass" recruited volunteer "host families" who, among other roles, prepared each week's prayers of the faithful after previewing the scripture readings for that mass. Sometimes during the homily, the congregation would be given reflection questions and asked to spend time discussing these among their own families and with those seated nearby.

What all these examples have in common is that lay believers are given an opportunity to articulate spiritual wisdom and questions they've encountered through ordinary life, including marriage and family relationships. The attempt to articulate and share one's faith in public (or perhaps, one's religious doubts and questions) is a valuable opportunity and challenge for adults who, all too often, haven't had any sort of "religion class" since they were teenagers. Both lay speakers and those who hear them could be edified through such practices. Moreover, these exercises could provide adults a "safe" forum to talk about their daily lives in connection with one's faith, and the practice may make people more at ease reflecting upon faith in ordinary conversations outside liturgy. A small faith-sharing outside mass might provide a similar opportunity, but the reality is that many Catholics have difficulty dedicating time to attend Sunday mass, let alone fitting extra appointments into their schedules. Moreover, there may be some in the congregation who may be inspired to join a small faith-sharing group for the first time, *precisely because* the Sunday testimonials provoked them to take that step. Yes, there's a certain novelty for Catholics, and perhaps a certain risk, in allowing lay people to speak unscripted during worship. The professional experts aren't in control of the message. But I believe we can take that risk, trusting that God's Spirit will guide lay people in sharing authentic spiritual wisdom and guide the "professional" presider to provide interpretation and friendly correction of what is said, as need be. There's no less risk in the status quo, just different sorts of risk: the risk that churchgoers will continue to presume that holiness isn't something lay people can aspire to; the risk of continued dichotomizing of "sacred" and "secular" life; and the risk that some Catholics — particularly those of an age for proximate or immediate marriage preparation — will stop attending mass altogether because it strikes them as monotonous and irrelevant. Let's not forget that Bishop Kurtz invited us to find "fresh, bold ways" to promote the rich teachings of the church related to marriage.

Besides testimonials during liturgy, I've stumbled upon other strategies to get spouses and parents to reflect upon their faith and moral priorities, with each other and with their kids. When I've taught marriage or family spirituality courses in a college setting, the final project has always been an interview exercise. Having moved to the high school setting, I've discovered that my students absolutely love any project that involves interviewing people. Maybe they all dream of growing up to be talk-show or reality-TV show hosts! I capitalize upon their enthusiasm by giving homework assignments that have them design questions connected with course materials; discuss these with family, friends, or even strangers; and analyze the results. Students have developed some fine questions: "How would your daily life be different if you were a polytheist rather than a monotheist?" "Do you think there are any unforgivable sins?" "Do you think most people have more difficulty believing they are sinful or believing their sins can be forgiven?" When we cover Anabaptists in my church history course, I have students interview their parents to find out why the parents chose to baptize their son or daughter, or not to do so. In most instances, this is the first time parents and children have ever had that conversation, and the same was generally true for my college students in their interview projects. Many of my college students have remarked that they chose to interview friends and family members whom they thought they knew well, but they had never before discussed Christian family in relationship to marriage and family life.

Morality courses present plenty of opportunities for students (whether in college or high school) to discuss moral discernment as it relates to real-life Christian marriages and families. In the "Messy House Case" (drawn from a dilemma of my own), parents who keep their house clean must decide what to do about their child's friendship with a playmate whose home is extraordinarily dirty. How should the "clean family" handle invitations for sleepovers, after their son comes home from a playdate and reports that there are cat droppings in his friend's bed? What would Jesus do in this situation, considering that this playmate has few other friends, precisely because people consider him smelly and dirty? In the "Ellen and Dan Case," based on the experience of my aunt and uncle, a woman whose husband is permanently disabled in an accident (both mentally and physically) must decide whether she will divorce her husband or remain his caretaker. In a third case, a young husband and father finishing law school must choose, in consultation with his wife, between two job offers — one at a high-paying, high-powered law firm and the other for a nonprofit legal clinic serving low-income clients. In the economic section of my high-school morality course, students must imagine themselves at thirty-five years old and complete a household budget based on a median family income for Louisiana and a time budget of a month's worth of hours. Before budgeting, they must first imagine how many people they hope to have in their household by the time they're thirty-five — already an important ethical decision. Will I have children at all, if it means I must curtail my shopping and vacation habits? Will my husband and I have a third child, if it means we won't be able to afford Catholic schools? Students are instructed to review their budgets with their parents, to see how realistic they are, and then to write an essay reflecting on what they've learned. The students' eyes are opened to the reality of prioritizing values as an adult. Once more, it seems these conversations are a first for many of the students and their parents.

For an exercise I've used in undergraduate and graduate courses while introducing the concept of sacrament, students are invited to bring a "show and tell" item that for them is a "visible sign of God's invisible grace." Very few students have brought items associated with institutional religious devotions. Far more often students have brought items that remind them of their families. What strikes me about this exercise, juxtaposed with the "holiness" class discussion cited earlier, is a default mode disconnect between students' most profound experiences of God on the one hand and, on the other, their experience of institutional religion, and models of holiness presented to them in religious upbringing. Yet in a context where a skilled facilitator can help illumine connections with Christian tradition, this exercise holds great potential to help people understand the relationship between so-called secular and religious life. I could even imagine this exercise included in an interactive homily at a Sunday liturgy. Among the more memorable show-and-tell items, one girl brought a stuffed duck, a gift from a family member, which kept her company in her hospital incubator for weeks after she was born prematurely. She said the duck reminded her to thank God for being alive. A nursing student brought the last paper cup her mother drank from before she died (at a relatively young age) of breast cancer. Their last few precious minutes together were a gift from God. One person brought a poem her husband wrote for her while they were dating in college. The poem described how he was coming to realize that he was growing up and falling in love with the woman he would marry. A married man brought a photo of his youngest child, the result of a "surprise" late-in-life pregnancy. The name her parents chose for her was Grace. An undergraduate brought a "sobriety coin" from Alcoholics Anonymous. She explained that her mother had seen success in her struggle with alcohol addiction, and the student said her mother's sobriety was a gift from God. Another student, a mother of several children, brought a large ceramic bowl. She explained a family tradition wherein an entire carton of ice cream was emptied into the bowl, and everyone used spoons to eat out of the same bowl together. To her, these community-building celebrations were moments filled with grace.

I've been asked to speak about spirituality throughout the marriage and family life cycle. I haven't given a lot of thought to the mature, empty-nester stage of marriage, because I'm not there yet. But I can attest that in my reading of the literature, this topic begs for attention. Increased life expectancy means that married couples can enjoy a relationship that far outlasts fertility and time with children at home. In a marriage of fifty or sixty years, twenty or thirty may be spent as postmenopausal empty-nesters.[10] Surely this "sign of the times" ought to profoundly impact Catholic reflection on marriage, for until the 1960s, Catholic teaching called procreation and nurture of children the *primary* purpose of marriage; other purposes were called *secondary*. In the past few decades, even with both purposes considered equal, Catholic discourse on marriage is slanted disproportionately to the earlier years of marriage and parenting. Medical advances give us added reason to assume that the lifelong marriage vocation can be quite multidimensional. Couples may be grateful for prompting from pastoral ministers to think intentionally about how to refocus their vocation and dedicate their energies for these twenty or thirty years. Donald Miller provides excellent insights into the shift in vocation that mature married couples will likely experience:

> While a couple may no longer be rearing their own children, they very likely may be in significant contact with their grandchildren or the children of relatives and friends. Thus, the couple's role as socializer and educator of dependent children does not necessarily end when their last child leaves home. Likewise, their parental role with their adult children continues, and as the theories concerning family lifecycles note, may go through numerous stages as both the parents and their offspring mature. The Church's vision of family challenges the post-childrearing couple to maintain a creative and dynamic sense of ministry appropriate to their new life stages.... [Furthermore] since the economic necessities of twentieth-century family life require that both parents in many families work outside the home, the financial, temporal, psychological, and physical realities of family life may make involvement in extra-familial activities difficult if not impossible during the childrearing years. Thus the engagement in social services and apostolic ministries may not be a practical possibility for a couple until their children are grown, or even until they reach the age of retirement. The relationship of the family as a social unit and as a domestic church to the larger society and the Church may very well find its most productive external expression in a couple's later years.[11]

There is so much untapped potential for Catholic parishes and educational institutions to help members become attentive to the spiritual, moral, and religious dimensions of marriage and family life. I've listed just a sampling. I'd like to close with a quote from Karl Rahner, whose work has been invaluable for me in probing these realities. In an essay titled "How to Receive a Sacrament and Mean It," Rahner elaborates on the relationship between the work of Christ, everyday Christian witness, the "Liturgy of the

World," and the church's official liturgy. It is easy to relate his comments to the frustrations and joys of marriage and family life:

> Grace is not a particular phenomenon occurring parallel to the rest of life, but simply the ultimate depth of everything the spiritual creature does when he realizes himself — when he laughs and cries, accepts responsibility, loves, lives, and dies, stands up for truth, breaks out of preoccupation with self to help the neighbor, hopes against hope, cheerfully refuses to be embittered by the stupidity of daily life, keeps silent not so that evil festers in his heart but so that it dies there — when, in a word, man lives as he would like to live, in opposition to his selfishness and to the despair which always assails him. This is where grace occurs, because all this leads man to the infinity and victory that is God.
>
> Something else must be said about this grace.... It attained its clearest manifestation in Jesus of Nazareth, and precisely in the kind of life in which he became like us in all things, in a life full of ordinariness — birth, hardship, courage, hope, failure, and death....
>
> The whole length and breadth of this monstrous history, full of superficiality, stupidity, insufficiency, and hatred on the one side, and silent dedication, faithfulness unto death, [and] joy...on the other side, constitutes the liturgy of the world, and the liturgy of the Son on his cross is its culmination.... It must be clarified and brought into reflex awareness in what we call ordinary liturgy.[12]

Chapter Seven

Marriage among the Spiritual but Not Religious

JAMES HEALY

AN INCREASINGLY COMMON PHENOMENON is the number of people who report themselves to be "spiritual but not religious." Indeed, the term has become a cliché; people feel they can use the term without explaining what they mean by it. For people completely uninvolved in formal religion it appears to mean that the persons consider themselves to have a deep inner sense of God or of transcendence, but they tend to experience it in what they consider to be nonreligious settings — through nature, through relationships, through spontaneous prayer, through sexuality, through service. In other cases, one hears this term from people who are marginally involved or relatively uninvolved in institutional religions, but it is given as the reason for their lack of any further involvement.

In its pure form, the term seems to suggest that spirituality and religion are directly opposed to each other, as I have pictured in Figure A.

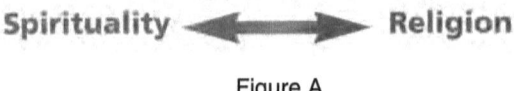

Figure A

This general attempt to separate inner spiritual experience from commitment to a specific religious community, creed, or tradition is new in its pervasiveness, but it has a much longer history, since it corresponds to a deep human need to balance autonomy and communion, agency and surrender. This tendency toward separation achieved greater momentum early in the nineteenth century, perhaps after the events of the French Revolution. It was spurred on by the Romantic movement in England, and, at about the same time, the Transcendentalist movement in America, which had its beginnings with Bronson Alcott, Ralph Waldo Emerson, and Henry David Thoreau.

As Figure A illustrates, for many people, spirituality and religion are antagonistic. In other words, the more spiritual I am, the less religious I need to be, and the more religious you are, the less spiritual I suspect you to be. Indeed, from their point of view, organized religion is a threat to their spirituality. Some research suggests that perhaps 20 percent of Americans hold this viewpoint in a rather uncompromising way.[1] However, many more individuals have some sort of uneasy foothold in religious communities and structures, but remain ambivalent about their involvement.

By "spirituality" I mean the inner impulse toward God and transcendence, experienced continually or intermittently in response to a wide range of natural internal and external stimuli, such as loving relationships, nature, sexuality, service, and spontaneous prayer. "Religion" comprises the codes, creeds, churches, traditions, and organized communities that intend to order spiritual experience and transmit it to the next generation in ways essentially similar to what they experienced. This would be how these two are often described, but in reality, the two cannot be separated, because everyone's spirituality is formed from birth by community and cultural experiences, and because very few religious settings are truly devoid of spirituality.

My own effort has been to enter into dialogue with those people who see spirituality and religion as opposed, and to suggest a different relationship between the two, as pictured in Figure B.

Figure B

Seen from this perspective, one can be high both in religion and in spirituality, or can be low in one and high in the other, or low in both.

Figure C shows the relation of spirituality and religion as Cartesian coordinates, with Spirituality on the vertical y axis and Religion on the horizontal x axis.

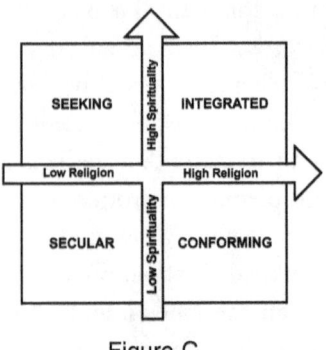

Figure C

Those high in both spiritual and religious experience I call Integrated, those high in religious experience and low in spiritual experience I call Conforming, those low in religious experience and high in spiritual experience I call Seeking, and those low in both I call Secular.

By taking an assessment of where a person has been at different points in their life, and tracking those spots on the two axes, I believe you can get a sense of a person's "faith journey," which I operationalize as the interplay of spirituality and religion in a person's life. It would be impossible to generalize the faith journeys of the people who are considering marriage, planning marriage, or are actually married. They describe every sort of development: circles, plateaus, dizzying ascents, steady states, precipitous drops. Four possible "faith journeys" are represented in Figure D.

Figure D

At the risk of oversimplifying, let me describe one possible path, which is imaged in the upper right box in Figure D. A person has been in a religiously observant household, but without experiencing a tremendous sense of spirituality. When this person leaves the controls of the parental home, there is a retreat from religious activities because they are seen as inauthentic, and perhaps for a period of time also a retreat from spiritual reflection — the "baby is thrown out with the bathwater." However, for any number of reasons, at some point there is a new recognition of the importance of the spiritual in life and a realization that the best place for most to find that is within a community of fellow believers, who support and affirm the spiritual search and offer a way of seeing and living spirituality through a structured religious community. There is a return to religious life and hopefully an increase in spiritual experience also.

It would be safe to say that many individuals are lower on the religious scale than in previous generations. Those of us involved in ministry in the Catholic Church would hope to call people to a life in which their spiritual and their religious experiences are mutually reinforcing, and, when, the incredible diversity is averaged out, look to be something like Figure B. How do we help people to achieve this? How do we help nurture involved, spiritually awake and growing Catholics, deeply connected to parish and Catholic organizational life, imbued with the traditions, beliefs, and doctrines of the church?

Let me apply this analysis to one particular issue in the church, that of interchurch and interfaith marriage.[2] For the purposes of this discussion, I use the term "interchurch" to refer to marriages between two baptized Christians and "interfaith" to mean a marriage between a baptized Christian and an adherent of another faith, such as Judaism or Islam.

Despite our efforts to be helpful to these couples, we may not be looking at the data adequately. We may not always have made the proper distinctions. We will focus on interchurch marriages, where both parties are baptized Christians. The definition of a true ecumenical marriage is one in which both parties share core Christian beliefs but are deeply committed to their own denominational tradition in which each intends to continue living out that tradition in vital and consistent ways. That definition, which would put those who fit it well into the "Integrated" quadrant, probably applies only to a small percentage of marriages where a Catholic marries a non-Catholic. The Creighton study *Ministry to Interchurch Marriages*,[3] found that only about 15 percent of the interchurch respondents registered "high" in religiosity, but much of our pastoral care — both marriage preparation and in the few cases where marriage enrichment is specifically offered to these couples — assumes that the couples sitting in front of us are all part of that 15 percent who found and married each other. The interchurch couples

Table 1. Self-Reported Involvement in Church

____ I go to Mass every Sunday, and I am involved in other things at the parish besides.

____ I go to Mass at least two or three times a month, but I'm not involved otherwise.

____ I might go to Mass every other month.

____ I get to Mass at Christmas or Easter, or maybe for a wedding, but that's about it.

____ I'm not Catholic anymore.

Out of ten men and women who were in their twenties or thirties at the millennium, and who had been confirmed, **how many would you put in each category?**

Adapted from Dean R. Hoge et al., *Young Adult Catholics: Religion in the Culture of Choice* (Notre Dame: University of Notre Dame Press, 2001).

---

who speak at our marriage preparation programs or act as sponsor couples are usually true ecumenical couples, and the issues discussed — raising the children when both parents are actively involved in different churches, harmonizing Sunday activities, etc. — are of the most interest to that group. We offer much less to those who are not of high religiosity. The study notes that "different approaches are needed to strengthen the marriages of those of high, medium, and low religiosity." There is a large group of couples in which one person has relatively high religiosity and the other doesn't. There is another group in which both are relatively low in religiosity. Along with the strategies they suggest, I would suggest focusing directly on the spiritual but not religious phenomena with these couples. For a relatively small number of Catholics who marry non-Catholics, the core issue is religious differences. For the much larger portion of this group that we are trying to reach, the core issue is not religious differences, but religious indifference. By and large, these are not couples trying to negotiate active differences in religious life, although that of course is present to some extent. These are couples in which one or both of them are not convinced that institutional religion has anything at all to offer them. Granted, life itself may convince them otherwise in the form of children, illness, life changes, and spiritual awakenings, but the argument is much deeper than Catholic versus Baptist — it is often church involvement versus no church involvement.

Many couples and individuals find it easy to see why high religion and low spirituality are limiting: harsh judgment of others, little flexibility, an experience of security but not of joy, little ability to connect with others at deep levels, limited ability to grow through crises, difficulty with forgiveness. These are resources crucial to a marriage. However, it is much harder for many of them to see why high spirituality and low religion can be equally limiting: dangers of self-deception, ego inflation, lack of accountability, little support for developing spiritual disciplines, little community support during crises, and the temptation to justify one's actions by constructing a set of religious beliefs from various sources in consonance with your own prejudices.[4] One is cut off from the self-balancing and self-correcting power of following a particular religious tradition, which I call the most powerful and only true democracy — even long-dead people get to vote.

Attitudes toward the Catholic Church

One very helpful book for the present discussion is *Young Adult Catholics: Religion in the Culture of Choice*.[5] Dean Hoge and his associates studied both Anglo and Latino Catholics then in their twenties and thirties who had been confirmed. The results of their survey placed the respondents in one of five different categories, which, for the purposes of this essay, I have personalized in Table 1.

I would ask you to look at the five categories in the table, and then visualize at random ten previously confirmed men and women who were in their twenties and thirties at the time of the millennium. Out of the ten, how many would you place in each category? The actual number, going down from the most active category to the least, is roughly, 1, 4, 2.5, 1.5, and 1. Now, depending on their assumptions and expectations, people find these results to be either good news or bad news. The comments of Hoge et al. on these results are very instructive. First, only about 11 percent say they are no longer Catholic, so the rest are still potentially swimming somehow in the Catholic ocean. Second, Anglo and (relatively acculturated) Hispanic Catholics do not differ significantly from each other in the makeup of these categories, despite our fears that Hispanics are leaving the church at a particularly high and unprecedented rate. Third, they want lay involvement, more empowerment of women in the church, church involvement in social issues, and they definitely want religious education for their children. Fourth, being Catholic is important to these people, even if it often seems more a matter of identification than of full and active participation. Finally, it would seem that this generation is not so much angry at the church. To use a current phrase, "They're just not that much into us." This survey was carried out before the last, most publicized round of sexual abuse reports, beginning with Boston in 2002, so it is possible that the anger level has risen.

I would have some further comments. First, very clearly, a large percentage of these Catholics could be characterized as spiritual but not religious. Sixty-four percent agreed with the statement that one could be a good Catholic without going to mass. Because of the centrality of the Eucharist in Catholic self-understanding, it is likely that many other facets of Catholic religious life would also be considered unnecessary if the Eucharist was so disregarded.

Second, I would encourage us not to downplay the role of Catholicism even in people who return only for Easter and Christmas, and perhaps for weddings and funerals. Although one wonders whether their children will be connected at all, for this generation the Catholic Church still functions as an anchor, even if they only drop the anchor a couple of times a year. Third, and most crucial for this discussion, out of all five of these categories, it seems quite likely that when the time comes for these people to either get married or to have their child baptized, all the people but the 11 percent in the last category ("I am no longer a Catholic") could potentially return for those services. Even people who return only on Christmas or Easter will normally be interested in these sacramental moments, unless there is a fiancée or spouse who strongly objects. To talk in salesmanship terms, these couples and new parents are "prequalified" for focused evangelizing efforts. This highlights the importance of both marriage preparation and baptismal preparation. When parishes talk about creating evangelization programs for young Catholic families, I tell them that the heart of any such effort should be marriage and baptism preparation programs as effective as possible.

As a church we appreciate the importance of marriage preparation even as we debate what combination of skills, theology, and community involvement is optimum. The Creighton study on Marriage Preparation, *Getting It Right*,[6] found that 92 percent of the participants found marriage preparation to be at least to some extent helpful soon after its completion. Although we can plan for and hope for more, we want to make at least "positive memories" for those who are only marginally connected with church life. There is a sociological term called "The Strength of Weak Ties," originally coined by Mark Granovetter in 1973 in an essay by that name. We certainly create some strong ties at these times, but simply creating a weak tie can also be important. You can pull a freighter into a harbor with a thread if you're careful enough. Now, no human being is careful enough, but God is. Our job is to at least "make memories" of a positive, adult church experience at the time of marriage, so that when people are disposed at some later time in their lives to give church another try, they remember some positive moments.

Joanne Heaney Hunter and I discussed our contributions because we didn't want to overlap, but there is one place where we do intentionally want to overlap, and that is in the area of baptism preparation.[7] The Creighton study *The First Five Years of Marriage*,[8] asked newly married couples, a group not normally tied in much with church life, when they would be most open to overtures from the church, and they said it would center around the areas of "pregnancy, new parenthood, and meeting other new parents." Baptism preparation represents a time when those sorts of encounters are "hard-wired" into church life. There is an additional reason why baptism preparation packs a greater punch: so many people are cohabiting now that some of them don't experience a qualitative change in their relationship, at least at the psychological level, until the birth of the first child. This may be the moment of decisive change, when they really "feel" married. While we would wish it were otherwise, baptism preparation is a tremendous opportunity for connecting with and deepening our relationship with these new parents — and what in reality do we do with this opportunity? We often squander it. To my knowledge, there has never been a national survey of infant baptism preparation programs, as there has been for RCIA, Eucharist, Reconciliation, Confirmation, and preparation programs for marriage and for holy orders. That alone suggests its relative neglect. We conducted our own study in the Joliet Diocese, and discovered that 90 percent of our parishes had baptismal prep programs that met just one time, and that the usual length of time was about seventy-five minutes. This means the programs were usually not even long enough to require a break period. Most couples can hold their breath through such a short meeting. What is the alternative? It is a program that lasts long enough to make a difference, so that at least memories can be created. The best recent baptismal programs, such as Mary Jo Pedersen's *Welcome Your Child* (second edition pending from Loyola Publishing), Charles Balsam's *What Do You Ask of God's Church?* (Liguori), and the older *Infant Baptism Basics* (OCP) by Christopher Heller, are longer, more engaging, and considerably more focused on the dynamics of marriage and family life.

In some ways baptism preparation is now situated where marriage preparation was fifty years ago. It exists in a backwater in many parishes, far away from the mainstream of religious education or of family ministry. It may be under the sway of a single volunteer or a single deacon and may not have been reviewed for a long time. There is often a distinctively apologetic tone: "We know you new parents are busy, so we'll try to get you out of here as soon as possible." Far too often, they take us at our word. We need to raise the bar here dramatically.

Finally, we look at attitudes toward marriage. Based on the research and from my own experience, it would seem that people still very much desire a lifelong marriage; what has changed for many is their belief that they will be able to achieve what they desire. The difference between what we want and what we're afraid we are going to get is called anxiety. For this generation, the anxiety gap regarding marriage is huge, due in large part to the prevalence of divorce, but also to a society that seems at best ambivalent toward long-term commitment. Many romantic movies end now not with marriage, but with some kind of liaison, and if it's a series, in the next movie, that romantic partner is gone — we're not sure where. Many in our culture, despite their hopes, seem resigned to accepting any kind of present relationship that feels right.

Decision theory says that when we make decisions anxiously, we tend to either take gigantic risks, or we take no risks at all. We may not even attempt marriage, feeling that there is not a good enough chance of things working. And indeed, the marriage rate is dropping. Or instead of following the careful process of mate selection described in John Van Epp's *How to Avoid Marrying a Jerk*,[9] we lunge; we take large chances and marry people we shouldn't. Cohabitation could be considered one such "lunge." Even as it becomes more institutionalized, cohabitation does not fill the need of the human heart for commitment, although for some it is a step toward it. There are some indications that the word is getting out regarding the inadvisability of cohabitation if one wants a lifelong marriage. For the first time last year, there was a drop in the number of high school seniors who said that cohabitation was a good way to prepare for marriage.[10] How do we help accelerate that mini-trend? My own decision has been to spend more time talking about cohabitation and marriage with young adult groups and in college settings. However, the argument must be made, and made strongly, in the high schools.

Research about cohabitation has become more sophisticated; researchers are less willing to make blanket statements as they find more distinctions among the cohabiting population. The consensus is still that there is no evidence for cohabitation increasing the likelihood of a long-term happy marriage and considerable evidence that cohabitation harms one's chances significantly. However, the conclusions are not unanimous, and the statistical differences between the groups have shrunk in some studies. One problem is that the more conventional cohabitation becomes, the more conventional couples do it. Therefore the selection factor (unconventional couples who are less disposed to traditional marriage tend to divorce at higher rates) has lessened. Couples who get engaged publicly before they cohabit seem to divorce at the same rates as those who don't cohabit. There is some evidence that women who live only with the man they eventually marry are at less risk. And, as the marriage rate continues to drop, it may be that some couples who might have married and divorced lived together and split up instead. In general, though, it would seem that cohabitation remains a substantial risk factor for those who go on to marriage.[11]

Regarding another kind of attitude toward marriage, there is another phenomenon that our Catholic tradition speaks against mightily. As Popenoe and Whitehead have pointed out in their latest *State of Our Unions 2007*[12] there is a real danger of two bifurcated Americas developing. These Two Americas would be divided not just by education level and income, but by family structure — one relatively well off with a subsiding divorce rate, and the other one impoverished, with a rising divorce rate and high levels of children born out of wedlock. Table 2 is from the *State of Our Unions 2007,* and the data in the table is obviously meant to be good news for those reading the report.

However, if one is on the negative side of those statistics, the prospects for a happy marriage are bleak indeed. Granted, there are personal factors operating in everybody's life, rich or poor, such as commitment in relationships, self-reliance, a virtuous life. But the societal factors impinging on the poor do indeed make it more difficult for them to sustain marriage. The efforts brought about by the government's Healthy Marriage Initiative are indeed laudable and praiseworthy. Bringing a variety of programs to Fragile Families and other disadvantaged groups is certainly part of the answer to the challenge. But our church teaches us that both private and social responsibilities are to be part of our response to Christ's call. Better health care, a more realistic minimum wage, job opportunities in communities that have none, and immigration laws that do a better job of keeping families together are all more universal ways of also helping marriages, and, in Dorothy Day's words, helping create a society where "it is easier to be good." Our preferential option for the poor must also be a preferential option for poor families.

Table 3 describes a three-level framework for Caring for Marriage. It includes the specific pastoral suggestions made in the body of the essay and adds more as examples. Using such a framework helps us to be both comprehensive and more specific in our response.

Table 2. Factors Affecting Risk of Divorce

Factors	Percent Decrease in Risk of Divorce
Annual income over $50,000 (vs. under $25,000)	–30
Having a baby seven months or more after marriage (vs. before marriage)	–24
Marrying over 25 years of age (vs. under 18)	–24
Own family of origin intact (vs. divorced parents)	–14
Religious affiliation (vs. none)	–14
Some college (vs. high-school dropout)	–13

From Matthew D. Bramlett and William D. Mosher, *Cohabitation, Marriage, Divorce, and Remarriage in the United States,* National Center for Health Statistics, Vital and Health Statistics, 23 (22), 2002. The risks are calculated for women only. Quoted in David Popenoe, *The State of Our Unions, 2007.*

Table 3: Caring for Marriage

The following outline is based on "The Three Levels of Prevention" — a public health concept first applied to the mental health field by Gerald Caplan in 1964. It gives us a way of thinking about the way that a community takes care of its members.

Primary Prevention

- Focus is on improving marriages by affecting society as a whole; doesn't focus on targeted groups or high-risk populations
- Dental Health Comparison: *fluoridating the water*
- Examples:
  - Public service announcements and billboards
  - Marriage education in all public schools and/or private schools
  - Legislative activity to protect favored status of marriage
  - Efforts to increase the economic well-being of families in general through political or legislative action — improved access to health care, reducing the extraordinary disparity between what line workers and CEOs make, raising of the minimum wage, etc.

Secondary Prevention

- Focus is on individual couples, or chosen groups of couples deemed to be at higher risk or with more specific needs
- Dental Health Comparison: *teaching good habits like brushing teeth, flossing, annual checkups*
- Examples:
  - Communication and conflict resolution skills programs
  - Marriage conferences
  - Special programs for interfaith marriages, second marriages, newlyweds, retirees, empty nesters, grieving couples, engaged couples, "spiritual but not religious" couples
  - Skills programs and modeling for "Fragile Families"
  - Expanded and improved baptism preparation programs
  - Marriage Encounter
  - Retorno

The Third Option: Tertiary Prevention/Intervention
- Focus is on the couples at high risk of divorce
- Dental Health Comparison: *filling cavities, pulling and replacing teeth, fitting for full dentures*
- Examples: "pro-marriage" guidelines for marriage counseling, Retrouvaille, The Third Option

---

In conclusion, I have attempted to review current attitudes, among those considering marriage, toward church, toward the Catholic Church, and toward marriage itself. In some cases, where these attitudes are based on what I consider faulty assumptions, such as the opposition of spirituality and religion, our response must be persuasive in nature. In other cases, such as the relative lack of focus on a key potential moment in a young couple's attitudes toward the church — the birth of their children and baptism preparation — a more wholehearted catechetical approach is required. Finally, if we are to strengthen marriage in America not just for the relatively well off, we marriage proponents must be challenged to join with the rest of the church in supporting the social change that makes an enduring marriage not only a dream but a goal that is broadly attainable.

Chapter Eight

Layers of Marriage Preparation and the Family Life Cycle

JOANN HEANEY-HUNTER

WHEN ONE WALKS THE STREETS of Florence, Italy, it is impossible to miss the beautiful cathedral at the center of the city, Santa Maria del Fiore.[1] This magnificent building, with a façade of white, pink, and green marble, and an even older baptistery, which showcases Lorenzo Ghiberti's beautiful bronze doors depicting biblical scenes, is a breathtaking sight. Upon learning about the cathedral, one realizes that its story is as complex as the structure is beautiful. While construction of the cathedral itself began at the end of the thirteenth century, the façade visible to the public is a product of the nineteenth century.[2] Moreover, we learn that Santa Maria del Fiore was not the first cathedral on the site; underneath the majestic building is a smaller, older church probably built in the fifth or sixth century called the cathedral of Santa Reparata, dedicated to a saint whose story may be more legend than fact.[3] When one digs even deeper into the history of this cathedral, one learns that Santa Reparata probably sat on top of the home of an unknown Roman nobleman.[4] The layers of the cathedral reveal different stages in the development of the city of Florence, the church in Florence, and European society at a number of points in history.

I use this image because it reminds me of how faith formation takes place for individuals, families, and faith communities. Like any ancient cathedral, built layer upon layer, the faith formation of an individual, family, and church continues to change, develop, and grow over the course of many lifetimes. We build on existing foundations, examine old structures of thinking and behavior, and continuously create new realities. The task of this essay is to explore how this building process takes place in the context of ministry for marriage and family life. In particular, it will explore these questions: When does marriage preparation begin, and how can it be most effective? Can ministry that takes place at other stages of life serve as formation for married life? In particular, what can be gained by using teen and young adult ministry — and even parent preparation for infant baptism — as opportunities to shape attitudes and values about Christian faith and the vocation of marriage? The answers to these questions will serve as one more layer in the process of forming individuals and couples in faithful marriages and families.

Part of the task of family ministry is to ask how the church facilitates an environment that invites and supports families through various stages of faith formation. In particular, we must develop more opportunities to support faith transmission as a lifetime process that flourishes when parents grow in faith themselves and share that growth with their children. Moreover, we must ask how faith formation contributes to a spiritual development that nurtures future generations of families.

A further task is to support these growing families of faith through a lifetime of partnership with local faith communities. One could argue that creating these partnerships is the task of religious education and youth/young adult ministry; I suggest that it is the responsibility of the entire community. Coordinating these opportunities certainly represents a challenge; I suggest that the benefits to families and local faith communities are well worth the effort. Pastoral leaders who support family faith formation throughout the life cycle can work together to support and enrich all families in their communities. Building these programs can be a daunting task, and as with building a cathedral, it is better to tackle the task one section at a time. For this essay, therefore, I limit the discussion to ways that parent preparation for infant baptism and ministry with teens and young adults can serve to build up faithful marriages and holy families. Adapting John Paul II's argument that marriage preparation takes place in three stages — remote, proximate, and immediate[5] — I explore the ways that faith formation through the life cycle provides support for marriage and contributes to the overall development of family faith.

Setting the Stage: Some Background Information

As one considers the attitudes of U.S. Catholics toward their religion today, we see significant changes from a few decades ago. Many U.S. Catholic adults, especially those born and raised after Vatican II, view the necessity of external religious practice differently from those who came of age before Vatican II.⁶ For example, according to one study, less than 40 percent of Catholics born after 1961 attend Eucharist more than a few times a year.⁷ Moreover, American Catholic teenagers are among the least engaged of all teens expressing a religious affiliation.⁸ More Americans than ever consider themselves to be spiritual but not religious and more Catholics believe wholeheartedly that one can be a church member in good standing without participating regularly in church practices.⁹

Catholic attrition also raises a concern. A recent *Pew Forum Religious Landscape Survey* noted that while 31 percent of Americans were raised in the Catholic Church, 24 percent describe themselves as Catholic today.¹⁰ As sharp as this decline is, the study also notes that attrition rates would be even higher except for the Catholic immigrants who boost numbers in the United States. Pastoral leaders ask: Can we do anything to reverse these trends? Can we encourage people who are loosely if at all connected to the church to see it as a resource for developing spiritually and living faithfully?

Despite the weakness of connection to the church, most adults marrying today still seek religious ceremonies for validation of their marriage. Those in pastoral ministry know that many young people appear in church for the first time as adults when they come for marriage preparation. Can we, as did John Paul II in *Familiaris Consortio,* recognize that even the most secular motivation for coming to the church for marriage can be an opportunity for God's grace to act on a person or a couple?¹¹ Moreover, can we capitalize on this desire, and use it as a stepping-stone for building another layer in the structure of faith?

The fact that so many young adults come to the church for weddings, major holidays, and sacraments for their children indicates that somehow faith traditions do mean something significant to them. This is a cause for hope. If they are willing to participate in a faith community at key points in their lives, perhaps parishes and dioceses can find new ways to strengthen their involvement during the "in-between times."¹² If we continue, however, to reach out to them in old ways, with strategies that do not correspond to the experiences of this generation, we will undoubtedly fail.¹³

Parent Preparation for Infant Baptism as Marriage Enrichment

Over the years, I have advocated parish-based, spiritually rich marriage preparation as one way to connect young adults with a faith community.

Even if a couple has been separated from the church for a number of years, they can form a bond with a vibrant parish through marriage preparation sessions and rituals. As important as it can be as an evangelization tool, however, many family life ministers agree that even the best marriage preparation is not a magic bullet.[14] When couples are consumed with wedding preparations, even those most active in the church may not appreciate fully the sacred in their relationship, regardless of how inspiring their marriage preparation might be. And sadly, we all have met couples who politely sit through our programs, walk down the aisle, and never return. Despite the discouragement, most of us continue to search for new ways to reach out to the engaged in our communities.

Perhaps the time is ripe to ask: How do we provide faith formation for marriage *after* the time of immediate marriage preparation? At what *other* points in the life cycle can we support and enrich marriage through connections with faith communities? For many adults, the times of sacramental preparation for their children are crucial times, because even if parents do not participate regularly in their parish community, they often want their children to celebrate sacraments.[15] Sacramental preparation becomes an opportunity for parent evangelization and a chance to support adult faith. I also argue that it can become a chance to help the parents build their own relationships, especially in the area of shared spirituality. Preparing parents for a child's baptism, for example, can invite parents to think about their shared faith life in the context of both the home and the parish community.[16] While focusing on all sacramental preparation is beyond the scope of this essay, I propose to highlight parent preparation for infant baptism as an example of how adult faith formation and support for married life can occur beyond traditional marriage enrichment programming.

Most parishes and dioceses offer a variety of programs to support marriages, and most require some parent preparation for infant baptism. It does not appear, however, that many make the link between the two. An informal survey of diocesan and parish websites throughout the United States revealed that few websites had extensive information about parent preparation for infant baptism; those that did specified minimal requirements — an hour-long meeting, a DVD presentation, registering in the parish, etc. Rarely do published resources indicate a connection between infant baptism preparation and parent spirituality.[17] While looking at websites is not necessarily the best way to get an in-depth perspective on a parish or diocese, it can give a glimpse into its workings. A purposeful connection is missing between baptism preparation and the faith life of parents; this connection can make clear the links between bringing up children in faith and shared spirituality between the parents.

My presupposition is that parent preparation for infant baptism can serve as a means to provide adults with a tool to support faithful marriage commitments. A key moment of sacramental formation after marriage, parent preparation for infant baptism can serve as a vehicle for marriage enrichment through the faith formation of parents.[18] Seen from this perspective, effective parent preparation for infant baptism programs can both enhance the faith of parents and provide opportunities for them to share that faith with their children.

Using an RCIA Model to Facilitate Parent Preparation for Infant Baptism

I believe that when adults welcome a child into the midst of a family, they may be more open to exploring spirituality than they were at the time of a marriage celebration, when they may have been overwhelmed by the details of the wedding day. Prospective parents awaiting the birth or adoption of a child may concentrate on meaningful questions such as: How does this child become a part of our family? What does it mean for us to grow as a family with this child? How can we develop as a family of faith? Through preparation for a child's baptism, parents can become more aware of how God can be at the center of their family lives and can grow in their ability to share more deeply in the mystery of their relationship — of two becoming one to build a family of faith. Baptism preparation ministers, therefore, are invited not only to educate about baptism, but to draw parents more deeply into the richness of their Catholic faith traditions and personal spirituality.

Is there an existing vehicle for accomplishing this goal? Evidence demonstrates that the *Rite of Christian Initiation of Adults* (RCIA), which has as its foundation faith-sharing rooted in scripture, provides an outstanding framework for nurturing adults on their faith journey and can be adapted for use in preparing for other sacraments.[19] One must note, however, that there is never a perfect correlation between the RCIA and other sacramental preparation modeled on it. This is because in the RCIA people freely choose to enter the process. With other sacramental preparation, including marriage or infant baptism, persons sometimes participate only because they are required to do so if they want to "get a sacrament." The task of ministers is to find ways to move beyond the negative perception of a requirement to help participants enter into the faith journey presupposed by an RCIA model of sacramental preparation.

A simple strategy for implementing a brief RCIA-style process for parent baptism preparation is to invite a small group of couples to come together for four meetings including: (1) a session focused on the history of baptism in the Catholic Church. Why is it so important to our tradition? How did it evolve? What is its significance in the church today? (2) a session helping parents to understand how and why baptism is connected with the overall faith life of a family, (3) a prayer and blessing for baptismal families in the midst of the community's liturgy, and (4) a practical session that educates parents about the key elements of the baptism ritual.[20] The sessions should be designed to involve the parents in faith sharing and should provide excellent content. Moreover, it should be sensitive to the constraints of families with infants and young children; for example, might Sunday mornings after mass be more convenient than evenings for families with infants and young children?

The Process

The first two sessions, ideally, take place with enough time for parents to process the input and consider how they might take a step forward in faith. In all likelihood, this means they should occur several months before the baptism, even if this is before a baby is born. The first session can be devoted to helping parents understand the history of Catholic traditions surrounding baptism. Video resources, lecture, discussion, and questions and answers can constitute the format for the first session.

The second session might simply be guided scripture reflections on what it means to bring new life into a family.[21] Encourage parents to share their thoughts and feelings about how scripture passages speak to them at this stage of their lives. Invite them to reflect on how a passage speaks to them about the impact of a child on their relationship: Does the experience of Mary and Joseph remind them of the great responsibilities associated with bringing a child into the world? Does Psalm 139 help them understand the awesome privilege of co-creating life with God? Assure them that the parish wishes to walk with them as they prepare for their child's baptism.

For the third session, invite families to a Sunday liturgy to be presented to the community and prayed for in the midst of the assembly. If they are regular churchgoers, they can be introduced at the liturgy they usually attend; otherwise, they can come to a parish-designated liturgy. Parents and children are welcomed just as catechumens and candidates are during their preparation for adult initiation. By drawing families into the community's liturgy, parents and other family members get a sense of the way the parish worships, and a taste of the parish's commitment to faith formation at all stages of the life cycle. The parish could conclude the liturgy with hospitality to further introduce parents and their children to other members of the community.[22]

The fourth session focuses on the baptism ritual and how its elements connect with faith-filled family life. Parents can be asked to reflect on these questions:

1. There is a similarity between the water bath of baptism and the bathing of children in the home. How do these actions of loving care in the church community and the home connect with each other?

2. Anointing a child with fragrant oil reminds us of the joy permeating a home when a child becomes a part of the family. How does the atmosphere of a community or a home change with a new child?

3. The white baptismal garment is a powerful reminder that parents are called to clothe their children in all that is good, and that the church takes care to clothe all God's children with the love of Christ. How will we find ways to clothe our children with love?

4. The baptismal candle reveals the light of Christ, present every day in the church community, in the love between parents and children and in the parents' relationship with each other. How do we keep the light of Christ burning brightly in our parishes and in the hearts of all family members?

The questions make explicit the link between the baptismal celebration in church and a household of faith, and help parents understand what it means to build the domestic church each day in their homes.[23] For some parents, this aspect of the preparation may be challenging because they have never considered that their ordinary life can be a source of sanctification. The time of parent preparation for baptism, as with marriage preparation for couples in diverse circumstances, can be an opportunity to accept people as they are and help them take another step in faith. Infant baptism preparation may be the beginning of a welcoming process for parents who have been distant from the church.

If parents are prepared for a child's baptism using this approach or something similar to it, they may become more connected to a parish community and desire to take a more active part in it. Consider ways that opportunities for involvement can be built:

1. Invite families to have their child baptized at a Sunday liturgy, which the *Rite of Christian Initiation of Children* holds up as the ideal time and place for baptism.[24]

2. Recognize that parent preparation for infant baptism can afford the opportunity to enhance programming for young families with children.

3. Make extra efforts to integrate parents into existing ministries and programs — and encourage them to support these activities in manageable ways. Every effort made by an individual or family contributes to the success of parish life.[25]

4. Create specific programs to support the marriage commitment of couples with young children.[26]

To increase chances of success, draw young families into the planning process; ask what they would like and what they would come to! Don't presume to know what will work for them. For example, which might be better for your couples — a night out without the children or an event that allows for baby attendance? Find out what keeps them from coming to events and make efforts to correct problems. Do young families face bad timing, high cost, or lack of interest? Each reason for nonattendance may demand a different response. Try planning and scheduling a few events in the first year, and see what happens. If programmatic ideas come from parents and they participate in event development, there is a greater chance of success.

As we work with families bringing children to the faith community for baptism, let us continue to ask how we might help them grow as households of faith in our midst. These few suggestions do not represent the full range of what we can do, they simply point to ways that parishes can enhance existing baptism preparation opportunities to help families recognize the holiness of their lives and become more active members in parishes.

Teen and Young Adult Evangelization as Proximate Preparation for Marriage

According to *Familiaris Consortio,* proximate preparation for marriage

> ... from the suitable age and with adequate catechesis, as in a catechumenal process — involves a more specific preparation for the sacraments, as it were, a rediscovery of them. This renewed catechesis of young people and others preparing for Christian marriage is absolutely necessary in order that the sacrament may be celebrated and lived with the right moral and spiritual dispositions. The religious formation of young people should be integrated, at the right moment and in accordance with the various concrete requirements, with a preparation for life as a couple.[27]

We face a number of challenges as we attempt to evangelize teens and young adults in parishes today:

1. How do we reconnect young people with the church from which so many of them "graduated" in their early teen years, shortly after Confirmation?[28]

2. How do we help them "rediscover the sacraments" when so many have not discovered them in the first place?

3. How do we provide proximate formation about the vocation of married life when so many have been affected negatively by experiences of marriage in their families of origin and in those of their friends?[29]

As the layers of the cathedral build one upon the other, the experiences of teens and young adults have accumulated to form a perception about faith and church participation. Sometimes that perception is quite negative. Creating an atmosphere that truly welcomes teens and young adults into the hearts of our communities will demand that we set aside our preconceived notions and meet them in ways that will nourish their faith.

One of the greatest difficulties associated with teen and young adult ministry today is that due to early adolescent celebrations of Confirmation and subsequent cessation of formal religious education, young people often are deprived of the opportunity to address spirituality and morality at a more mature level.[30] While their intellectual development continues to grow at a rapid pace, young people's spiritual and religious development often is stunted because developmentally appropriate spiritual activities have ended for them. Many young people "drop out of church" because they neither have been deeply rooted in faith nor connected to the church more than minimally throughout their lives. Often they see the reception of Confirmation as the last stop in their religious development.[31] Many of these young people end all religious education on Confirmation day and do not return to a parish community until they begin marriage preparation.

In particular, teens and young adults often drift from the externals of religious practice[32] and engage in often risky, unsatisfying sexual behavior that contradicts Catholic beliefs. For example, the notion that sex is a commodity rather than a constitutive element of a permanent relationship prevails as much among Catholic young people as any other group.[33] Surprisingly, though, the teens and young adults who participate in church activities are often attracted by pre–Vatican II traditions and devotions.[34] Pastoral ministers should reflect on how we work with these young men and women trying to define their religious identities and affiliations. We're also confronted with how we help these young men and women plan for a future that includes a commitment to a Christian vocation. In relationship to the stated scope of this essay: Can ministry with teens and young adults be a tool for marriage preparation?

High-quality teen and young adult ministry that promotes discussion of serious faith issues and helps young men and women to grow in faith is necessary to help facilitate mature attitudes toward Christian life in general and Christian vocations in particular. It is necessary to make every effort to help our young people recognize what it means to be a follower of Christ in the world today. Moreover, in all ministry programming, it is critical to devote some time to relationship education. By intentionally working with young people on topics such as communication and negotiation skills, family of origin, Catholic values on sexuality, and family spirituality, we can help them enter into a process of adult faith development and proximate preparation for marriage in the overall context of faith formation.

Renewing the Vision: A Framework for Catholic Youth Ministry (the U.S. bishops' 1997 document on ministry for and with teens) and *Sons and Daughters of the Light* (the 1996 pastoral plan for working with young adults) present an ambitious vision for helping young women and men grow in faith and develop as adult disciples of Christ.[35] Both documents support the notion that young men and women need assistance as they engage in discernment regarding their vocational choices, including marriage.

One way that faith communities can incorporate greater awareness and respect for the mystery of human sexuality and married life is to provide teens and young adults with a coherent approach that supports church teaching. While there are a number of different ways to do this, John Paul II's *Theology of the Body* and all the programs flowing from it are growing in popularity. The primary purposes of *Theology of the Body* are to explore the dignity of marriage and sex in a world that often devalues them, to highlight spousal love as a key ingredient of God's plan for humanity, and to reaffirm the intrinsic connections between life and love. It also recognizes the multifaceted dimensions of love as *eros* and *agape*, a theme further developed in Benedict XVI's *Deus Caritas Est*.[36] The approach has weaknesses, to be sure.[37] It can, however, serve as a tool to facilitate teens' and young adults' ongoing reflection on sexuality and the church's official teaching on it.

What is the usefulness of *Theology of the Body* for teen and young adult ministry? To begin, it represents an authoritative teaching of Pope John Paul II on a subject that was dear to his heart, human love and marriage. Moreover, it explores the human person as the culmination of God's creation and emphasizes the need to preserve the sanctity of sex, marriage, and family life.[38] Furthermore, it reflects the tradition of the inseparability of love and life as a principle of natural law and an articulation of God's divine plan for humanity.[39] Throughout *Theology of the Body*, John Paul makes use of scripture texts to illustrate his points about human love and sexual relationship, reflecting on their truth regarding human relationships and God's plan for sex and love.[40]

From a programmatic perspective, *Theology of the Body* is helpful in the following ways:

1. It gives a coherent explanation of why Catholics see sexuality as a gift from God and as a total gift of self[41] and insists that it is a precious gift not to be treated lightly.

2. It helps young people understand that the body is a constitutive element in the call to holiness.

3. It highlights the dignity of the human person, created in God's image.[42]

4. It demonstrates that the fullest image of God is found in loving human relationships[43] and that the perfect community, the Trinity, can be embodied by the life of a loving couple.[44] While we certainly do not image the Trinity perfectly, the person in loving communion stands as

a symbol of the love between the persons of God and the love of God that reaches out in generosity to others. Young people are challenged to recognize that in their relationships they are called to manifest the love of God each day.

5. It articulates the sacramentality of marriage as an expression of human love as found in God's plan and provides a concrete application of that love in today's contemporary life.

If we present *Theology of the Body* in a jargon-free way that engages young people, it can be used well to present the church's official teaching on the dignity and beauty of sexuality. For most effective use, as an evangelization tool that facilitates proximate preparation for marriage, I recommend breaking *Theology of the Body* into manageable segments, much as John Paul did in his weekly addresses. Try focusing on key themes such as "spousal love," "sacramentality of marriage," and "inseparability of life and love." Many young people who have not had opportunities to talk about sexuality in a faith-based context will benefit from programs based on *Theology of the Body* because they give clear reasons for Catholic sexual teaching and reinforce that young people are precious gifts from God, so valuable that they deserve to be treated with dignity and respect at all times.

Besides youth faith formation programs, how else do we enhance proximate preparation for marriage? As with parent preparation for infant baptism, we must turn to the family—the household of faith.

Building a Household of Faith and Proximate Preparation for Marriage

In 1993, the U.S. bishops' landmark letter *Follow the Way of Love* declared that a family is our first community and the most basic way in which the Lord gathers us, forms us, and acts in the world.[45] For better or worse, it is in the family that we first learn about life. We experience parental roles, gender expectations, problem-solving skills, relationships with adults and children first and foremost in a family of origin. Inevitably, these experiences affect our lives.

In addition, the family of origin shapes faith. Does the family discuss faith on a regular basis? Is shared worship a part of the family experience? Is religious experience exclusively limited to what goes on in a church building, or does the family perceive itself as a place where faith is built? For so many young people today, the parental decision to be disconnected from a faith community has had an impact on them. One ministry goal for those working with young people is to supplement the family faith experiences (or lack thereof) with other opportunities for shared faith in the context of parish communities.

What does family holiness mean? Is it about how many hours are spent in prayer and community service? That may happen, but as we've already seen, family holiness primarily means that families take on the attitudes of Christ — generosity, openness to God, a stance of prayer, concern for justice — and live them each day in the midst of their homes. While they may never name it as such, families such as these enter into the paschal mystery each day. Through ordinary life events, they enter into the dying and rising of Christ. In the midst of family interactions, all members are asked to die to selfishness and rise to generosity, die to unrealistic expectations and rise to new outlooks, and die to narrow-mindedness and rise to openness. In other words, every loving action in the family reveals the death and resurrection of Christ in its midst. In all these acts of dying and rising and in the many other activities that take place within ordinary family life, God's Spirit is present and active. Holiness, as Mother Teresa reminded us in her 1979 Nobel Peace Prize acceptance speech, is not necessarily centered on doing great things; instead, it focuses on doing small things with great love.[46] These ordinary activities lay the foundation of holiness for households of faith. Moreover, all members, regardless of age, are called to make the connections between their life of faith at home and the celebration of faith within the wider church community. Just as surely as Christ is really present in the Eucharist, He truly is present in the loving interactions, challenges, problem solving, anxiety, and, yes, even arguing that takes place in the home. Families aware of their call to holiness participate in the mission of Christ twenty-four hours a day, seven days a week in the context of their homes and local communities.

As those engaged in the enterprise of building faith at home, families must learn to appreciate and use the gifts of young people. All too often in our society, and sometimes in our families and church communities as well, young people are experienced as problems to be solved or challenges to be faced. Yet day in and day out, they enhance and enliven family life with their experiences and fresh perspectives. Families can grow in faith together by sharing the new world vision experienced by teens and young adults. Rather than adults thinking that they have all the answers, part of what must happen in families and faith communities is to hear the new voices of young people. Just as Jeremiah was a young man, called to be a prophet by God,[47] and just as Mary of Nazareth, a young woman, was chosen to be the mother of Jesus,[48] the teens and young adults in our midst can reveal God's love in homes and parish communities. The task of the entire faith community is to listen to their voices and encourage them to be apostles, sent forth by Christ as evangelizers in the world.

Proximate Preparation in the Parish Community

After the church of the home, the local parish is often the next place where young people's lives of faith are shaped and shared. Parishes can serve as sanctuaries where we meet God and go forth to serve God's people. As parish teams work with young people, they must ask how well they welcome them and integrate them fully into the faith life of the community, how often they consider them to be subjects of mission rather than simply objects of it, how much they encourage meaningful participation and a leadership voice at every table in the community. "Young people are more likely to gain a sense of identity in the community if they are regarded as full-fledged members."[49] But what does this mean? For too many years, we have, in well-intentioned but often unsuccessful ways, tried to make young people feel "special" by separating them from rather than integrating them into the life of the parish. While it certainly is important to provide programming that will nourish and develop the spiritual lives of young people, it is just as crucial to make sure that these same young people have opportunities to work within the community to help build up the entire body of Christ. Rather than keeping teens and young adults on the margins of the community, parishes should ask how they can draw them in.

Parish communities can play an important role in the lives of young people by engaging them in efforts that will support their faith and encourage healthy relationships. Parish communities can support young people through:

1. presence and enthusiasm at liturgies and events led by teens;
2. hospitality for and with teens as they integrate into the life of the parish;
3. multiple opportunities of prayer for young people;

4. opportunities for meaningful conversation about important life issues such as vocation choice, moral decision making, social justice, liturgy, and the range of topics that are priorities for the young people in our midst;

5. service that helps them make connections between prayer and life.

Teens and young adults provide a witness of energy and enthusiasm within a parish; conversely, the parish supports young people through their own witness to Christ and loving support for them. As part of any effort to evangelize teens and young adults, conduct an inventory of a parish. Does the parish have the following characteristics that support teen and young adult involvement?

1. *An open, welcoming community.* If a parish has a strong sense of community, it will be likely to see the value of welcoming young people into its mainstream. In a parish with a weak experience of community, it may be easier to engage in defensive behavior and find excuses why teens and young adults can't be integrated into the life of a parish.

2. *A strong spirit of faith formation at all levels.* If a parish community understands what it means to foster lifelong faith formation it will be better able to see the faith formation needs of teens and young adults. Through processes of faith sharing, service, and community prayer, young people will begin to see the importance of becoming disciples in a parish.

3. *Willingness to enter into a continuing process of team development and support.* Are those involved in teen and young adult ministry willing to grow in their ministry through training, shared prayer, and community building?

4. *Inclusion of new young people in all ministerial roles in the parish.* Reach out to recruit some new people to minister for and with the youth of the parish — young marrieds, recent college grads, older teens. They'll like the invitation, and you'll get different people involved in the community. Be sure, however, to be aware of all requirements for screening and training volunteers.

5. *Willingness of the parish leadership to support the faith formation of young people.* Teen and young adult faith formation is not a quick fix;

it is a commitment to creating disciples through ongoing pastoral care. This takes time and effort to be successful.

Teens and young adults are gifts to our communities. Through our welcoming and their willingness to participate, entire faith communities are enriched. Along the way, we can help teens and young adults by supporting them in their faith formation, and inviting them to think about the ways that their faith is closely linked to their vocational choices.

Conclusions

The layers of the cathedral in Florence give us a metaphor for examining a lifelong process of faith formation and continuing preparation for and support of the vocation of Christian marriage. Just as structures were added, deleted, and modified over a long period of time, insights, support, and education for the lifetime of marriage takes place over many years — from the sacramental preparation of young couples through faith formation and education of teens and young adults. The cycles of faith formation and marriage preparation then flow to the next generation.

On paper, this may sound like a simple process, but as we have shown, it is a complex building process that includes revisions in original plans, replacing structures when necessary, and even tearing out what's already been built because it doesn't meet needs anymore. As scholars, pastoral leaders, and faith community members, it is necessary to consider how we facilitate the building process. We invite people into this life of faith, show them how their family lives contribute to its overall structure, nurture them as new structures of faith involvement emerge layer by layer, and gently encourage them to grow and develop as true foundations of faith who will serve as the bedrock for the next generation. By working to develop outstanding faith formation at key points in a family's life, and in all the in-between times, in particular when welcoming a child into the family and helping young men and women realize their potential as faithful adults, we can contribute to building a structure of faithful people, called to holiness in their daily lives, and challenged to transmit faith to those around them — their partners, children, and those in the wider Christian community.

Through the life cycle, we walk with these families and take advantage of those things that help them focus more clearly on the message of faith. We contribute by adding layers to their structures, supporting the places that are weak, and removing the debris that has tumbled down, knowing that we do this only with God's help and that of the community. We see beautiful families in our midst and know that the process of building faithful disciples, like the construction of the magnificent cathedral in Florence, is a complex and rich process that takes place over the course of a lifetime, and from generation to generation.

Chapter Nine

Learning from the Liturgy

PAUL COVINO

For most of my twenty-six years in lay ecclesial ministry, my major area of interest, research, writing, and pastoral practice has been the celebration of Christian marriage. Beginning with a wonderful experience of helping to plan and then participating in a parish-based marriage preparation program at Holy Trinity Church in Washington, D.C., in the early 1980s, I have worked with countless couples as they prepared for the celebration of their marriage, I've had the privilege of working with colleagues and parishioners throughout North America whose interests and expertise have covered the myriad aspects of ministry to the engaged and newly married, and I have benefited greatly from the insights of theologians whose writings have focused on marriage. Like the group gathered for this symposium with diverse areas of expertise but a common dedication to life-giving marriage ministry in the Catholic Church today, the couples and colleagues that I've encountered in my work relating to marriage have convinced me that effective marriage ministry needs all of us working collaboratively and together: bishops, priests, deacons, family life ministers, catechists, theologians, musicians, and liturgists. I have grown immeasurably from graced opportunities over these years to work with people who have transcended their particular specializations in marriage ministry for a commitment to cohesive pastoral care of engaged, married, and separated or divorced members of the Body of Christ, and I sense that same spirit among the group that has gathered here.

The liturgical celebration of marriage can, and should, be a vital part of effective Catholic marriage ministry today as well as a source of theological reflection on the sacrament of marriage. Let me begin with a story that I first heard in a class many years ago during my first semester of graduate school at Notre Dame. The story has stuck with me over these years partly because, as the professor was recounting it, a storm was visibly brewing outside and, as a northeasterner unfamiliar with such midwestern storms, I was sure that

I was going to be sucked up into a tornado's vortex and deposited miles away in a cornfield, like a bad replay of the storm scene from *The Wizard of Oz*. More important, this story has stuck with me for what it says about the interplay of theology and liturgy for us Catholics and, for our purposes today, for what it suggests about the value of considering what the wedding liturgy has to contribute to our discussion of marriage.

Many years ago, a bright young theologian from the West was fascinated with the Eastern Orthodox churches. He applied for, and was granted, a sabbatical from the university where he was teaching to study the Orthodox faith. Pulling together all the money he had been saving, he purchased round-trip passage to Russia. During his journey there, he designed the focus of his research: he decided not to go to the universities or the monasteries, but to go directly to the people, to learn what they believed. And so the theologian spent his time among the peasants of the Russian villages. "Tell me," he would ask, "what is it that you believe in your religion? I'm a theologian from the West and am here to study the Orthodox faith. Can you explain your faith to me?" To his surprise, the answers he received were brief and, to his scholarly mind, incomplete. The days and weeks went by, and he found himself with very few notes, very little information.

Finally, the day of his departure came. The theologian walked disappointedly to the small station in the village where he would catch the train that would take him to the port and the ship back home. As he was walking, an old woman in a horse-drawn cart came along and offered him a ride. It was a Sunday and she, like many others in the town, was on her way to church. "You look so sad, young man," the woman remarked. He responded, "I have been here for weeks to study your faith. I have talked to many people, but no one has been able to explain what you believe. Now I have spent all my savings, and I have nothing to show for it." The old woman stopped the cart in front of the church and said to the theologian, "Come into the church with me." "Oh, I can't," he replied. "I'm not a member of your religion and, besides, I'll miss my train." The old woman got down from the cart, looked up at the theologian, and said, "Young man, it seems to me that you have only two choices: you can get on the train and go home empty-handed, or you can come into this church for our liturgy and see what we believe."

In a profoundly simple way, the woman taught the theologian something quite basic and essential not only to Orthodox Christianity, but also to Roman Catholicism and other religious traditions with a strong liturgical identity: if you want to know what the church believes, then come worship with the church. It's a maxim attributed to Prosper of Aquitaine in the fifth century: *legem credendi lex statuat supplicandi*, or in its more common abbreviated form *lex orandi, lex credendi*, which has been translated to mean that the law of prayer is the law of faith, the church believes as she prays, the liturgy expresses the belief of the church and shapes the faith of the assembly. The *Catechism of the Catholic Church* cites this maxim and explains it this way: "The meaning and grace of the sacrament... are clearly seen in the rites of its celebration. By following the gestures and words of this celebration with attentive participation, the faithful are initiated into the riches this sacrament signifies and actually brings about."[1] Approaching the liturgy as a primary source of our theology, the *Catechism* devotes several paragraphs in the chapter on each sacrament to describing how the faith of the church is expressed in the signs and symbols of that particular sacramental celebration.

All of this suggests that the liturgy itself is a form of *primary theology*, that is, an unfolding of the church's faith in the very experience of the texts, rituals, and symbols of the liturgical celebration.[2] The same could be said about the married life. The experience of married couples is another form of *primary theology* insofar as we see the church's faith about marriage broken open in the lived reality of the marriage covenant. *Secondary theology*, which has its own unique and equally important contribution, is the more systematic reflection on the church's faith contained in catechisms and the writings of theologians. I want to suggest that the text and symbolic actions of the church's *Rite of Marriage* (and the revised *Order for Celebrating Marriage*, which was published in Latin in 1990, but has not yet been approved for use in the United States) and the actual use of these texts and celebration of these symbolic actions in wedding liturgies represent a *primary theology* of the sacrament, that is, an understanding of marriage drawn from the liturgical rite itself. At the same time, the first section of the introduction to the ritual text entitled the "Importance and Dignity of the Sacrament of Marriage"[3] provides a *secondary theology* of marriage, a summary of the church's doctrine on the sacrament. These points are considered "the fundamental elements of Christian doctrine" that form the foundation for catechesis with people preparing for marriage.[4]

Before proceeding, let me acknowledge a caution that some have raised to this line of thinking. In our not too distant past, Catholic marriage theology and ministry were heavily focused on the wedding whereas less attention was devoted to the unfolding of the sacrament in the lived experience of marriage. Movements such as Marriage Encounter have helped to broaden our focus with their reminders that "a wedding is a day, a marriage is a lifetime," and our marriage theology and ministry have benefited from the wide variety of perspectives and insights that are represented here at this symposium. What I am advocating here is simply that, given our sacramental and liturgical tradition, the wedding liturgy needs to have a fundamental place at the table when it comes to our conversations about marriage ministry in the church today. This, I believe, is what the bishops at the Second Vatican Council meant when they said that "liturgy does not exhaust the entire activity of the Church ... [but] nevertheless the liturgy is the summit toward which the activity of the Church is directed; it is also the fount from which all her power flows."[5] In the years since the Council, we've seen this vision enfleshed most profoundly in the *Rite of Christian Initiation of Adults*. As with Christian initiation, our marriage ministry is most effective when theology and catechesis, marriage preparation and enrichment, and the wedding liturgy are experienced as inseparable components in a cohesive whole.

In suggesting implications for us and for the bishops' pastoral letter, I envision theologians and catechists drawing on the wedding liturgy itself, as well as the lived experience of married and formerly married Christians, as sources of theological reflection and catechesis. I'm suggesting an approach in which marriage ministers would see the wedding liturgy as a culminating moment in the marriage preparation process and would be concerned about the careful preparation and life-giving celebration of every wedding liturgy celebrated in the parish. And I'm imagining musicians and liturgists who understand their role with engaged couples as part of an overall marriage ministry and are, therefore, more concerned with the unique journey that has brought these two people to this point in their lives and less with simply enforcing a blacklist of prohibited music.

Returning to the story of the theologian and the old woman, then, the question I want to pose is this: What contribution does the liturgical celebration of marriage make to the theological foundations for marriage ministry today? What understanding of marriage is reflected in our current rites of marriage, as celebrated in American parishes? What would the theologian have learned about American Catholic attitudes toward marriage if he had been present at the 10:00 a.m. wedding at the local parish? Or, closer to home, what message about Christian marriage today will be left with the millions of worshipers at the thousands of weddings to be celebrated this year in the Roman Catholic parishes and chapels in the United States? Will they find a hope-filled alternative to society's despair about committed relationships in the church's proclamation of marriage as "an intimate partnership of life and love,"[6] or will they exit the church, like the groom in a poignant Jack Ziegler cartoon, saying "not bad for a ceremony steeped in meaningless symbolism."[7]

As a sacramental church, we Catholics know that every word, gesture, symbol, and ritual action in the liturgy conveys meaning. There is no such thing as a meaningless symbol, no such thing as a neutral ritual. The question is: Are the messages and the values conveyed in our liturgies consistent with what we believe about what is taking place? More important, the nature of symbol and ritual is such that they shape our impressions and form our understanding of what it taking place. The question is: Are they forming an understanding that is consistent with what the church believes about what is taking place? These are important questions because it is commonly acknowledged that weddings are great opportunities for evangelization.

If we were to ask these questions honestly of our current rites of marriage, I think we'd have to give a mixed response. I say mixed because the answer would vary if we were talking about the "rite in print" or the "rite in action." By the "rite in print," I mean simply the texts and rubrics of the ritual book. The "rite in action" is the actual liturgical celebration. There is often quite a difference between the two. Part of that difference is due to inculturation, the manner in which Catholics of a particular culture enflesh and ritualize the faith. Thanks to the work of scholars like Anscar Chupungco, we have come to understand how natural and necessary the process of liturgical inculturation is, and the *Rite of Marriage* makes generous provision for adaptation.[8] At the same time, there is a difference between faithful inculturation and subsuming the church's faith to prevailing cultural norms. The liturgy, at its best, not only dons the garments of each culture, but also challenges cultural norms that may be contrary to the Gospel and the faith of the church. Part of our task as marriage ministers serving the church in the United States is to ask how the rites of marriage might find expression in the wonderful diversity of American culture while, at the same time, challenging American customs surrounding marriage that obscure and even contradict the church's faith concerning this sacrament.

We turn first to the "rite in print." The *Rite of Marriage* has served the church in the United States since its promulgation in 1969, and we await the U.S. edition of the *Order for Celebrating Marriage*. The introduction in the Latin edition of the *Order for Celebrating Marriage* weighs in at forty-four paragraphs, more than double the size of the eighteen-paragraph introduction to the *Rite of Marriage*. The eleven paragraphs that outline the fundamental elements of Christian doctrine concerning marriage in the *Order for Celebrating Marriage* also more than double their counterpart in the current rite. As in the *Rite of Marriage*, this section in the *Order for Celebrating Marriage* draws heavily from the chapter on "The Dignity of Marriage and the Family" from the Second Vatican Council's *Pastoral Constitution on the Church in the Modern World*, along with references to the *Dogmatic Constitution on the Church* and the scriptures. New references in this section of the *Order for Celebrating Marriage* are to Pope John Paul II's apostolic exhortation *Familiaris Consortio*, the *Code of Canon Law*, Tertullian's *Ad uxorem*, and the text of the nuptial blessing, the last of which is particularly noteworthy since it represents the kind of primary theology I mentioned earlier.

There are several doctrinal principles that appear in the *Order for Celebrating Marriage* that are not addressed directly in the *Rite of Marriage*. Before reviewing these, let us look at the points that are common to both editions of the rite.

1. The marriage of Christians is a symbol of the unity and love between Christ and the church.[9] While the *Rite of Marriage* states this as a matter of fact, the *Order for Celebrating Marriage* provides several concrete examples of this self-sacrificing love: e.g., "Just as Christ loved the Church and gave himself up for it, so Christian partners work to nurture and foster their union in equal dignity, mutual dedication, and an undivided affection that has its source in divine love."[10]

2. Christian marriage is established by the covenant that the partners freely give to and receive from each other.[11] The two editions speak of the marriage covenant in similar terms, but the *Order for Celebrating Marriage* amplifies the significance of this covenant by referring to God's "covenant of love and fidelity"[12] and "Christ's covenant with the Church."[13]

3. Christian married couples cooperate with their creator in the procreation and education of children.[14] This aspect of Christian marriage is emphasized much more strongly in the *Order for Celebrating Marriage,* which echoes the *Rite of Marriage* in stating that children are the couple's "crowning reward" and "the most outstanding gift of marriage."[15] The revised rite goes on to add that, in raising children, spouses "help each other

toward sanctity," cultivate "a spirit of sacrifice," and "fulfill their human and Christian responsibility."[16]

4. There are several purposes of marriage.[17] Like the *Rite of Marriage*, the *Order for Celebrating Marriage* does not limit the purpose of marriage to the procreation and education of children. Noting that its emphasis on children is "not to disparage the other purposes of matrimony,"[18] the *Order for Celebrating Marriage* specifies in much more detail than the *Rite of Marriage* those other purposes: "an intimacy of life and community of love,"[19] helping "each other toward sanctity,"[20] nurturing and fostering "equal dignity, mutual dedication and an undivided affection,"[21] and "public witness before everyone."[22]

Several additional principles appear in the *Order for Celebrating Marriage*. Consistent with the introductions to the *Order of Christian Funerals*, the *Rite of Christian Initiation of Adults*, and the *Pastoral Care of the Sick*, the first eleven paragraphs of the *Order for Celebrating Marriage* display a more comprehensive understanding of sacrament than appears in the *Rite of Marriage* and other texts from the first round of postconciliar revision of rites. These additional principles paint a much richer and more complete picture of Christian marriage.

1. Marriage is part of the order of creation taken up and renewed in Christ.[23] The "intimacy of life and community of love"[24] that are the basis of marriage are portrayed as part of God's plan in creation. Far beyond the Pauline begrudging tolerance of marriage,[25] the *Order for Celebrating Marriage* speaks of marriage as divinely ordered,[26] renewed in Christ, and raised by Christ to the dignity of a sacrament "so that it could signify more clearly and be an easier example of his marriage with the Church."[27]

2. The sacramental nature of marriage is rooted in baptism.[28] Through baptism, the spouses are already "inserted permanently into Christ's covenant with the Church... so that their conjugal community is taken up into Christ's love and is endowed with the power of his sacrifice."[29] Marriage is a graced way in which the spouses live out their baptismal commitment and, in doing so, serve as icons (or sacraments) of Christ. The sacrament has as much to do with who the spouses are (i.e., human beings taken up in Christ and joined to Christ's covenant with the church through baptism) as with what they do (i.e., freely and mutually give and accept each other, help each other toward sanctity).

3. The sacrament of marriage unfolds over time.[30] Although not as explicitly as the *Rite of Christian Initiation of Adults*, the *Order for Celebrating*

Marriage seems to suggest a view of the sacrament as more than a specific, definable moment. While the consent and vows are proclaimed at a given time, thus establishing the marriage, the purposes and characteristics of Christian marriage only become evident over time. Drawing on Tertullian and Pope John Paul II, the *Order for Celebrating Marriage* speaks of marriage as "a binding of two believers in one hope, one discipline, and the same kind of service," a public witness lived day by day, a continuous call from "the same God who calls spouses to matrimony" in the first place.[31]

Proceeding beyond the introduction, we can list the theological themes in the scriptural and prayer texts of the rite. Since the U.S. edition of the *Order for Celebrating Marriage* is not yet available, I will limit myself to the texts in the current *Rite of Marriage*. Beginning with the scripture readings, we see the following motifs:

In the Old Testament: marriage as part of the order of creation; husband and wife become one body in marriage; the place of prayer in marriage and family life; the goodness of the sensuality of love; marriage as a covenant.

In the New Testament: the love of God in Christ; the reflection of love in the married couple's concerns for the needs of others and in their hospitality to others; the body as a temple of God's Spirit; the countercultural nature of love exemplified in its attributes of patience, kindness, and humility; the deference that spouses are to show one another; love and the various other virtues of the Christian life.

In the Gospels: the beatitudes as guiding principles for married life; the married couple as salt of the earth and light to the world; the practice of the Gospel in married life; love as the greatest commandment; the inseparable nature of what God has joined in marriage; Christ's concern for married couples as exemplified in the wedding feast at Cana; marriage as symbolic of Christ's union with God and the church.

Turning to the *prayer texts* in the current rite, we see an equally rich portrait of marriage. Like the scripture readings, these texts are primary theology, the engagement by the worshiping assembly in proclaiming the church's faith concerning marriage. Among the theological motifs that are found in the prayer texts are the following:

1. Love as fundamental to Christian marriage. God is praised for the love that has brought these two people to this point, and God is asked to bless their love.

2. Covenant as a pattern for the marriage relationship. Just as God entered into a covenant with the people, so husband and wife are enjoined to undertake marriage as a covenant.

3. Faithfulness as a hallmark of the marriage covenant. God's covenant with the people and Christ's union with God and the church are marked by fidelity. The marriage covenant mirrors these relationships by the life-long fidelity of spouses.

4. The couple serves as co-creators with God as they develop this new family in the church and as they bring children into that family.

5. Husband and wife help each other to grow in faith. The family that this couple begins is, in this sense, the "domestic church."

6. The equality and complementarity of wife and husband in the marriage relationship.

7. Service to others and simplicity of lifestyle as characteristic of the Christian family created by marriage.

8. The Christian community as the context for celebrating marriage.

9. The unfolding of the grace of the sacrament throughout married life, not just limited to the wedding celebration.

The scripture readings and prayer texts of the rite are fruitful sources of theological insight into the sacrament. Just as importantly, they can serve as a rich source of reflection on the Christian married life for engaged couples as they prepare to enter into the marriage covenant and for married people as they discover, through good times and bad, the graces and challenges of marriage. As we have learned from the *Rite of Christian Initiation of Adults*, the mystagogical unpacking of texts and ritual actions after the liturgical event can yield entirely new insights. Married couples can see more and more of the wisdom in the texts and ritual actions of the *Rite of Marriage* as their marriages develop over the years.

As Catholics, though, we are well aware that texts are only one component of the liturgy. As powerfully — and often more powerfully — than the texts, the symbols and ritual actions of the liturgy tell the story of what the church celebrates and believes. When we get beyond scripture and prayer texts, we also begin to see how the "rite in action" often diverges from the "rite in print." Here, in the actual celebration of marriage, is where the basic form of marriage catechesis and evangelization take place. Here, in the weddings celebrated week in and week out at parishes all over the country, is the privileged opportunity for us to proclaim and celebrate what we believe about marriage. Here, in this particular church with this particular couple, the pastoral decision is made as to how much of our Catholic story of marriage we will tell, how much we will share with this assembly. When we make these pastoral decisions, more is at stake than "How can I make it through this wedding with the least hassle and the fewest calls from an angry mother of the bride?" What is at stake is whether the church's faith concerning marriage is going to have a life beyond books on our shelves and whether we will take advantage of the opportunity that the wedding liturgy presents for evangelization about Christian marriage.

Let us turn, then, to some of the nonverbal ritual elements of the wedding liturgy to see what theological message is conveyed in them.

1. The texts of the *Rite of Marriage* present hospitality as one of the hallmarks of the Christian couple. The wedding liturgy presents a unique opportunity for the couple to practice hospitality, especially considering the mix of people who often make up the assembly at weddings. Yet the potential for offering hospitality is often lost as it is reduced to the task of seating people, a task delegated more often than not to a group of guys who may have been out way too late the night before the wedding, that is, the ushers. The potential is that this could be a true act of hospitality by the couple and their parents to the people who have supported the couple throughout their engagement and their lives and who now gather to witness and celebrate their marriage. In a growing number of places, this is happening as the couple and their parents are at the door of the church before the wedding to greet arriving worshipers while their male and female attendants cordially seat people. For this practice to become more common, we have to proclaim boldly that our faith simply does not admit of any superstition that would keep the bride and groom from seeing one another in the time leading up to the start of the wedding liturgy.

2. For almost forty years, the *Rite of Marriage* has presented a single instruction for the entrance procession at Catholic weddings: "The ministers go first, followed by the priest, and then the bride and the bridegroom. According to local custom, they may be escorted by at least their parents and the two witnesses."[32] There is no mention of the custom whereby the bride enters with her father and the bridesmaids and meets the groom who appears out of the blue at the head of the aisle. Unlike the common American form of the procession, which suggests that the bride is given away by one

man to another man, the faith of the church holds that the bride and groom enter marriage mutually and as equal, complementary partners. This is why the tune known as "Here Comes the Bride" is not recommended for the procession: its focus on the bride alone contradicts the church's emphasis on the couple.

In addition to both bride and groom, the *Rite of Marriage* includes the parents of the bride and groom in the entrance procession. Once again, the ritual action enfleshes the church's faith: mothers *and* fathers contribute to the formation of their sons and daughters. In their document *A Family Perspective in Church and Society*, the U.S. bishops remind us that marriage creates a new family from two existing families. The wedding liturgy marks not only the new union between husband and wife, but in a very real way, their taking leave of their parents and family of origin. The entrance procession as outlined in the *Rite of Marriage* gives ritual expression to our Catholic reverence for our families of origin and to the need for leave-taking.

In this scenario, the father of the bride is not left out; he is simply joined in his happy role by the bride's mother and the groom's parents, the latter of whom are often overlooked in the common American approach to weddings where, as one commentator remarked, they are expected to "wear beige and be unobtrusive." The entrance procession, in the vision of the church, is not intended to reflect who is footing the bill for the reception; it is intended to be a ritual movement into a new state in life and a new order within the church, a movement supported by the parents who have helped their son or daughter on the journey to this day.

3. The Second Vatican Council challenged us to understand and experience sacraments as "celebrations of the Church."[33] Quoting the Council, the *Catechism* reaffirms that "liturgical services pertain to the whole body of the Church. They manifest it, and have effects upon it.... Rites which are meant to be celebrated in common with the faithful present and actively participating, should as far as possible be celebrated in that way rather than by an individual and quasi-privately."[34] Nowhere has this been a more elusive goal than at weddings.

Weddings are parish celebrations, as Fr. Austin Fleming reminds us in his book *Parish Weddings*.[35] Just as we invite engaged couples into more active participation in the life of the parish, we also invite parishioners to support engaged couples through prayer. The *Book of Blessings* provides an order for blessing engaged couples at a parish gathering.[36] Parishioners should always feel welcome to participate in weddings in the parish, with or without a formal invitation. Why couldn't parishes list upcoming weddings in the bulletin, with an invitation to parishioners to keep these couples in their prayers and to participate in the wedding liturgy? The *Order for Celebrating Marriage* goes so far as to offer the possibility of celebrating marriage within Sunday Eucharist as a visible sign of the ecclesial context of marriage.[37]

4. The longstanding teaching of the church in the West is that the bride and groom are the ministers of the sacrament of marriage. They marry each other; the priest or deacon is the church's chief witness. The very positioning and posture of the couple and the priest or deacon during the marriage rite should reflect their unique roles. This theological insight is lost when the bride and groom turn their backs to the assembly during the marriage rite. In no other postconciliar sacramental rite does the minister of the sacrament do this. It is more appropriate to their role as minister of the sacrament for the couple to stand in such a way that the entire assembly can see and hear them exchange their vows and exchange their rings. In many places now, the couple stands to the front of the sanctuary for the marriage rite while the priest or deacon stands in the aisle at the front of the assembly. Since the proclamation of the vows is part of the sacramental action with which the bride and groom marry each other, it is better for the bride and groom to say their vows directly to each other rather than repeating phrases after the priest or deacon or simply responding "I do" to the question form of the vows.

In some of what I have discussed above, we confront the tension that exists between dominant social and cultural norms for weddings and the vision of the wedding liturgy that is contained in the church's rite. This is no small challenge, and it points out how easily the "rite in print" can get overwhelmed by peripheral items. Twenty years ago, Fr. Bob Hovda made this point in speaking about baptism: "I remember a pamphlet on baptism which contained innumerable suggestions for the celebration of that rite but did not once mention the actual bathing in water. To miss the point of a thing — that totally takes some doing. Immersion in baptism, conviction and reaching out to the hearers in the proclamation of the word, eating from the common plate and drinking from the common cup — these are essentials. Start with them! Don't leave the shriveled and neglected essential elements untouched while concentrating on the periphery!"[38] There are many wedding resources that do the same disservice to weddings that the pamphlet that Fr. Hovda mentions did to the baptismal rite. The result is that some of the most important insights into Christian marriage and some of the most basic principles of good liturgy are obscured by well-intentioned, but peripheral, social customs. When that happens, the "rite in action" does not proclaim or celebrate the fullness of the church's faith concerning marriage. When that happens, the great opportunity for evangelization that weddings present is either lost or greatly diluted.

Recommendations

1. Encourage theological reflection on the church's marriage rite and the celebration of the wedding liturgy. As we continue to prepare for the revised *Order for Celebrating Marriage,* the church could benefit from the reflections of systematic theologians who explore the theological riches and shortcomings of the revised rite. In particular, theological reflection on the proposed order for the celebration of marriage in the presence of a lay presider[39] will be needed if this option is to receive serious consideration for the U.S. edition of the *Order for Celebrating Marriage* and if pastoral ministers and engaged couples are going to understand the rationale for this form of the rite. The insights of theologians could also be a tremendous help to our bishops in the preparation and review of the translation of the *Order for Celebrating Marriage* for use in the United States.

2. Include the wedding liturgy as an essential consideration in the upcoming pastoral letter on marriage from the U.S. bishops and in marriage preparation programs and resources. Present the wedding liturgy as the summit toward which the activity of marriage preparation is directed and the fount from which the grace of the sacrament flows for the lived experience of the marriage covenant. Draw on the texts and ritual actions of the marriage rite to illustrate the church's understanding of marriage and encourage couples to pray with and reflect on the texts of the wedding liturgy during their period of engagement. Most couples only peruse the scripture and prayer texts of the *Rite of Marriage* to decide which of these texts will be used at their wedding liturgy. Long before decisions have to be made about which texts will be used in the liturgy, give couples these texts and encourage them to pray with them together. This would be a particularly pertinent way to encourage couples to develop a habit of prayer together. After the wedding, these texts can be used mystagogically to help the couple reflect on the lived experience of marriage in light of the church's understanding of marriage.

3. Let the energy surrounding the bishops' pastoral letter on marriage be an opportunity to reinvigorate the process of translating and adapting the *Order for Celebrating Marriage* for use in the United States. The Latin *editio typica* of the *Order for Celebrating Marriage* was published in 1990, and a couple of committees have contributed time and energy toward the bishops' efforts to produce a U.S. edition of the *Order for Celebrating Marriage,* but seventeen years after the revised *editio typica,* we are still using the *Rite of Marriage* from 1969. In the production of this revised rite for use in the United States, let us take our inspiration from the *Rite of Christian Initiation of Adults,* the *Pastoral Care of the Sick,* and the *Order of Christian Funerals,* which give us models for how catechesis, pastoral care, and liturgy can be integrated. We can certainly do the same with marriage.

4. Offer additional rites for marking the movement from the single life to engagement through the various stages of marriage. I'm not suggesting a formal catechumenate-like structure for marriage preparation, although others have presented excellent models for this,[40] but I do believe that the *Rite of Christian Initiation of Adults,* the *Pastoral Care of the Sick,* and the *Order of Christian Funerals* show us how prayers and rites of varying solemnity can celebrate the grace present in various moments along the way and call on God's blessing for the next stages. In particular, I would encourage the U.S. bishops to seek more generous provisions for the public celebration of "The Order for the Blessing of an Engaged Couple" that is already contained in the *Book of Blessings.* Rubrical directives currently prohibit celebrating this blessing within mass, yet engaged couples could benefit from the grace and support that comes from the prayer of the gathered community, and it would benefit the public character of Christian marriage if the local community were more aware of who is preparing for marriage.

5. Let the wedding liturgy be an opportunity for evangelization about Christian marriage. Encourage couples to resist the consumerism evident in much of the wedding industry and to choose options for the wedding liturgy that encourage the participation of the entire assembly and that reflect an authentically Christian understanding of marriage. There is tremendous pressure on engaged couples to spend beyond their means in order to have "the perfect day." Pastoral ministers, feeling helpless in the face of such societal pressure, sometimes bracket the wedding liturgy as "just one hour" that doesn't make or break a marriage and so unwittingly give tacit approval for a consumerist extravaganza that is clearly at odds with most of what the

texts and ritual actions of the wedding liturgy actually proclaim and celebrate. Wedding liturgies can be festive celebrations that joyfully proclaim the church's faith regarding marriage, while not buying into the commercialism that pervades many current American assumptions about weddings. In particular, give attention to those current, but largely ignored, provisions in the *Rite of Marriage* for texts and rituals that most clearly reflect the church's faith regarding marriage, such as the entrance of the bride and groom together with their parents and the encouragement of active participation in the liturgy by the assembly, which acts as witness to the marriage.

Part Three

COMMUNITIES

Chapter Ten

Marriage and Family Ministry among Hispanic/Latino Catholics

ALEJANDRO AGUILERA-TITUS

IN 1983 THE BISHOPS of the United States wrote a pastoral letter on Hispanic ministry titled *The Hispanic Presence: Challenge and Commitment*. The pastoral letter brought great joy to Hispanic Catholics as they heard the bishops say: "At this moment of grace we recognize the Hispanic community among us as a blessing from God." The bishops went on to say that Hispanics exemplify and cherish values that are central to the service of the church and society: A loving appreciation for God's gift of life; a marvelous sense of community that celebrates life through fiesta; an authentic and consistent devotion to Mary, the Mother of God; and a deep and reverential love for family life, where the entire extended family discovers its roots, its identity, and its strength. Today these gifts are shared by millions of Hispanic Catholics in more than four thousand parishes where Hispanic ministry is present. In particular, the love of family makes itself quite visible through the countless Hispanic children of all ages present at Sunday Liturgies in Spanish across the nation.

The strength of Hispanic marriages and families is rooted in a profoundly Catholic culture that can thrive even in the most difficult of situations. Data from the U.S. Census Bureau shows that out of the 9.9 million Hispanic families residing in the United States, 67 percent consist of a married couple and 44 percent of a married couple with children under age eighteen. On the same note, 66 percent of Hispanic children live with two married parents (2007). These percentages are significantly higher than the median average for families as a whole in this country. However, this relative "success rate" should not be taken for granted. Hispanic couples and families are not immune to the many societal factors that erode marriage and family life today. Moreover, many Hispanic families have to face the direct impact of forced emigration from their native countries that leaves spouses and entire families divided by borders. They suffer further division under a broken immigration system that not only hinders their efforts for reunification; it also separates spouses and children from their parents due to deportations, often done without regard for family life or human dignity. Newspapers are filled with stories of children getting home from school to find out that one or both of their parents have been taken into custody for alleged lack of documentation to reside or work in the United States.

These notes aim to start a conversation on this question: How can the church better support couples and families who are Hispanic today and in the future? The conversation begins by looking at who the Hispanics are and what challenges they face today. It follows with practical steps that promote Catholic identity, a sense of belonging, and a commitment to ministry among Hispanics. Finally it offers specific pastoral recommendations to strengthen Hispanic couples and families in the context of increasingly culturally diverse parishes.

Who Are the Hispanic/Latino Catholics?

As we look at the challenges faced by Hispanic/Latino couples and families today, it is important to keep in mind the rich diversity that exists within this ever-growing community. With roots in some twenty-three different Latin American countries, variations in the use of language, cultural expressions, and religious traditions are evident from one group to another. Economic status, citizenship, and educational differences are also evident as Hispanics are present in every strata of life in U.S. society. More recently, being native-born or foreign-born has meant a very significant difference given the high percentage of new immigrants and their own particular experiences, needs, and aspirations. According to the 2000 Census, four out of ten Hispanics residing in the United States were foreign-born.

Despite their particular lived realities and cultural accents, most Hispanics share three significant things in common: language, culture, and faith. In regards to language (or should we say languages), 32.2 million Hispanic U.S. residents age five and older speak Spanish at home while more than half also speak English very well. In regards to culture, Hispanics share a *mestizo* culture: that is, a culture born out of the fusion of two or more cultures giving birth to a new culture, and a new people, in whose veins runs the blood of Native American, European, and African ancestors. In regards to faith, about 70 percent of Hispanics call themselves Catholic. Most others identify themselves with different Christian denominations, and yet *anecdotal evidence* suggests that many of them continue to practice certain aspects of Catholic faith and life, particularly those related to popular devotions. This is not surprising since Hispanic culture is shaped by Catholic values, symbols, and expressions.

The Challenge of a New Beginning in a Foreign Land

The social sciences tell us that the main responsibility of parents is to protect and provide for their children and to empower them into a positive relationship with the institutions of the society in which they live. But what happens when parents don't know how to relate to these institutions or, even worse, are afraid of them?

Being a new immigrant couple and parents can be extremely difficult and even painful. Stories abound of Hispanic parents agonizing as they see their children slip away from their arms into a world that they don't understand, a culture that more often than not tells new immigrants that they don't belong, that they just aren't good enough. One can only imagine how frustrating it is for new immigrant parents, regardless of where they come from, not to be able to advocate for their children in school, on a doctor's visit, or in the local sports league. Even more dramatic is for parents to depend on their children as translators at stores, government agencies, and schools. Such disadvantages keep Hispanic parents from being perceived by their children as role models on how to be a spouse or a parent. This frustration can also exist between spouses as one of them may be more bilingual and better acculturated in U.S. society, thus adding a layer of dependency on the other.

New immigrants wanting to get married also face major challenges. Depending on their immigration status, their knowledge of English, and their degree of mistrust in the government, these couples may look at the road leading to marriage as an endless obstacle course, filled with signs warning: *deportation, harassment,* and *waste of time and money.* New immigrant couples wanting to get married in the church face even more challenges. Getting a copy of their baptismal certificate from the parish in their small town somewhere in southern Guatemala or Ecuador is not an easy task. Issues of previous marriages and annulments are even harder to resolve, particularly in parishes without a Spanish-speaking priest.

The Challenge of Cultural Identity

All children growing up in the United States are impacted by the way we deal with racial and cultural differences as a society. For Hispanics in particular, the issue of race is marked by ambiguity since Hispanics can be of any race. Along with being *mestizos,* Hispanics/Latinos face an open-ended cultural identity process that adds a second layer of ambiguity to their personal and cultural identity, particularly for children of immigrant parents. This being "in-between" was captured by a role-play presented by Hispanic teenagers during a retreat some time ago. The role-play began by showing how teens were expected by their parents to carry themselves, speak, and even eat as if they were living in Mexico, Puerto Rico, or El Salvador. Not being able to fully please their parents, they would often hear how they were losing their roots and becoming distant from their own parents. On the other hand, the same teenagers were told in school that they were too Mexican, too Puerto Rican, or too Latino and that they needed to be more like everybody else.

The tension of living between two cultures and being told that you have to choose one over the other is one of the most confusing and even dramatic aspects of growing up as a first-generation Hispanic/Latino. This confusion plays a significant role in how Hispanic couples relate to one another. Bridging the gap between different sets of expectations, values, and roles ranging from housework to sexual intimacy is a challenge. Women working outside of the home, men having to take on housework, sharing authority in the decision-making process as a couple, reaching agreement on how to raise the children, and dealing with religious differences are some areas of tension between Hispanic spouses.

The Challenges of Culturally Diverse Parish Communities

A growing number of the 68-million-plus Catholics residing in the United States today live in culturally diverse parishes. New waves of Catholic immigrants representing many races, languages, and cultures live and celebrate their faith under one roof and share the same spiritual home with post-immigrant Catholic communities in parishes across the country. This is particularly true for Hispanic Catholics, as 97 percent of parishes with Hispanic ministry are culturally diverse parishes.

The perceived image of the United States has shifted from a melting pot to a multihued tapestry[1] (RVYM, 22). The images of a "pizza supreme," a salad, or even a stew also began to be used to illustrate this shift that recognizes cultural differences as a gift that enriches the whole in transforming and unifying ways. On the other hand, the temptation of expecting Catholics from different cultural backgrounds to simply assimilate into a one-size-fits-all program, group, or activity continues to linger.

The Catholic Church has been the great advocate for immigrants in the United States. It has also developed models to respond to the challenges faced by new immigrants and their families. Examples of these models are the national parish of the late 1800s and early 1900s, and Hispanic ministry as articulated by the U.S. bishops. These models have been built upon an understanding of culture as a fundamental part of people's personal, communal, and religious identity. As such, this understanding distinguishes and makes a choice between cultural assimilation and ecclesial integration. Through a policy of assimilation, the bishops said in 1987,

> new immigrants are forced to give up their language, culture, values, and traditions and adopt a form of life and worship that is foreign to them in order to be accepted as parish members. This attitude alienates new Catholic immigrants from the Church and makes them vulnerable to sects and other denominations. By [ecclesial] integration we mean that our Hispanic people are to be welcomed in our church institutions at all levels. They are to be served in their language when possible, and their cultural values and religious traditions are to be respected. Beyond that, we must work towards mutual enrichment through interaction among all cultures. (National Pastoral Plan for Hispanic Ministry #4)

This statement by the bishops resounds loud and clear in the historical memory of the Catholic Church in the United States. The same principle of ecclesial integration versus cultural assimilation propelling Hispanic ministry was at the very root of the national parish model that safeguarded the Catholic identity of European Catholic immigrants. This model provided each community with the ecclesial space they needed to live their faith, to pray and to worship, and to build community in the context of their own language, culture, and traditions. The bishops were very much aware of this when they wrote *The Hispanic Presence* in 1983: "We are called to appreciate our own histories.... The Church in the United States has been an immigrant Church whose outstanding record of care for countless European immigrants remains unmatched. Today that same tradition must inspire in the Church's approach to recent Hispanic immigrants and migrants a similar authority, compassion, and decisiveness."

The Challenge to Reach Out to Hispanic Catholic Young People

There are more than four thousand parishes with Hispanic ministry in the United States. However, many of them lack a ministry with Hispanic young people. If there is one element that can strengthen Hispanic couples, marriages, and families it is a sound and vibrant ministry among Hispanic youth and young adults. Such ministry needs to be incarnate in their lived reality and within their specific cultural and linguistic context.

Ministry among adolescents found definition in 1976 when the pastoral statement *A Vision for Youth Ministry* was issued. Since then, youth ministry has experienced a tremendous growth, becoming a sophisticated and professionalized ministry among mainstream Catholic adolescents. During that same time, Hispanic ministry had successfully welcomed and developed ministers and ministries among adults, following an ecclesial integration model within culturally diverse parishes.

Unfortunately, Hispanic young people have only benefited marginally from the impressive growth of youth ministry or Hispanic ministry for adults. The unspoken assumption that children of new immigrants knew English, or were in the process of learning it, made the development of culturally specific catechetical programs for them quite difficult. In the area of youth ministry, this assumption was even more prevalent as adolescents from these communities were simply expected to assimilate into the existing mainstream parish youth group, programs, and activities. This assumption has proven to be incorrect, as a large segment of the young Catholic population outside of mainstream Catholics has gone without appropriate pastoral attention.

In their document *Encuentro & Mission: A Renewed Pastoral Framework for Hispanic Ministry* (E&M), 2002, the bishops of the United States make a direct reference that helps explain why Hispanic Catholic adolescents have been falling through the cracks between successful youth ministry and Hispanic ministry.

In the case of Hispanic ministry, the principle of ecclesial integration versus cultural assimilation was consistently applied to ministry only with adults, leaving adolescents in a kind of cultural and ministerial limbo. Regarding youth ministry the bishops say that "The traditional [mainstream] model of parish youth ministry has not, for the most part, reached Hispanic adolescents because of economic, linguistic, cultural, age-range, and educational differences" (E&M, #70). In the same document the bishops note that the majority of parish youth ministry programs serve adolescents of well-established families mostly of European descent. They are part of mainstream culture, English-speaking, and tending to be middle class or upper middle class. Many of them live in the suburbs, are more likely to attend Catholic schools, and are college bound. In contrast, Hispanic adolescents can be monolingual in Spanish or English, or bilingual. They can be U.S. born of many generations or new immigrants, working-class or middle class, white, black, or brown. Most of them go to public schools, a significant number have a low educational attainment, and less than 15 percent are college bound.

Such contrasting economic, linguistic, cultural, racial, and educational differences explain, to a good extent, why most Hispanic adolescents living in culturally diverse parishes don't participate in mainstream youth ministry. It also explains the emergence of alternative youth groups and apostolic movements for Hispanics and by Hispanics to fill the pastoral void created by a policy of assimilation.

Inculturation of the Gospel as Paramount

The concept of inculturation of the Gospel is pivotal to guiding Hispanic couples and parents through the promising and yet challenging waters of racial and cultural ambiguity. It involves following Jesus' example to become gracious hosts for one another, as we acknowledge and embrace our cultural, ethnic, and linguistic diversity and God's unique presence in each of our lives, histories, and cultures.[2] It also describes a truly Catholic understanding of ministry among diverse communities that focuses less on how mainstream culture looks at and relates to "minority communities," and more on how to have meaningful conversations and build meaningful relationships among all the culturally and racially diverse members of the parish community.

In the *General Directory for Catechesis* (GDC), the church speaks of inculturation of the Gospel message in the following words:

The Word of God became man, a concrete man, in space and time and rooted in a specific culture. Christ by His incarnation committed Himself to the particular social and cultural circumstances of the men [and women] among whom he lived. This is the original "inculturation" of the word of God and is the model of all evangelization by the Church, called to bring the power of the Gospel into the very heart of culture and cultures. (GDC, #109)

In the context of a culturally diverse parish, inculturation comprises all the riches of the different cultural and ethnic communities that have been given to Christ as an inheritance. It is a profound process that touches every culture deeply, going to the very center and roots of each culture, taking from each what is compatible with Gospel values while seeking to purify and transform beliefs, attitudes, and actions that are contrary to the Reign of God. The challenge to inculturate the Gospel reminds us that the most fundamental mission of the church is to evangelize, to bring the Good News of Christ to every human situation (*Go and Make Disciples*, 2).

The Church Making a Difference in Healthy Hispanic Marriages

The support Hispanic couples find in their parishes and other faith-based communities can be the key to a solid marriage and a healthy family. Studies show that Hispanic families with strong ties to their faith community are more likely to achieve a higher level of education as well as economic and social success. How can the church provide a healthy environment and a sense of community for Hispanic couples and families growing up in culturally diverse parishes today and in the future?

The answer to this question is not only found in what we do, but in who we are and how we interact with one another. In the document *Encuentro & Mission: A Renewed Pastoral Framework for Hispanic Ministry* (2002), the U.S. Bishops articulate a pastoral response calling for Hispanics and all ministers to be bridge people, to be faithful to the message of Christ and to the people they are called to serve on his behalf, and to be mindful that how we do things is as important as what we do.

First, priests and lay ecclesial ministers need to become more aware and committed to the call to welcome Hispanics, embrace them, and journey with them, leaving behind the *we-they* language and moving into the *all-of-us-together* language. We must make the church the home and the school of communion (*Novo Millennio Ineunte*, 43).

Second, what we do as Catholic ministers should be rooted in the double commitment we have to the message of Christ and to the people with whom we live and minister. This requires solid knowledge of Christ and his message, as well as interpersonal knowledge of Hispanics in our parish, and the cultural, religious, social, and economic context in which they live. Such knowledge is born from our efforts to be good listeners — sensitive to and authentically interested in people's lives, needs, aspirations, and ideas.

Third, ordained and lay ministers need to be effective communicators of the message of Christ among people who speak Spanish and have a particular culture and way of doing things. This includes understanding how Hispanics make decisions, how they learn, and how they organize and come together with other groups. Such awareness and commitment help us welcome and empower them to develop and exercise their leadership.

Pastoral Recommendations for Ministry with Hispanic Couples and Families

Striking a balance between the needs and aspirations of families from different cultural and ethnic communities is not an easy task. Equally challenging is accepting each other's differences and confronting each case of prejudice, cultural stereotype, and expression of racism present in our society.

At the convocation of the *Encuentro 2000*, the national event celebrated in Los Angeles in the Jubilee Year, the bishops spoke of the need to acknowledge and embrace our cultural, ethnic, and linguistic diversity and God's unique presence in each other's lives, histories, and cultures. The increase of cultural diversity challenges all Catholics to achieve ecclesial integration, to discover ways in which we, as Catholic communities, can be one church yet come from diverse cultures and ethnicities (*Many Faces in God's House*, 4).

This twofold commitment to unity in diversity is highlighted in various pastoral statements marking the beginning of the twenty-first century. The common thread in all of them is a call for a ministry that requires the commitment to welcome and foster the specific cultural identity of each of the many faces in the church, while building a profoundly Catholic identity that strengthens the unity of the one body of Christ (*Encuentro & Mission*, 2002). In *Renewing the Vision: A Framework for Youth Ministry* this call emphasizes "the need to focus on a specialized ministry to youth of particular racial and ethnic cultures and, at the same time, promote mutual awareness and unity among all young people" (RVYM, 22). It is in this context of unity in diversity that specific programs and pastoral practices on marriage and family among Hispanics can be relevant and effective.

The following pastoral recommendations speak of five important areas or principles that can guide ministry efforts in the parish setting.

1. Articulate a vision of marriage and family ministry among Hispanics based on ecclesial integration.

    - Be willing to listen to the stories, perspectives, and preferences of people from the Hispanic community in your parish.
    - Recognize and affirm cultural, linguistic, and racial differences as a gift from God, not a problem to be solved.
    - Promote the right of Hispanic couples and families to have their own space to live and practice their faith in the context of the one parish community.
    - Avoid the temptation to expect Hispanics to assimilate into a one-size-fits-all marriage preparation program or activity.
    - Commit to achieve unity in diversity, not uniformity, in your programs and events.

2. Foster the inculturation of the Gospel in all cultures.

    - Be aware of your own cultural heritage and relate to Hispanics with respect and appreciation of differences and commonalities.
    - Use the concept of inculturation of the Gospel as a point of reference in all ministry efforts.
    - Be willing to be a bridge builder between people from cultures rather than a gatekeeper of your own culture.
    - Avoid the tendency to see your culture as better or more valuable than the cultures of others.
    - Avoid *we-they* language.
    - Commit to the spirit of mission of the New Evangelization and its ongoing transformation of all cultures by the Gospel values.

3. Plan with people, not for people.

   - First, listen and welcome the unique perspectives of Hispanics regarding marriage and family.
   - Include them, from the beginning, in the development of plans, programs, and activities.
   - Use the language of ministry *to, with,* and *for* Hispanic young people and couples as regards marriage preparation and family.
   - Avoid planning for others and judging them when they don't show up for your activity.
   - Build community in everything you do within the Hispanic community and with all the members of the parish.

4. Broaden your understanding of youth ministry groups, programs, and structures, and cast a bigger net.

   - Recognize the unique lived experiences, needs, and aspirations of Hispanic young people.
   - Understand the existence of more than one marriage preparation program in your parish as a blessing and as the first step toward ecclesial integration among all couples.
   - Promote the formation of culturally specific programs and activities, and of apostolic movements for marriage and family life as effective means of evangelization, catechesis, and community building.
   - Avoid the perception that allowing the formation of culturally specific programs and activities creates division or separation.
   - Make a commitment to create welcoming spaces for Hispanics living in your parish.

5. Empower Hispanic couples into leadership positions.

   - Understand the way in which different groups view leadership, organize themselves, and make decisions.
   - Identify Hispanic young leaders and couples and mentor them into ministry within their own cultural community and in the parish as a whole.

- Advocate the inclusion of young people and their families in leadership positions within youth ministry and in the parish.

- Avoid a mentality of scarcity when growth in ministry generates demands for more resources.

- Commit to the awesome mission of weaving a vibrant Hispanic marriage and family ministry in your parish.

Seven Steps to Develop a Marriage and Family Ministry in Your Parish

The following seven steps are a road map to develop a marriage and family ministry among Hispanics in your parish. Each step marks a new development and has its own central task to accomplish as Hispanics go from being guests to becoming stewards of the parish community. The seven steps also describe an ongoing process of ecclesial integration that builds unity in diversity.

First Step: Meet Hispanic couples where they are

This step involves becoming aware of the Hispanic presence in the parish and their need for marriage and family ministry. The task is for the parish leadership to see and relate to Hispanic couples in a true spirit of mission, just like Jesus did. Hispanic couples are not going to simply show up, register, and join in parish activities and programs already in place. They need to hear the good news in the streets, their neighborhoods, and their homes. They need to know that God loves them and that by virtue of their baptism they are members of the Catholic Church and invited to share in the grace of a marriage blessed by God and supported by the parish community.

Second Step: Welcome them and make them feel at home

Establishing a group for couples is the most concrete step to have them feel at home and develop a sense of trust.

Third Step: Develop ministries and ministers

Once Hispanic couples have the ecclesial space to share, learn, and pray in the context of their own cultural context they are frequently extremely successful in building community among themselves. This includes the development of plans and programs as well as the formation of apostolic movements like Engaged Encounter, Marriage Encounter, Movimiento Familiar Cristiano, Small Ecclesial Communities, and others.

Fourth Step: Build relationships across cultures and ministries

This step focuses on building relationships across cultures and ministries. Its central task is to bring couples from different cultures together for specific activities. The following are some examples of common experiences that can bring a diverse faith community together.

- *Liturgy and prayer:* Bicultural or multicultural celebrations throughout the liturgical calendar year are essential to fostering unity in diversity.
- *Community building:* Parish social events and activities are great opportunities for building community across cultural boundaries. Multicultural festivals where couples from different cultures bring a dish and share a cultural expression such as dances are quite popular in many parishes.
- *Formation and leadership development:* Workshops on communication and skills development, retreats, and faith formation programs for Hispanic couples are a must.
- *Advocacy and service:* Visits to couples and families in migrant camps, ESL programs, and ministries with homebound and disadvantaged couples and families are unique opportunities to strengthen marriages.

Fifth Step: Champion leadership development and formation

This step calls for the parish to commit resources to the leadership development and formation of Hispanic couples. Its central task is to develop a Hispanic leadership base for marriage and family ministry within the Hispanic community and in the parish as a whole. The hiring of a person as coordinator for Hispanic marriage, family, and youth ministry, at least part time, is also a benchmark.

Sixth Step: Open wide the doors of the decision-making process

The main focus of this step is to secure the participation of Hispanic couples in the parish's decision-making process. It involves making room for Hispanics to sit at the table where decisions are made not only within Hispanic ministry, but also in the life of the parish community as a whole.

Seventh Step: Strengthen a sense of ownership

Parishes that have reached this level of development are equipped with a committed, well prepared, and vibrant Hispanic leadership team for marriage and family ministry. Hispanics move from having a sense of belonging to achieving ownership. Pastoral planning is done taking into consideration the needs, aspirations, and contributions of all parishioners, Hispanic and others.

Chapter Eleven

Marriage and Family Ministry among African American Catholics

ANDREW LYKE

MARRIAGE MINISTRY in the Catholic Church in the United States is mainstream with the church's outreach. That is, it is directed toward and relevant to those who are in the mainstream of the church. The resources developed in the area of ministry are also relevant and directed to the mainstream. Despite the growing number of African Americans in the mainstream of U.S. society, African American Catholics, in general, are marginal in the church in the United States. And the outreach to marriage by the Catholic Church misses the mark in addressing the issues of the rapidly declining family life in the African American communities across the country.

This essay attempts to address the struggles, cultural impediments, and structures that systemically frustrate effective marriage ministry with African Americans by the Catholic Church. Drawing insights from my personal experiences as a lifelong Catholic who is African American, from more than twenty-five years of service to the church in various areas of ministry, and from my experience as a father and husband who has struggled with and benefited from Catholic marriage ministry, I hope to shed light on structures and systems that will assist the church in the twenty-first century in effectively ministering with African Americans.

My Personal Journey

I am currently the coordinator of Marriage Ministry in the Family Ministries Office of the Archdiocese of Chicago. My employment began in 1999. But my service to the church through the Family Ministries Office extends back to 1981, when Terri, my wife of then six years, and I, with a team of couples and clergy, initiated Pre-Cana for the African American community. This program was the first diocesan marriage preparation program by and for African Americans.

Ancillary to this work was our ongoing effort to promote Marriage Encounter in the African American community. We had attended a Marriage Encounter weekend retreat in 1978 and found it to be transformative to our marriage and our faith life. That initial experience and the subsequent ongoing formation in the form of monthly sharing groups were socially and culturally challenging. And we grew significantly from it. Facing those challenges was part of an enculturation and assimilation process that had begun for us individually through school and work experiences. Our collective enculturation and assimilation into the "mainstream" had picked up momentum with our moving from Chicago's Southside to suburbia in 1977 in our second year of marriage. The subsequent experiences with Marriage Encounter were part of our "suburbanization" in the early years of our marriage. Our efforts to proliferate the profundity of our Marriage Encounter experience among African Americans were done with naiveté and a certainty that other African Americans would find the same magic we had found. Such surety came from other African American married couples who joined us in that effort, few though they were, who acted from a similar naiveté.

In the 1980s, Worldwide Marriage Encounter (WWME) experimented with the short-lived African American Expression weekend under the leadership of Ken and Gretchen Lovingood of Santa Barbara, California. Terri and I were privileged to be a part of its maiden voyage in Los Angeles. We also assisted in bringing the program to Chicago.

Despite the rubrics as designed by WWME to ensure a qualitative marriage enrichment experience, we observed dynamics among the African American couples that were beyond what we had experienced with the "standard" Marriage Encounter. The prescription against couple-to-couple interactions and the stressing of intra-couple dialogue seemed naturally violated by the African American couples. And rather than it diminishing the marriage enrichment experience, our breaking of the rules enhanced it. Loyal to a fault, our assessment of this phenomenon was to imagine how even more powerful the experience could have been if we had stayed within the rubrics.

It was after getting consistent feedback from African American couples who were persuaded by us and others to attend standard weekends (Worldwide, National, and Joliet Marriage Encounter) that we began to rethink our roles as promoters of Marriage Encounter in the African American community. Feedback suggested that the experience was stifling, that it was "too white," and that they didn't relate to the middle-class, white, suburban mind-set upon which the teams' heartfelt testimonies were based.

However, it was our participation in a monthly "Community" group of "encountered" African American couples that gave clarity to the couple-to-couple dynamics we experienced with other African American couples. The prayerfulness and playfulness within the group, the importance of music and inter-couple dialogue, and facilitation that flows with the energy of the group rather than the structure of an outline all had us consider what Marriage Encounter would be like if it were designed with African American proclivities in mind.

In the mid-1980s, Terri and I were invited to address the governing board of WWME to report our experiences as promoters of Marriage Encounter among African Americans and make recommendations for future actions. We shared with them our frustrations and suggested that they "tear up the outline" and create a process with African Americans in mind. We discovered quickly that our suggestions were tantamount to blasphemy, and we were abruptly asked to leave. This was a moment of liberation for us. We no longer felt obliged to work within the Marriage Encounter structure. With the encouragement of the priests with whom we had collaborated, namely, Father Larry Duris, Father Wilton Gregory, Father Tom McQuaid, and my uncle, Bishop Jim Lyke, and with the assistance of our marriage ministry team, John and Pam Ashford, Martin and Pat Redd, Leonard and Beverly Richardson, Martin and Helen Dumas, and Maurice and Dorothy Carter, we designed marriage enrichment programs for the African American Catholic community in the Archdiocese of Chicago. The earliest programs were titled "The Best Is Yet to Come" and included elements borrowed from Marriage Encounter, but stressed inter-couple sharing and included well-prepared prayer services and rich, prayerful music.

In 1993 we inaugurated Arusi, a marriage enrichment retreat that incorporates African American cultural elements, in Milwaukee with a group of African American married couples. We had refined the design of the program to include principles for facilitating, which include the principle of process over content.[1] The process was the gathering of the couples, the respectful listening and sharing, table discussions during meals, and our openness to the movement of the Holy Spirit in our midst. The content was the program outline, time frames, and the structured aspects of group sharing. The principle demands that when there is a clash between the two, we should always let the process win. An important element of the program was reconciliation as an ongoing process in marriage as a means of restoring the relationship — restoration from major breaches, certainly, but also forgiveness for our not meeting the original promise of the earlier marriage and expanding ourselves to make room for our flaws and to live well with them. Fifteen years later we are still conducting Arusi, which means "marriage celebration" in Kiswahili, in dioceses around the country.

While the Arusi model has proven to be effective with African Americans, we have also found it very effective with other cultures. In January of 2007 we presented it for several white couples for a parish in Libertyville, Illinois. Most recently in Beaumont, Texas, six white couples were among a group of nineteen couples who attended an Arusi. For whites Arusi is not only an effective marriage enrichment, it is also culturally enriching.

Despite our being convinced that our approach to marriage enrichment with African Americans is better than Marriage Encounter's, we don't claim to have a formula to absolute knowledge on the matter. I am reminded of what Jacob Bronowski said in *The Ascent of Man:* "There is no absolute knowledge, and those who claim it, whether they are scientists or dogmatists, open the door to tragedy."[2]

Why Does Culture Matter?

White people and black people are culturally different, and it is naïve to proceed in the serious work of the church without an appreciation of those differences. Within ethnic cultures are verbal and nonverbal communication patterns that may be easily misread by a person outside that culture without an understanding of those patterns. To complicate matters even more, those patterns are nuanced by other cultural layers, i.e., regional, generational, religious, and so on.

This is true of any culture. However, in the United States of America, at least among the majority, there is a hidden culture that exists in the guise of being generic. It is perceived by its constituents as noncultural and the basic empty shell from which culture contrasts. I am referring to white culture. For white people, generally speaking, white culture is enigmatic. However, it is hardly so for people of color. Again generally speaking, people of color can readily identify white culture — white speech patterns, white walking, white dancing, white facial expressions, etc. — though doing so may very well express unflattering stereotypes and may cross the line of what is deemed socially acceptable interracial discourse. What's important here is the contrast of perspectives between white people and people of color. The differences are such that it would be unwise to ignore them.

Edward T. Hall in his book *Beyond Culture* writes the following:

> It is possible to live life with no knowledge of physiology, speak a language well without knowing linguistics or even schoolteacher's grammar, or use a TV set, a telephone, and an automobile without a clue to electronic or mechanical know-how. It is also possible to grow up and mature in a culture with little or no knowledge of the basic laws that make it work and differentiate it from all other cultures.[3]

There are "mechanics" of culture that we can't explain but we know they exist.

Hall also outlines the differences between high context cultures and low context cultures. Generally speaking of African Americans in varying degrees, they are of a high context culture. That is to say that there is much in the interplay of a conversation that is "understood" without explicit words spoken or written. The context of the culture is part of the message. There are some things that just don't have to be stated. There is a community base of wisdom, knowledge, and understanding that is generated from shared histories and common experiences.

On the other hand, and again generally speaking, white people are of a low context culture. The content of messages communicated is more explicit in words and obvious gesturing than what is implicit in the community base.

This cultural difference alone, if taken into consideration, would have us approaching marriage ministry with African Americans differently than with whites. When a program is designed and presented without consideration of the high context of African American culture, it's easy to dismiss it as for "white folks."

The experiences of Terri and myself presenting programs and facilitating processes with African Americans and "general" audiences illustrate this well. There are striking differences in facilitating a group of African American couples and a group of white couples. An example: when presenting our retreat program with whites, proceeding without providing a written agenda or itinerary induces anxiety in the group. Creating safe space is enhanced by providing even a skeletal outline of the program, whereas having a written agenda doesn't matter as much with African American groups.

With mixed groups, whites are more assertive in group sharing. Making use of the "Mutual Invitation"[4] process helps to balance group dynamics in multicultural settings. Below is an explanation of this process.

Objectives: To facilitate sharing and discussion in a multicultural group.

Type of Group: Any

Size of Group: 4–15

Setting: Participants should sit in a circle.

Materials: Newsprint and markers.

Time Required: Depending on the size of the group. A good way to tell how much time will be required for each round of sharing is to multiply the number of participants by five minutes.

How to Proceed:

   a. Let participants know how much time is set aside for this process.

   b. Introduce the topic to be discussed or information to be gathered or questions to be answered. Write this on newsprint and put it up on a wall so everyone can see it.

   c. Introduce the process by reading the following: *In order to ensure that everyone who wants to share has the opportunity to speak, we will proceed in the following way. The leader or a designated person will share first. After that person has spoken, he or she then invites another to share. Whom you invite does not need to be the person next to you. After the next person has spoken, that person is given the privilege to invite another to share. If you don't want to say anything, simply say "pass" and proceed to invite another to share. We will do this until everyone has been invited.*

If this is the first time you use this exercise with the group, it will be very awkward at first. The tendency is to give up on the process and go back to the whoever-wants-to-talk-can-talk way. If you are persistent in using this process every time you facilitate the gathering, the group will eventually get used to it and will have great fun with it. A good way to ensure the process goes well the first time is to make sure there are a couple of people in the group who have done this before and, as you begin the process, invite them first.

Problems to Anticipate: This process addresses differences in the perception of personal power among the participants. Some people will be eager for their turn, while others will be reluctant to speak when they are invited. If a person speaks very briefly and does not remember to invite the next person, do not invite for him or her. Simply point out that this person has the privilege to invite the next person to speak. This is especially important if a person "passes." By ensuring that this person still has the privilege to invite, you affirm and value that person independent of that person's verbal ability.

Making use of this process honors cultural and personality differences and helps facilitate groups, even when participants are of the same culture. This demonstrates how benchmarking at the margins can serve the center.

Racism in the Twenty-First Century

The U.S. Bishops in 1979 stated: "Racism is an evil which endures in our society and in our Church. Despite apparent advances and even significant changes in the last two decades, the reality of racism remains. In large part it is only external appearances which have changed."[5] This statement is as true today as it was in 1979.

Nonetheless, the strides gained in race relations since the civil rights era are significant. Personally, I reject notions that "things are the same" because of what I have observed and experienced in the world since the end of the civil rights era. However, I also reject any notion that work necessary to end racism in the United States is completed. While strides from whence we have come are great, there are yet as great strides to make to accomplish the goals of racial equality and Dr. King's dream of a new social order.

The bishops state further:

Racism is a sin: a sin that divides the human family, blots out the image of God among specific members of that family, and violates the fundamental human dignity of those called to be children of the same Father. Racism is the sin that says some human beings are inherently superior and others essentially inferior because of race. It is the sin that makes racial characteristics the determining factor for the exercise of human rights. It mocks the words of Jesus: "Treat others the way you would have them treat you." Indeed, racism is more than a disregard for the words of Jesus; it is a denial of the truth of the dignity of each human being revealed by the mystery of the Incarnation.[6]

Today's "battlefield" against racism is not the Jim Crow South. That's abolished, though vestiges of it insidiously remain in the culture in some communities, e.g., the Jena 6. Still, the struggle against modern-day racism is not about exposing cross burning or hooded horsemen intent on preserving a social order of white supremacy. A clear, definitive result of civil rights is that legally sanctioned apartheid is extinct in this land. When we look at the externals of American culture there is evidence that African Americans are in significantly larger numbers among people of economic privilege. Gone are the days when the telephone "grape vine" would go abuzz within African American communities because Sammy or Ella or Duke or Diahann or Sidney was on TV. Especially among young people today, American entertainment culture, including sports, news, theater, screen, and music is well bridged into the African American community.

The struggle today is primarily wrestling with systemic issues through which racism maintains its grip on American society. Racism that is manifest within the structures of institutions and systems is our new focus. Cardinal Francis George, archbishop of Chicago, addresses institutional racism in his 2001 pastoral letter on racism, "Dwell In My Love":

> Patterns of social and racial superiority continue as long as no one asks why they should be taken for granted. People who assume, consciously or unconsciously, that white people are superior create and sustain institutions that privilege people like themselves and habitually ignore the contributions of other peoples and cultures. This "white privilege" often goes undetected because it has become internalized and integrated as part of one's outlook on the world by custom, habit, and tradition. It can be seen in most of our institutions: judicial and political systems, social clubs, associations, hospitals, universities, labor unions, small and large businesses, major corporations, the professions, sports teams and in the arts. In the Church as well, "... all too often in the very places where blacks, Hispanics, Native Americans and Asians are numerous, the Church's officials and representatives, both clerical and laity, are predominantly white."[7]

Sometimes, with a genuine desire to be more inclusive, one or two black, Hispanic, Asian, or Native Americans are asked to fill leadership positions in order to change the internal culture of an institution. But the racist disposition of the institution can remain largely unaltered when the nonwhites do not acquire full participatory rights. Without rising to levels of influence that can change the entrenched attitudes, approaches, and goals of the institution, they live with and even have to preside over policies, procedures, and regulations that leave the institution in a basically racist mode. Often when these select few people of color exhibit qualities of morality, intelligence, and skills, which contradict the low expectations of the racial stereotypes applied to their cultural groups, they are viewed as "exceptional anomalies."[8]

The Catholic Challenge

In the Catholic Church in the United States, having that one black bishop in New Orleans, Harold Perry, S.V.D., was an anomaly in 1966 that intrigued black Catholics. Today there are fourteen living African American bishops, of whom six are active ordinaries of their dioceses and two are retired ordinaries. Since Harold Perry's episcopal ordination in 1966, there have been twenty African American bishops ordained for dioceses in the United States.

Currently there are approximately 1,300 African American Catholic parishes in the United States; 250 African American priests; 300 African American sisters; and 380 African American deacons. All are in service to a church with about 3 million African American Catholics.[9]

Despite these significant strides and numbers in the church in America, African American Catholics are still marginal. In my home diocese, the Archdiocese of Chicago, in a city that is so very Catholic and with such a strong and vibrant African American political base (the current and past presidents of the Cook County Board are African American Catholics) being black and Catholic is still an experience in the margins and not the mainstream. It's a paradox that exists in communities around the United States. I dare not try to unravel the complexities that create this paradox. It's far beyond our agenda for this symposium. But I would like to address one aspect that contributes to this situation and is central to our purpose: structural impediments to effective outreach by the Catholic Church to African American families, particularly married couples.

In my opinion, African American families are on the front line of the cultural assault on American families. Forty-one percent of African American adults are married, compared to 62 percent of whites and 60 percent of Hispanics (2000); 23 divorces per 1000 African American couples per year, 19 for whites (1990); 69 percent of African American births are to unmarried women, compared to 25 percent for whites and 42 percent for Hispanics (1998); 55 percent of African American children live with single parents, compared to 23 percent of white children and 31 percent of Hispanic children (1998).[10]

In short, the institution of marriage is broken in the African American community. And despite our Catholic understanding of marriage, which elevates it as a sacrament of service to the world and for which the church and society give support and protection, Catholic marriage ministry hasn't made any significant inroads into African American communities and the families that comprise them.

At the 2005 National Association of Catholic Family Life Ministers Twenty-fifth Anniversary Conference in Chicago, I presented the opening keynote in which I highlighted past accomplishments of the organization and presented some challenges for the future. In that presentation, I quoted the Rev. Dr. Howard Thurman, who was considered the spiritual director of the civil rights movement. Please pardon the lack of inclusive language that typified texts of this era:

> It seems to me that experience reveals a potent half-truth; namely, that the world can be made good if all men in the world as individuals become good men. After the souls of men are saved, the society in which they function will be a good society. This is only a half-truth. Many men have found that they are caught in a framework of relationships evil in design, and their very good deeds have developed into instrumentalities for evil. It is not enough to save the souls of men; the relationships that exist between men must be saved also.
>
> To approach the problem from the other angle is to assume that once the relationships between men are saved, the individual men will thereby become instruments of positive weal. This is also a half-truth. The two processes must go on apace or else men and their relationships will not be brought under conscious judgment of God. We must, therefore, even as we purify our hearts and live our individual lives under the divine scrutiny, so order the framework of our relationships that good men can function in it to the glory of God.[11]

Before sitting to write this essay, I contacted several African American Catholic directors of Offices for Black Catholic Ministries (OBMs) in dioceses across the United States. The conversations that ensued from that letter suggest to me that while there is general consensus among the OBMs regarding the verity of my assertion, there are examples of successful collaborative ventures. Those collaborations emanated from personal relationships between personnel of those agencies. Still, what is lacking is the mainstreaming of those programs into the central work of those agencies. Yet to be explored is the general resistance exercised by diocesan workers in Catholic parishes that serve in the African American communities.

Those conversations have inspired hope. I intend to enlist the assistance of and collaboration with the National Association of Black Catholic Administrators (NABCA), of which most with whom I spoke were members. We in the African American Catholic community are also encouraged by the prophetic words of His Holiness John Paul the Great who addressed an assembly of black Catholics in New Orleans in 1987:

> I am sure that you share with me a special concern for that most basic human community, *the family*. Your faithful Christian families are a source of comfort in the face of the extraordinary pressures affecting society. Today, you must *rediscover the spirit of family life,* which refuses to be destroyed in the face of even the most oppressive forces. Surely that spirit can be found in exploring your spiritual and cultural heritage. The inspiration you draw from the great men and women of your past will then allow your young people to see the value of a strong family life. Know that the pope stands united with the black community as it rises to embrace its full dignity and lofty destiny.

What Can We Do?

Following the logic that says that if we continue with our current strategies we will get the current results, "thinking outside the box" is what is needed. We need to challenge conventional ways of doing things and reconsider partnerships, delivery systems, and general assumptions about marriage and family life. How might what is thought to be culturally generic be in fact white? How open are we to the "stranger" whose ways are foreign to us? With whom should we be collaborating? How is our hospitality presented and received? These are just a few questions to consider as we do the work of marriage ministry with African Americans in the twenty-first century.

No matter how profound our expressions of the "Good News," if the people we are serving don't relate to our analogies, idioms, and premises, even though we all may speak English, we might as well be speaking a foreign language.[12] This work should be perceived as mission work. There are characteristics of mission that should be fully appreciated and operative, i.e., expression of the superordinate role of the host and subordinate role of the guest — the *stranger*. Let me explain: To be a host assumes a role that has an upper hand, one who has something to give — hospitality. Another assumption is that to be a host is to be in relationship with another who is the stranger. That relationship is inherent in the definition of being a host. There are rights and duties for being a host, the one who holds the initiative. For the host there is a *home team advantage*. There is an indebtedness the stranger has to the host. This is intrinsic to the relationship between host and stranger.[13]

The role of the stranger is as defined by Anthony Gittins:

> To become a stranger effectively and with dignity entails two unfamiliar processes. First, the learning process that transforms us as we encounter a new reality. This involves *understanding* and *standing under*: the former, the familiar absorption of external information; the latter, the willingness to be absorbed into another world, even if one does not fully understand it. The second process required of us as strangers is the suffering process that allows us to grow as we negotiate the necessary discomfort and distress. This involves both risk and trust.[14]

Gittins outlines in greater detail characteristics of the roles of the host and the stranger in *Ministry at the Margins*. I leave it to the reader to explore more fully those characteristics. For the purpose of my recommendations for future actions, I succinctly summarize that for effective mission work both roles need to be mutually owned by those who minister and those who are ministered to.

In this interplay of mission as both host and stranger all parties involved benefit and are benefactors, give and receive, teach and learn, and grow as a result of the encounter. Certainly there is much in what the Catholic Church offers in marriage ministry from which African Americans can benefit. Catholic theology resonates with the history, lived experiences, and proclivities of African Americans. The African American understanding of *village* and community accountability fits well with Catholic understanding of *sacrament* and communal character of human vocation.[15] As many African American Catholics can attest, the experience of being both authentically black and authentically Catholic is not a stretch of the imagination.

Nor does it require remedial approaches in catechesis and evangelization. Being black and Catholic is a natural fit. The African American community, churched as well as unchurched, is a vineyard with much promise for Catholic evangelization.

I believe that African Americans, precisely because of their history and current experiences as oppressed people, have a prophetic role in the broader society. Just as the civil rights movement transformed the American conscience and recalibrated America's moral compass, the legacy of African Americans also belongs to all other Americans. Theirs is a story of promise and hope that serves all who claim it for themselves. Being prophetic is not just about attending to those who come to us — those who are present, those gathered. Avenues and processes of ministry designed for the mainstream are often ineffective and rejected in the margins. Good ministry in the church of the twenty-first century also recognizes who is not present. It reaches to the margins to benchmark the work. For when we serve the margins well we serve everyone better. What we learn on the edge is put to good use in the center. To do this we need to consider new ventures with new partnerships.[16]

The dyadic relationship between the Catholic Church and the African American community is one where African Americans play a prophetic role as host and where the church is the stranger. This role reversal is necessary to live out the mission. This mutual exchange is what is commonly felt deeply by African American Catholics and white Catholics who serve in those communities.

Conspicuously absent among those *strangers* ministering with African Americans are Catholic family life ministers. Thinking outside the box for family life ministers might mean seeking new partnerships with whom we collaborate for the sake of serving African American families. The Administration for Children and Families of the U.S. Department of Health and Human Services, through its Healthy Marriage Initiative (HMI) and African American Healthy Marriage Initiative (AAHMI), is indeed a strange bedfellow in the effort to strengthen African American marriages in partnership with Catholic family life ministers. Despite this being a promising opportunity to advance the church's mission on behalf of marriages and families, and despite the fact that the Special Assistant for Marriage Education at ACF who is the lead person in the HMI and AAHMI, Bill Coffin, is a former director of Family Life for the Archdiocese of Washington, D.C., the participation of Catholics in these federally funded initiatives is well below what was anticipated when the initiatives were taking shape. Among Coffin's initial overtures for forming coalitions to qualify for federal funding for serving at-risk families in general and African American families in general were to his former colleagues in Family Life Ministry in the Catholic Church.

Our future promise for effective outreach to African American marriage is in saying "yes" to such opportunities and reshaping our work and our vision to make these new ventures central to what we do. This is what is happening in the Family Ministries Office of the Archdiocese of Chicago. We are partners in two coalitions, both of which have placed demands on our human resources, which has had us question at times whether it was worth it. However, the ministry experience itself has been so profound that we have found ourselves learning new and better ways (stranger) of doing that for which we are perceived to be the experts (hosts). This work is now becoming central to what we do and transforming us into better service providers on the margins as well as the mainstream.

These kinds of new opportunities can be the needed common ground for diocesan Family Life Offices, OBMs. Therefore, the challenge is not just for us in Family Life Ministry. These new partnerships should include OBMs and their functional equivalents. Formal conversations with members of NABCA may fuel this. But if we are to really think outside the box, partnerships may include Offices of Peace and Justice, and perhaps even Offices for Catechesis and Offices for Ecumenism.

Our Spirituality and Its Gifts

Below is an excerpt from the 1984 pastoral letter on Evangelization by the then ten African American Catholic bishops, *What We Have Seen and Heard*:

"Black Spirituality" has four major characteristics.

1. Black Spirituality is contemplative. Prayer is spontaneous and pervasive in the Black tradition. Our ancestors taught that we cannot run from God, we must lean on him and surrender to his love.

2. Black Spirituality is holistic. The religious experience is one of the whole human being — feelings, intellect, heart, and head.

3. Black Spirituality is joyful, a celebration in movement, song, rhythm, feeling, and thanksgiving. This joy is a sign of our faith.

4. Black Spirituality is communal. In African culture individual identity is found within the context of the community. The good of the community must come before personal profit and advancement. In the same way worship is a celebration of community with no one being left out or forgotten. Community also means social concern and social justice. Our spiritual heritage always embraces the total human person.

The Family

The heart of the human community is the family, and the black family has been assailed. In the African tradition, family has always meant "the extended family" — grandparents, uncles, aunts, godparents, all related kin, and close friends. Circumstances often required childcare to be the responsibility of many. Despite the erosion of our family life we as a people still have a strong sense of family bonds. This carries over to our church, where we see ourselves as brothers and sisters to one another.[17]

The bishops express well the gifts from the African American community available to the Catholic Church. The mutual gifts of church and community make for "good church," and a wealth of opportunities strengthens families.

Conclusion

Part of the richness in being Catholic is universal membership that gives "ownership" beyond our local experience. For me this is an invitation to reach beyond myself, beyond my culture, and even beyond my own traditions to at the very least acknowledge my brothers and sisters who are strangers, and perhaps be enriched by their culture and traditions. It invites me to be a gracious host in reaching out to others. It encourages me to risk being the stranger and be open to learning from others.

It is from this stance that Catholic marriage ministry will find its place with African Americans. From this stance the systemic impediments for such ministry will organically crumble. The frightening downward spiral of marriage among African Americans indicates a state of crisis that demands Catholic Family Life ministers and Offices of Black Ministry to take action to transform those structures and collaborate for the sake of all of the People of God, for whom it is our privilege to serve.

Because we are an evangelizing church we need to always reach out to the margins. Adapting our work to be effective on the margins will strengthen our work and make us more authentic as a one, holy, catholic, and apostolic church. Amen!

Chapter Twelve

Marriage and Family Ministry among Asian American Catholics

JONATHAN Y. TAN

THIS ESSAY SEEKS TO EXPLORE the issues and challenges that surface in contemporary Asian American marriage ministry in typical urban and suburban contexts. First, it discusses the term "Asian American" and examines the principal demographic data from the United States Census Bureau. Second, it introduces Asian American Catholics and their presence in the United States. Third, it identifies the unique and distinctive sociocultural issues that affect Asian American marriages. Finally, it considers the pastoral responses to the challenges of doing Asian American marriage ministry and suggests five possible strategies of responding to these challenges.

Defining "Asian American"

The term "Asian American" is often used in contemporary discourse as a generic and convenient shorthand to categorize all Americans of Asian ancestry and heritage, with their diverse languages, cultures, and traditions.[1] Nonetheless, this term masks distinct racial-ethnic communities under the facade of a rigid, homogenous, and monolithic pan-Asian American identity that exists more in theory than in reality.[2] In reality, the category of "Asian Americans" encompasses groups of peoples of diverse languages, cultures, spiritual traditions, worldviews, socioeconomic classes, and generational levels, such that all attempts at generalizations run the significant risk of error.[3] Moreover, the concerns of first-generation Asian immigrants are very different from those of subsequent generations of Asians born and bred in the United States.

Since the passage of the Immigration and Nationality Act of 1965 (Hart-Celler Act), which abolished the restrictive measures that limited Asian immigration, Asian Americans collectively comprise the second fastest-growing and most diverse racial category in the United States. The statistical data from the 2000 census reveals that as of April 1, 2000, Asian Americans comprise 4.2 percent (11.9 million) of the total U.S. population of 281.4 million. The largest Asian American ethnic group are Chinese Americans (2.73 million), followed closely by Filipino Americans (2.36 million), Indian Americans (1.90 million), Korean Americans (1.23 million), Vietnamese Americans (1.22 million), and Japanese Americans (1.15 million), respectively (United States Census Bureau, Census Topic Report #9, 2002a:9).[4]

In the context of U.S. Catholicism, the two major Asian American ethnic communities, namely, Filipino Americans and Vietnamese Americans, are heavily Roman Catholic. Indeed, the massive influx of Filipino and Vietnamese immigrants in the past forty years has contributed significantly to the diversity of the U.S. Catholic Church. While accurate statistics are hard to come by, the United States Conference of Catholic Bishops' pastoral letter *Asian and Pacific Presence: Harmony in Faith* (2001) estimates that some 83.0 percent of Filipino Americans (1.54 million), 29.0 percent of Vietnamese Americans (0.33 million), 17.0 percent of Indian Americans (0.29 million), 12.3 percent of Chinese Americans (0.30 million), 7.0 percent of Korean Americans (0.07 million), and 4.0 percent of Japanese Americans (0.03 million) are Catholic.

Defining Asian American Families

Just as there is no homogeneous and monolithic pan-Asian American identity, so too, a universal and normative definition of Asian American family does not exist. Nonetheless, amid such multiplicity and plurality, scholars and practitioners have identified five basic categories of Asian American families: (1) the "traditional" family, (2) the cultural conflict family, (3) the bicultural family, (4) the "Americanized" family, and (5) the interracial family.[5]

The first category of "traditional" family refers to Asian American families where all the family members are first-generation Asian Americans, i.e., they are born and raised outside of the United States and immigrated either voluntarily or involuntarily to the United States as children or adults. As first-generation families, many of them may have limited English-language skills and limited exposure to American culture (e.g., Indochinese refugees).

They usually live and congregate within their racial ethnic communities (e.g., Little Saigons). Family members, especially those who emigrate as adults, are often deeply attached to the land of their birth, as well as their native sociocultural traditions and values. They continue to speak their native tongues fluently, developing only rudimentary English skills at best. As a result of their language limitations, they often look to their families and their specific racial ethnic communities for support, socialization, validation, and stabilization.

The second category of family, cultural conflict, comprises intergenerational families in which Asian-born parents and their 1.5-generation or American-born children hold different and often conflicting cultural values. The term "cultural conflict" refers to the intergenerational stress and conflict arising from different cultural values and expectations between the Asian-born parents and grandparents on the one hand, and the 1.5-generation or American-born generation on the other hand. For example, parents and grandparents who were born in Asia often cling tenaciously to traditional sociocultural values and ethical mores. By contrast, their American-born children are more acculturated into an Americanized lifestyle. To worsen matters, the children or grandchildren may not be conversant in their traditional languages or know much about traditional values that are espoused by their parents and grandparents.

The third category, i.e., the bicultural family, refers to the well-educated Asian professionals who immigrate voluntarily to the United States with a familiarity with the American way of life and exposed to urbanization, modernity, and Western culture. Bilingual and bicultural, cosmopolitan and urbane, they are fluent in both English and their native languages. In most cases, they espouse a transnational worldview, going back and forth between their traditional and American cultures. Economically and socially, they usually belong to the upper- and middle-income brackets. Many Chinese Americans, Indian Americans, and Filipino American professionals would belong to this category.

The "Americanized" family refers to those Asian American families where parents and children are American-born and raised. This category covers mainly the third-, fourth-, and fifth-generation Chinese Americans and Japanese Americans. Unlike the "traditional" family, members of a typical "Americanized" family communicate mostly in English and adopt a more Americanized lifestyle, with an emphasis on personal autonomy and an egalitarian perspective of life. Typically, these families are culturally assimilated into the mainstream United States, speaking flawless and accentless English, and being at ease with a contemporary American lifestyle.

As second and later generations of Asian Americans engage in interracial dating, a new category of interracial families is emerging from the increasing number of interracial marriages. While many interracial families are able to integrate both cultures with some success, misunderstandings and conflicts often arise between the spouses and in-laws on the questions of values and traditions. Moreover, many interracial families face an uphill battle for acceptance from more traditional first-generation parents and older family members who are worried about the disappearance of their traditional racial ethnic heritages and identities in the United States.

General Characteristics of Asian American Families

An important characteristic that sets a typical Asian American family apart from a typical white American family with its nuclear family structure is the fact that the *extended* family structure is often the basic family unit across the various Asian American racial ethnic communities.[6] It is not uncommon to find unmarried adults continuing to live with their parents or older married siblings in an extended household in many Asian American households.[7] More important, this multigenerational setup of a typical Asian American extended family is often perceived as its principal strength, enabling children to have greater contact with grandparents and other relatives, family-based childcare rather than outsourced childcare, and the pooling of economic and other resources for the benefit of the family as a whole. Indeed, Asian Americans are often praised for their multigenerational family structure, where a son, usually the eldest, often takes care of his aged parents in his household.

On the whole, Asian American families also have lower rates of divorces than mainstream U.S. families. Statistics show that about 4 percent of Asian American men and 4.7 percent of Asian American women are divorced, compared with 8 percent and 10.3 percent of the total male and female population respectively in the United States.[8] This is due to the stigma associated with divorce in many Asian American racial ethnic communities. It appears that divorce is becoming increasingly acceptable and more prevalent among American-born Asian Americans compared with first-generation Asian Americans.[9]

Studies show that Asian American immigrants have retained many aspects of their native cultures, especially their traditional values of religion, family, marriage, and children, as well as the value system of traditional patriarchal hierarchy that defines the norms of gender roles and relations, places family interests over individual autonomy, and mandates obedience to parents (filiality). By contrast, the 1.5 and subsequent generations of Asian Americans are becoming increasingly restive and assertive in questioning and challenging these traditional values and ways of life. This is true of Indian Americans,[10] Chinese Americans,[11] Korean Americans,[12] and Vietnamese Americans.[13] Nowhere is this conflict and challenge more acute than the issue of marriage and family.

Marriage in Asian American Families Today

Across diverse Asian American racial ethnic communities, marriage is often perceived as the cornerstone of families and communities, especially in the eyes of first-generation Asian Americans. In their eyes, marriage confers the sociocultural identity of adulthood on their children. To put it another way, one is not an adult until one is married. As a result, married persons are more highly regarded and respected than their unmarried counterparts. In particular, unmarried persons are not only viewed as children despite their age and personal accomplishments, they are often nagged by their families about when they are going to get married. Not surprisingly, many first-generation Asian American parents often put an inordinate pressure on their children to get married. Thus marriage often generates a great deal of intergenerational stress and conflict among Asian American families, especially when parents demand the right to arrange their children's marriages.

In the preceding section, we saw how Asian Americans families are multigenerational and parents often expect to live with their children. What outsiders fail to realize is that this arrangement frequently adds an inordinate burden to a marriage, especially when the parents intervene in family matters. Indeed, tales of overbearing mothers-in-law, timid and cowering adult sons who find themselves powerless to define their own identity apart from their parents, as well as spouses who clash with their live-in in-laws are common fodder in Asian and Asian American popular literature, movies, soap operas, and television sitcoms.

More important, in the minds of the first-generation Asian Americans across the board, marriage is more than an individual choice between two consenting adults in love with each other. Instead, first-generation Asian Americans often perceive marriage as a fundamental means of ensuring the survival and continuation of a kin, clan, group, or family name. To put it in another way, when two Asian Americans get married, the reality is that their two families or clans are getting married too. Many Asian American racial ethnic groups celebrate this marriage between two families, groups, or clans with elaborate engagement rituals that comprise formal betrothal announcements, presentation of dowry, and gift exchanges. Hence, the typical prevailing attitude among many first-generation Asian Americans is that *one loves the person that one marries and does not marry the person one loves.*

While the colorful marriage rituals and pageantry are a sight to behold, what is often overlooked is the reality that the deep-rooted patriarchal worldview of many Asian American racial ethnic groups results in sons often deferring obediently to the wishes of their parents, thereby creating friction with their spouses. Here we see the conflict between self-sacrifice to the family ideals, subservience to one's elders, preservation of family line and honor, social conformity, and tradition maintenance being espoused by the older generation on the one hand, and the younger generation's yearning for autonomy, individuality, unfettered choice, compatibility, and romantic love on the other hand. When the first generation is neither ready nor willing to concede traditional paternal or patriarchal hierarchy of authority, the ensuing intergenerational conflict generates much disharmony and friction, threatening family ties and the continued viability of parent-child relations. Wrongly handled, this could lead to outright rebellion and, in extreme cases, children eloping to get married or parents disowning their children, thereby severing parent-child relations. Another sad reality that ensues is that many children associate the church and their Christian faith with their parents' faith, and this breakdown in parent-child relations often affects the children's continued practice of their family faith.

Hence, many marriages often become unstable and a source of major, recurring conflict, especially when children and their spouses begin to assert their independence, and both the older and younger generations lack the skills to negotiate between their ideals and polarized viewpoints. Rightly or wrongly, parents often accuse their children and in-laws of becoming "Americanized," perceiving them to have imbibed the American ideals of individualism, independence, and assertiveness. They think that their children and their spouses have become too Americanized, too assertive, abandoning traditional (read "patriarchal") gender and spousal roles. One hears of complaints of mothers-in-law accusing daughters-in-law of disobedience and their sons of not disciplining their wives. On their part, the sons and their wives would often counter that the parents fail to understand the changing expectations in marriage in the contemporary United States context, especially with regard to children, work, gender roles, and family roles. Hence, a new sensitive approach to navigating intergenerational strife on the issues of restrictive sociocultural traditions, as well as paternalistic and patriarchal gender and hierarchical roles in family and community is needed.

Regrettably, attention is often lavished upon the "model minority" image of Asian Americans, ignoring the underlying interpersonal relations between husband and wife, as well as parent and child. Intergenerational clashes between traditional arranged marriages vs. so-called "love" marriages, as well as *endogamy* (marriage within one's racial ethnic group, kin, clan, or caste) or *homogamy* (marriage within one's socioeconomic class) on the one hand vs. *exogamy* (interracial, intergroup, intercaste, or interclass marriages) on the other hand, are becoming increasingly common and divisive. Nonetheless, one must not forget that many first-generation Asian Americans also experience stresses and problems in their marriages. Many first-generation Asian American couples face challenges arising from their new status in the United States. This problem is especially acute in Indochinese refugees who have been forced to leave their countries because of war or persecution. Moving to the United States, many wives who stayed home in their native homelands find themselves entering the workforce to contribute to the family income. While this adds to the family's economic spending power, it also increases the stress level on the family due to the fact that many husbands are not willing to relinquish male authority. We will examine this issue in greater detail in the next section, followed by a discussion of the divisive issues of arranged marriages and endogamy.

Challenges to the Patriarchal Order of First-Generation Asian American Marriages

Wife abuse and domestic violence are not unique to Asian American communities. Other racial ethnic groups in the United States also experience these horrors that are inflicted on women and children. Nonetheless, they have different root causes within the Asian American communities. Within Asian American communities, wife abuse and domestic violence are rooted in the traditional norms of patriarchy that the first generation brought over from their countries of origin.[14]

Among Vietnamese Americans, the traditional family structure exemplifies the rigid Confucian patriarchal gender roles that define the relations and obligations between husband and wife, parents and children, as well as older and younger siblings.[15] Within a typical Vietnamese family, the gender roles between husband and wife are defined by the Confucian precepts of the "Three Obediences" (*Tam Tóng*), which subordinate a woman to her father when she is a minor, then to her husband when she is married, and finally to her eldest son when she is widowed. In other words, Vietnamese women are socialized into accepting a position of subordination to male headship and authority at every stage of their lives. In addition, the womenfolk are also taught from young to practice the "Four Womanly Virtues" (*Tứ đức*) of proper housework (*công*), proper appearance (*dung*), proper speech (*ngôn*), and proper ethical behavior (*hạnh*). Stephen Young explains these four virtues succinctly as follows:

> *Dung* is appearance, which should be neat and attractive. *Công* is industry, which should be precise and careful. *Ngôn* is speech, which should be submissive and respectful. *Hạnh* is character, which should be upright, filial, devoted, and trustworthy.[16]

When Vietnamese refugees arrived en masse to the United States, they experienced a gender relations framework that is completely different from that in Vietnam, shaped by a twofold socioeconomic force. On the one hand, first-generation Vietnamese American women acquired new socioeconomic power when they entered the workforce. On the other hand, many immigrant Vietnamese men experienced a loss of socioeconomic power.[17] In a similar vein, Tuyet-Lan Pho and Anne Mulvey identify three important factors causing problems in the marriages of Vietnamese Americans:

> (1) the restructuring of family relationships and expectations between wives and husbands and between parents and children in a new community and cultural context; (2) the conflicting demands and related personal dilemmas associated with the maintenance of traditional values and changing gender roles; and (3) the different approaches among community members to addressing and resolving social problems such as domestic violence.[18]

More significantly, Pho and Mulvey point out that when women "want to change this traditional structure by changing their roles and becoming more assertive in family affairs," they "were considered by their partners as being 'too Americanized' or were subject to domestic violence."[19]

On the one hand, Pho and Mulvey discover that the womenfolk "considered independence from their husbands or parents to be a major aspect of their lives since moving to the United States," equating economic self-sufficiency with self-empowerment. On the other hand, they also came face to face with the hostility of the husbands toward these changes: "five out of six husbands interviewed considered their wives' influence on major family decisions a 'win-lose' situation and saw themselves on the losing side. The friction between husband and wife usually stems from the husband's perception that his wife cannot attend to her responsibilities as a wife, a mother, and a working woman."[20] In other words, Vietnamese husbands' expectations concerning the gender relations and roles between husband and wife remain wedded to the traditional Confucian precepts of the Three Submissions and Four Womanly Virtues, creating discord and threatening marital relations and family harmony.[21]

In response to these socioeconomic pressures and strains, many Vietnamese men resort to wife beating, i.e., husbands exerting physical violence on their wives, which is accepted as the traditional expression and enforcement of patriarchal authority in Vietnam. Kibria notes that physical assaults by men on women in the family regularly occurred, "suggesting that wife beating continues among the Vietnamese in the United States."[22] Although it is true that Asian Americans have the lowest reported rates of domestic violence, this may be attributed to the fact of significant underreporting by Asian American women. According to Pho and Mulvey, unreported cases of domestic violence in Southeast Asian immigrant families in the United States are considerably higher than other racial ethnic groups for many reasons, including "adherence to traditional values and roles, fear of government and legal authorities related to political histories, fear of deportation, language barriers, and immigration status." They find that the "high domestic violence levels are attributed to war-related violence, post-traumatic stress disorder, and urban violence in the United States generally."[23]

Pho and Mulvey identify women who are at high risk of domestic violence: "women who were older, homebound, did not speak English, and were very isolated," as well as "women who were younger, spoke English, and were immersed in American culture."[24] They explain that effective outreach to "older Southeast Asian women is very difficult due to high incidences of trauma-related mental and physical health problems including post-traumatic stress disorder, memory and cognitive losses, and psychosomatic blindness," and these problems were exacerbated by language barriers and lack of participation in community groups.[25] Ironically, younger women also faced domestic violence, but for different reasons: "women working outside the home, loss of men's status that was often attributed to women's public roles and to American culture; gender-based norms for dating, family, and parenting roles; and power inequities associated with hierarchical family structures."[26]

The Challenges of Arranged Marriages

Traditional arranged marriages with their foundational understanding of marriage as union between two families, clans, or groups, stand in stark contrast to the contemporary American understanding of marriage as the union of love between two individuals. The first-generation Asian Americans who promote arranged marriages often view marriage as first and foremost a familial or parental process, where the wishes of the children are subordinated to those of their parents. While the practice of arranged marriages may seem out of place in contemporary United States, one must not forget that many first-generation Asian Americans come from countries in Asia where arranged marriage is still widely practiced.

By contrast, for many 1.5 and later generations of Asian Americans, the concept of arranged marriage in any form is not only inimical to their contemporary worldview, it also generates an inordinate amount of stress as a result of the dissonance between their ideals of personal autonomy, independence, and romantic love, as well as their freedom of choice and pursuit of individual goals with their parents' insistence on playing a very active role in determining or, at the very least, influencing their children's choice of marriage partner through the articulation of specific family goals, limitations, or restrictions on the possible choices of marriage partners.

From the parents' point of view, it is important that they select or at least approve the choice of marriage partners for their children because marriage represents a continuation of family name or lineage, as well as the continued preservation and survival of their traditional culture and way of life. Not surprisingly, parents often lament that their children are becoming too vocal and assertive, and in certain cases too rebellious against authority. From the children's perspective, they are increasingly rejecting any demand of unconditional submission to parental authority when they reject any call to give up their demand for individual choice in favor of family choice. They point to their different lifestyles, professional careers, values, and expectations.

Farha Ternikar notes that formal arranged marriages are still widespread among Indian American families, including Indian American Christian families. In this context, arranged marriages are practiced as a culturally acceptable mechanism to maintain and perpetuate ethnic and religious ties. Ternikar cites a female respondent whose family wanted to find her a marriage partner because they wanted her to marry within the Malayalam ethnicity and the Catholic faith. She further notes that arranged marriages will remain the norm in South Asian immigrant communities because "the traditional arranged marriage allows parents to have great involvement in the selection of their children's spouse, while ensuring the maintenance of ethnic and religious tradition and racial purity. There is a great emphasis in South Asian immigrant communities to maintain endogamy for both ethnic and religious reasons."[27]

The Challenges of Endogamy

For many traditional Asian American parents, race is an important element in identity construction, creating boundaries that define and demarcate a specific racial ethnic identity from others that are defined biologically, i.e., as a matter of "blood," such that marriage outside the group "carries with it the danger of impurity or contamination, as personified by the 'mixed-race' child.'"[28] Many first-generation Asian Americans firmly believe that arranged marriage is the key to ensuring the survival of their ethnic, cultural, and religious traditions in the midst of powerful forces of encouraging assimilation into a white American sociocultural ideal.[29]

The conflicts surrounding arranged marriages often center on the question of endogamy, or marrying within one's own racial, ethnic, caste, or social group. Among Asian Americans, endogamy is widely practiced by the Indian American Christians who belong to the Knanaya community.[30] Well-educated and ambitious, many Knanayas have immigrated to the United States since 1965 and settled in Chicago and other metropolitan areas. The Knanaya Catholics are distinct from other Indian Catholics (Latin Catholics, Syro-Malabar and Syro-Malankara Catholics) by the fact that they continue to practice one of the most restrictive forms of endogamy.[31] Raymond Williams explains the dilemma well when he writes:

> They are small and endogamous like some branches of the Amish, but they live in the world, not separate from it, distributed in urban areas across the country. They wish to preserve ethnic ties even though they do not follow traditional occupations. Exclusion results from marrying out of the community even though...the community is so small as to make it difficult to find marriage partners inside it. They prefer endogamy within the ethnic group to endogamy within the Church, although all recognized Knanaya are at least nominally Christians, albeit Orthodox and Catholic.... Members of the first generation value and pursue an ethnic purity that flies in the face of some contemporary American rhetoric and which leaves many young people uncertain about their individual prospects and the future of their distinctive community in America.[32]

As a result, the Knanaya American community faces two immediate problems, having to (1) justify the continued practice of endogamy to their skeptical children and equally skeptical public, and (2) find suitable spouses for their children. As Williams explains:

> Knanaya youth in America are just coming to the marriage age, so the issue evokes lively debate. Parents prefer that their children return to India for marriage within the community, but the youth look forward to marriage in the United States. A person who marries outside the community is no longer considered to be a practicing Knanaya, nor are the children enrolled. That creates a great deal of resentment and misunderstanding. Already, several young people have married out, some to other Syrian Christians and some into other ethnic groups. That is a grave threat because the very existence of the Knanaya depends on endogamy.[33]

More specifically, endogamy is also problematic for it is perceived by the younger generation of Knanayas as un-Christian, racist, and smacking of casteism, and therefore it has no place in the contemporary United States. Again, citing the findings of Williams:

> Young people question the rationale for maintaining such strict endogamy in America. Some believe that the claim to be "old Christians"

and part of an aristocracy requiring endogamy is casteism at its worst and should not be imported to America. The response in religious terms is to apply to the Knanaya all the injunctions regarding exclusiveness found in some Hebrew texts and in sociological terms is to show that other groups practice *de facto* endogamy. Even if the young people are convinced, it is difficult to find appropriate partners.[34]

A small minority of Knanayas marry outside of their community, but they usually end up being alienated and marginalized for doing so.[35] For those who accept the fact of endogamy, however grudgingly, the Knanaya Catholic Youth League of North America (KCYLN) sponsors singles events at their annual conferences, hosting dinners, picnics, etc., that are often used as venues for introducing singles to other singles by parents and family members.[36]

Pastoral Responses

Asian American Catholics face significant challenges in their quest to construct and shape a meaningful identity, peoplehood, worldview, and moral order as a minority community in the sociocultural environment of the contemporary United States, which may not always be sympathetic to their concerns. On the one hand, Asian American Catholics have a strong sense of marriage and family life that is often praised by outsiders. On the other hand, beneath the placid surface of family harmony lurks problems such as gender strife, spousal abuse, and domestic violence, as well as the American-born Asian Americans' rejection of sociocultural traditions that seek to maintain racial ethnic identity and purity, e.g., arranged marriages and endogamy. What follows next is a fivefold proposal for the church's consideration as it seeks to respond to the challenges of doing Asian American marriage and family ministry.

First Recommendation: Outreach to Asian American Catholics

Like many minorities, Asian American Catholics are often hesitant to wash their dirty linen in public. Rather than seek assistance for problems, they tend to minimize these problems in a defensive attempt to "save face." Further, many older Asian American Catholics may not be fluent in English and have limited skills and experiences in reaching out for help. Hence, the Catholic Church has to take the initiative to reach out to Asian American Catholics instead of waiting for them to come knocking on the church's door.

At the same time, church leaders would do well to avoid two common pitfalls that could derail their ministry in their outreach to these Asian American Catholics. First, church leaders have to avoid the temptation of adopting an uncritical and Orientalist approach toward Asian Americans, essentializing and idealizing Asian American sociocultural traditions and ethnic practices. Second, church leaders should also avoid an *assimilationist* approach, which presumes that if Asian American Catholics were more Americanized and assimilated into the norms of a presumed "white" American Catholic suburban family, their problems would disappear. Asian American Catholics argue that both viewpoints fail to consider the nuances and complexities of their life experiences.

Second Recommendation: Selection and Training of Pastoral Leaders

The Catholic Church would have to recruit and train pastoral ministers with the appropriate cultural, linguistic, and psychological skills to minister to Asian American Catholics and their families. In an ideal world, these pastoral leaders would be recruited from within specific ethnic communities. Where this is not feasible, outsiders could be trained for this purpose. While it is desirable that these pastoral leaders who are not members of specific ethnic communities are equipped with the appropriate language skills for their ministry, it is equally important that these pastoral leaders be trained to understand the sociocultural nuances of the people that they minister to, reading between the lines through the unspoken body language to understand what is really going on beneath the facade of normalcy. Moreover, pastoral leaders have to avoid *essentializing* Asian Americans into stereotypes, e.g., Asian Americans always stress family over individuality, Asian Americans always cling on tightly to their Asian cultural heritage, Asian Americans have no sense of a differentiated self apart from family, etc. In addition, they ought to be aware that all attempts to "change" the situation or to convey the "right" way of doing things would be viewed as interference or meddling by an "outsider."

Third Recommendation:
From Sympathizing to Empathizing

Pastoral leaders go beyond merely sympathizing with Asian American Catholics to *empathizing* with them and their communities in solidarity with their daily life experiences as Asians, Americans, and Catholics. They listen to the hopes and aspirations, as well as struggles and broken dreams of these Asian American Catholics, exploring the intersections of faith, ethnicity, and culture, as well as the interaction of social, gender, and generational identities. Though such empathy and solidarity, pastoral leaders help Asian Americans navigate the difficult waters between remaining loyal to culture and tradition on the one hand, and realizing that uncritical loyalty could be unhealthy and counterproductive in the long run.

Fourth Recommendation:
From Traditional Maintenance to Traditioning

Pastoral leaders should assist and encourage Asian American Catholics to go beyond idealized and essentialized constructions of identity, culture, and ethnicity, moving away from *tradition-maintenance* — i.e., clinging to ethnic-bound traditions, customs, and theological positions from the "Old World" at all costs — in favor of *traditioning*. Traditioning is the largely unconscious and ongoing process of shaping, constructing, and negotiating new traditions, practices, and norms that seek to address the issues and questions confronting all Asian Americans Catholics, immigrant or American-born. The process of *traditioning* is based upon the premise that tradition is not fixed and static, but rather, it is dynamic and contextual. As Jaroslav Pelikan explains:

> Tradition is not fixed for all time.... It is the perpetuation of *a changing, developing identity*. Tradition is the living faith of the dead; traditionalism is the dead faith of the living. Tradition lives *in conversation with the past,* while *remembering where we are* and *when we are* and that *it is we who have to decide.* Traditionalism supposes that nothing should ever be done for the first time, so all that is needed to solve any problem is to arrive at the supposedly unanimous testimony of this homogenized tradition.[37]

Pelikan's insights have far-reaching consequences for Asian American Catholics who are endeavoring to make sense of their cultural and ethnic traditions in the contemporary United States. Although he did not use the specific phrase "traditioning," it is clear from the extended quotation that the verb "traditioning" best describes what Pelikan had in mind when he spoke about a tradition that "lives *in conversation with the past,* while *remembering where we are* and *when we are* and that *it is we who have to decide.*" In other words, Pelikan unequivocally eschewed the static *traditionalism* that clings tenaciously to past precedents without any regard for the contemporary context and its specific needs, in favor of an active and dynamic traditioning that pays attention to contemporary social locations, needs, and challenges.

Moreover, Pelikan's statement highlights the fact that traditioning questions simplistic and uncritical reproductions of the past, rejecting all attempts at fossilizing or archaizing the present in a state of *stasis,* as well as challenging any notion that tradition is ahistorical, atemporal, and independent of sociocultural changes. Instead, traditioning entails critical reflections about a community's present and future. By going beyond mere replication of historical precedents, traditioning seeks to retell, reinterpret, and nuance one's traditions with new layers of meaningfulness that address the concerns of the present context. Traditioning also pursues strategic, dynamic, creative, and contextualized interpretations, mediating between historical precedents and current concerns, thereby endeavoring to create a coherent tradition that unites the rich legacy of historical precedents with contemporary needs and challenges. Rather than looking for a single normative, essentialist, and unchanging meaning, traditioning seeks hybridized and multiple *meaningfulness,* embodying and integrating both differences and consensus, past and present, precedent and innovation, authority and creativity, thereby facilitating the articulation of new meanings for the present and future. As a result, tradition is constantly being renegotiated, renewed, and nuanced.

Fifth Recommendation: Dialogue

Pastoral leaders would do well to adopt an approach of dialogue that seeks to understand and respect the problems, while gently encouraging all the parties to open up and talk to each other. Rather than a *deus ex machina,* a pastoral leader would be more effective as a collaborator who facilitates the process of dialogue between parties in conflict, gently prodding parties to go beyond what seems immutable to consider alternative meanings and understandings. Members of a family are in a good position to know about the competing worldviews, values, challenges, identity constructions, problems, and other issues confronting that family better than any outsider. They are the ones with the knowledge to change the problematic situation once they feel empowered through dialogue and finding a common ground.

A dialogical approach would enable pastoral leaders to overcome the defensive stonewalling by family elders who often hunker down with a bunker mentality in view of external sociocultural forces that threaten to change their ways of life. This is because changes come about not by direct intervention in altering the family dynamics, structure, or social conditions, but by facilitating conversation and dialogue. To put it another way, changes come about not by church leaders "changing" individual family members, but by getting those family members to dialogue about their issues and conflicts. In doing so, those family members can be empowered to change by finding a common ground for compromise. As new understandings are constructed in dialogue, new options and possibilities are opened up for these families.

Chapter Thirteen

Interchurch Marriages: Challenges and Blessings

Bonnie P. Mack

I SPEAK FROM THE PERSPECTIVE of a partner in an interchurch marriage as well as a marriage preparation minister. When I entered an interchurch marriage thirty-nine years ago, I had no concept of what that meant for me personally, for my relationship with my spouse, with our families, and with the universal church. Now, thirty-nine years later, I believe my marriage, our families, our churches, and I are all much richer because of this choice. Knowing that we have been witnesses to the unity that Christ talked about is both humbling and motivating. What the ecumenical movement is continually trying to do at a hierarchical level — honestly sharing commonalities and differences in pursuing peace and building up common life — interchurch couples do in their marriages for some of those same reasons.

Pope Benedict XVI stated in one of his addresses at the beginning of his pontificate that "a priority in his ministry would be the restoration of full visible unity among Christians."[1] Both at a grassroots level and in the truest sense, this is what the interchurch couple represents — a visible sign of Christ's unity.

Terminology

An initial challenge in writing about, working with, or talking to couples of two different faith backgrounds is understanding terminology. Canon Law uses the words "mixed marriage" to refer to any couple of two faith backgrounds. Interfaith, interchurch, interdenominational, ecumenical, and inter-religious — these are all terms I have seen and heard through the years. In the general Catholic population, these words refer to a wide variety of Catholic/non-Catholic marriages. The term "interchurch" has surfaced as the most common term used for all Catholic/Christian configurations.

The couple or individuals in the marriage might be inactive, marginally active, or fully immersed in two faith traditions. In addition, both parties might be "members" of their partner's faith community with varying degrees of participation. But to the Association of Interchurch Families (AIF) and the American Association of Interchurch Families (AAIF), the word "interchurch" has a very specific meaning.

The AIF/AAIF defines mixed marriage and interchurch families as including "a husband and wife who come from two different church traditions (often a Roman Catholic married to a Christian of another communion). Both of them retain their original church membership, but so far as they are able they are committed to live, worship, and participate in their spouse's church also. If they have children, as parents they exercise a joint responsibility under God for their religious and spiritual upbringing, and they teach them by word and example to appreciate both their Christian traditions."[2] Therefore the differences in terminology and subsequent ramifications can bring a sense of frustration and misunderstanding to these interchurch couples. These couples, although a small percentage of "mixed" marriages, are nevertheless rich resources in a parish. For the sake of this essay I will be using the word "interchurch," incorporating all the various meanings just mentioned and trying to craft a response with the meaning in that context. The exception in terminology will be for Catholic/Non-Christian unions, which I will refer to as "interfaith" marriages.

The results of the Creighton University Center for Marriage and Family study *Getting It Right* (1995) clearly revealed that couples who shared "joint religious activities" had lower divorce rates and believed that religion added cohesion to their marriage. These interchurch couples can offer much and desire to share their gifts and their uniqueness with the churches they attend. To minimize or ignore them hurts both the couples and the church. Therefore, it is important that Catholics prioritize the preparation of interchurch couples, both for their benefit and the benefit of the wider church family.

Immediate Marriage Preparation

One place in the marriage continuum where the Catholic Church can positively or negatively impact interchurch couples is in the immediate marriage preparation phase. Many engaged couples, no matter what faith tradition, are lukewarm in their faith walk. Making the transition from their parents' faith to their own is crucial in their ongoing church participation and formation. Family of origin issues often surface with interchurch couples as they try to build their faith life together. Helping couples step back from their particular church traditions and families to begin talking about their experiences with God, and situations or circumstances that have drawn them to God, are wonderful ways to surface faith commonalities and evangelize. Experience has shown that if and when interchurch couples discover a shared spirituality, one based on Christ, they have the mortar rather than the wedge in their faith journey.

This is where the church plays a critical role, I believe. As I thought about my lived experiences and sifted through input of interchurch and interfaith couples, the words "hospitality" and "welcoming" surfaced again and again. Hospitality and welcoming are essential because in many ways, our experiences and therefore impression of church, positive or negative, are tied to hospitality. Whatever the circumstances, if we have felt welcomed, included, and valued, our experience is richer, our impression more positive. Something as simple as checking our own attitudes and motivation toward those religiously different from us can be critical. Do we view them as spiritually inferior, someone to convert, or do we see them as someone to learn from and journey with? And how do we view specific interchurch and interfaith couples we know? With concern? Skepticism? Indifference? Tolerance? Appreciation? Therefore, woven into this section as well as most sections will be examples and suggestions for hospitality and welcome.

The Catholic Church must be bridge builders rather than gatekeepers at this critical juncture. If gatekeeping becomes the focus during marriage preparation, there might be long-term consequences for both the couple and the church. Too often, I have heard engaged couples share negative marriage preparation experiences with Catholic and Protestant clergy that have driven them into anger or apathy. It is not easy to strike a balance between being open and welcoming with maintaining the church's identity and integrity, sacrificing Catholicism or becoming Pharisaical.

It is also difficult to separate tradition and Catholic culture from religion. The church language that each tradition uses and that resonates with its members can be overwhelming and scary to an outsider. Sensitivity to religious language or culture is especially important when talking with someone from a different tradition and a practical way to be welcoming. I remember peppering my husband with language questions I was too embarrassed to ask at church. "Ambo," "Blessed Sacrament," "novena," and all the "catech...'s" were new to me. Even terminology that is understandable but different (e.g., readings versus scriptures, the Our Father versus the Lord's Prayer, homily versus sermon) can be addressed in an open, welcoming way. When marriage preparation ministers are talking to engaged interchurch couples, they should automatically assume that neither of them understands terms from the other's tradition and use terms from both traditions interchangeably. Helping engaged couples explore and negotiate this new territory is essential, and therefore interchurch couples should certainly be included in the marriage preparation process.

Experience after experience has shown me that normalizing the situation, addressing and answering some of the concerns, even asking the tough questions are extremely helpful. Anything that threatens a couple's unity at the engaged stage is scary and often avoided. Who better to challenge the unity than someone who is walking the walk? A part of each diocese's marriage preparation process should include at least one opportunity for engaged interchurch couples to address this issue. Talking with married interchurch mentors or including an interchurch session as part of a diocesan or parish program are examples of opportunities to help engaged couples look at their religious backgrounds as they relate to their forming a new family. However, it is best to instruct these mentors to raise the issues and identify areas to explore rather than simply sharing their story or giving pat answers.

A part of the immediate marriage preparation process generally includes a six-month or one-year follow-up with newly married couples. This would be an ideal time to again address interchurch issues, for example, with a mentoring couple or a parish gathering of interchurch couples. Interchurch couples could benefit immensely just having a neutral place to share and learn from each other. My experience has continually proven that if couples see others walking a similar path and sharing commonalities, they can successfully negotiate potentially rough waters. They realize they are not alone and are encouraged and helped by sharing with other couples. Try piloting a program inviting all interchurch couples to gather. With a few starter questions such as, "What do you find to be a challenge to you as an interchurch couple," or "What is one blessing you have received as an interchurch couple," you will provide a safe and helpful environment for all.

Affirming engaged or newly married interchurch couples wherever they are in their journey is another way of being welcoming. Obviously, there is a preference for a marriage between two people of the same faith tradition, but that does not occur in over 40 percent of Catholic marriages.[3]

Interchurch couples seek and desire the church's blessings, encouragement, and appreciation wherever they land on the spectrum of participation. Being hospitable and welcoming goes a long way in achieving this.

Remote Preparation

Within a few years, many newly married couples have children and face special challenges as an interchurch family. At this point the couple will encounter issues of faith practice. In addition, they are actually beginning to prepare their young children for marriage many years off. Remote marriage preparation (from birth to age twelve), "includes all those family as well as other environmental factors that influence and prepare a person in positive and negative ways for marriage."[4] Central to remote marriage preparation is the spiritual aspect. Oftentimes, delayed decisions about church attendance and participation can no longer be ignored. As marriage ministers, we know the importance of helping all families understand their holiness consists of just being a family. In addition, assisting interchurch families to see how their different traditions can strengthen the bond is essential whether they choose to worship in one or two churches.

In *Familiaris Consortio*, John Paul II uses the phrase, "family, become what you are," and this was affirmed by the bishops at their annual meeting in San Antonio, Texas, in 2004. The family was challenged in a number of ways to live out who they inherently are. Becoming the church in the home or the "domestic church" with the mission of being the foremost educators of children, being a sanctuary of life by welcoming children as gifts of God, being salt of the earth and light of the world to promote life, justice, and peace and completing the mission as "Good News" for all the world, are worthy goals for all families, interchurch included. This begins in families with very young children through remote marriage preparation. It is essential to encourage religious practice of some sort, especially the religious education of the children. Therefore, the local church should do everything in its power to support and encourage interchurch couples whatever place they are in their faith practice.

A positive result from an interchurch home can be that children usually emerge more tolerant of religious differences. A downside from the church's perspective could be less certainty of their own religious identity. Both results can be positive, however. When interchurch families attend and participate in each other's churches, they can be a living example of Christian unity and love. Unity doesn't necessarily mean conformity. The three Persons of the Trinity are one, yet each has a very different role to fill in God's ultimate plan of salvation. Helping families realize that ignoring religion altogether in the home with the idea that "the children can make their own choice when they are older" is faulty logic. In reality most children make no choice as we generally choose from a position of knowledge, not from a vacuum.

Because each child is being continually prepared for a possible future marriage (one with the same or different religious traditions), it is important to proclaim your faith tradition without demeaning others. This may come more naturally to an interchurch family because they are living out and proclaiming the diversity, while focusing on the commonalities. The commonality: Christ has called us into relationship with him and asks us to share his love with others, especially our children. This can be incorporated into every family's experience and built on in a variety of ways as the child grows. Establishing a value system of right and wrong based on Christian teachings, expressing needs, feelings and thoughts through simple dialogues of prayer with God, practicing respect for self and others no matter the differences are wonderful, healthy ways to remotely prepare very young children for marriage whether the children are growing up in an interchurch or same church family. As a child develops chronologically and spiritually, there is generally a deeper attraction to stories from scripture and a variety of opportunities for prayer and ritual celebration, again a time to recognize and celebrate the commonalities and diversity of all religions.

Although interchurch couples might not recognize the term "domestic church," my experience has found that Christ's church with its intended unity is often found in their homes, whether or not that is intentional. In order to build up the common faith, interchurch couples often draw on the strengths of a spouse's tradition, which can be very helpful in bringing Christ into the home. My love of scripture and spontaneous prayer helped shape my husband's and my decision to share this with our children in building Christ into our daily lives. Mealtimes usually included both, often in songs and poems. It is a treat to now watch these rituals being passed on to their children. The Catholic Church has such a love and appreciation of the sacraments, and my husband's joy for his children receiving these was evident. My understanding and appreciation of them and him grew as a result. Partnering with young families as they prepare for these sacraments can again support this home church which, in turn, strengthens the local community.

As marriage ministers, we are continually looking for opportunities and occasions to support and enrich marriages. We know that spirituality is a critical component. Sacramental preparation can be an opportune time for marriage enrichment, remote marriage preparation, and evangelization, all essential pieces of the interchurch ministry puzzle. Once again, the words "hospitality" and "welcoming" come to mind. Extending hospitality and welcome to interchurch families takes effort and planning but can produce big returns. Including interchurch couples on the various preparation teams or as consultants can serve a number of purposes well. The interchurch couple can assist the parish by providing the interchurch lens needed for sensitivity and welcoming hospitality and at the same time be encouraged and blessed themselves. It can also help fold in a couple when one of the two is marginally involved.

Partnering with young interchurch families and accompanying them on the journey can be extremely helpful. Generally, the first sacrament a married couple experiences is baptism, and most churches have some sort of preparation for it. What a wonderful opportunity interchurch couples have to experience the universality and unity of Christian churches in common baptism. Yet it is at this very juncture that interchurch challenges and family of origin issues might appear. In which church will the child be baptized? Will the parents choose baptism or infant dedication? Will the baptism involve pouring water or full immersion? These are among the questions that interchurch couples must tackle. Baptism classes, which help young families in faith formation, can incorporate a time specifically for interchurch couples. This time, perhaps led by an interchurch couple, can provide a safe place to discuss individual and particular concerns. How to blend two faith traditions may be the deeper, truer issue needing discussion rather than the sacrament of baptism. Often these couples simply need a venue to discover they are not alone on their journey. Although each couple's walk varies, there are common threads that, once identified, can be bonders rather than dividers.

Reconciliation is a sacrament that can help individuals and families develop skills of conflict management and communication through the gifts of honesty and forgiveness. Too often this sacrament is experienced in conjunction with First Communion only, and then overlooked by many, including interchurch families. Because of differing views on personal confession there might be less emphasis put on this sacrament by interchurch couples. An honest discussion with an opportunity for questions and answers can be helpful. My recollection of reconciliation for my children is vague, possibly because there was no parents' meeting about it or much emphasis placed on it. But certainly understanding the importance of asking for and giving forgiveness is a critical piece of being the domestic church.

First Communion can be a time of joy and growth or pain and isolation for interchurch families. Non-Catholics are often dealing with some level of recognized or unrecognized anxiety because of their lack of knowledge or experience with Eucharist. In addition, this sacrament can be very painful for interchurch families because of the divisiveness associated with it. Eucharist is called the Great Sacrament of Unity, yet it divides faith-filled interchurch families. The division existing in the churches results in the division of husbands and wives, one flesh, often resulting in pain and anger. At the present time the only way to sincerely respond to this deep spiritual need is through compassion and understanding, both essential. Pastoral, welcoming, and sensitive preparation ministers can help build bridges instead of walls for interchurch families.

I had two completely different experiences with our first two children, in two different parishes. When I attended the parents' meeting for our oldest child's First Communion, one obviously disgusted parent asked, "*When* are you going to start talking about being Catholic instead of being Christian?" The priest responding in a very kind way said, "I never knew the two were separate." He went on to explain his response but quite honestly, I was so moved and relieved by his initial remark, I did not hear the rest of the explanation. His hospitality from the beginning to the end of the meeting was inviting and welcoming and I have never forgotten it. I graciously thanked him after the meeting. A few years later, when our daughter was preparing for her First Communion, my husband, daughter, and I went to meet with the priest. His explanation of Eucharist was excellent until he began discussing Protestants and their level of understanding. "Because Protestants do not believe in transubstantiation (explained in child terms), they can just throw Jesus in the trash can." Demonstrating this with a host, he asked our daughter how Jesus might feel. I was mortified but said nothing at the time. When we were walking to our car after the meeting, our daughter looked up at me questioningly and asked, "Mommy, do you just throw Jesus in the garbage at your church?" My husband and I had a long talk with our daughter followed by a talk with the priest. This experience has also stayed with me for years. I remember worrying about getting the appropriate dress and how to attach the veil (boys were so much simpler!), not wanting to stand out and not *look* Catholic. I also wanted to be included by walking forward with our daughter when she received for the first time. Again, having the input of non-Catholics on sensitivity and welcoming issues might be especially helpful for this sacrament.

Proximate Marriage Preparation

Proximate marriage preparation follows remote preparation and covers preadolescents through young adults. Proximate marriage preparation can provide opportunities for deepening young people's understanding of themselves, of the sacraments, including the sacrament of marriage, and of their faith life. Just as in this stage young people explore qualities they desire in a spouse and begin to understand the importance of lifelong friendship with a marriage partner, they should also be learning that if God is in the marriage this three-strand cord can help sustain them. Often it is in this stage that young people are invited to answer the call to holiness by developing a personal relationship with Jesus Christ. In addition, helping incorporate the Gospel and church-based morals in decision making for particular moral situations is critical. If all these pieces of the faith puzzle are understood and internalized, an individual will be better prepared for the marriage whether same or mixed faith. There are several considerations for interchurch families at this place in the lifecycle. Children who are raised in an interchurch home might be more open and tolerant of various religious configurations and see Christ in the midst of it all, but they also might have a lot of questions surface regarding religious traditions as well. If a young person has been raised in an interchurch home where one of the partners has drifted away or otherwise been inactive the young person may either gravitate toward or harbor resentment with the active parent's church tradition.

Whatever the situation, spiritual opportunities abound at this stage. Hopefully, church staff members know the interchurch families and have laid the groundwork of hospitality, welcome, and acceptance during the remote period. If so, expressing a willingness to talk with the young person can be beneficial. Answering parents' questions and affirming them is also helpful. If parents and parish staffs are aware and responsive with open formal or informal opportunities to address concerns and pertinent issues, everyone benefits. School classes can help too by providing opportunities for young people to grow in their faith and understanding of the above. Having youth represented in the life of the parish, whether that is ministry or liturgy, is excellent. The church can learn much from its young folks. Encouraging families to create a hospitable and reconciliatory setting in their home or to demonstrate Christ's love by reaching out to others through service projects are tangible ways to bridge the differences in faith traditions. Interchurch families can especially benefit from having their children involved in the parish. Often adults learn more about their own spirituality through their children's experiences.

Gift or Challenge?

Fr. Gerard Kelly, a priest in the Archdiocese of Sydney, Australia, has written a challenging essay entitled "Pioneers not Problems."[5] He begins the essay by talking about how historically "mixed marriages" were viewed as problematic; people were discouraged from marrying someone outside their religious tradition. He goes on to explain the change he has witnessed since that time, now viewing interchurch couples as pioneers. Not only are interchurch marriages "witnesses to the possibility of unity in the Church, but also to a way of life that is enriched rather than torn apart by diversity." Does this statement challenge you? Do you see the diversity an interchurch couple might bring to the church as a gift or a problem? Perhaps both?

Interchurch families experience a wide variety of responses from their church communities, ranging from total acceptance to tolerance or avoidance, even rejection. Recently, a deacon told me about a new phenomenon he is seeing, which may be a result of couples' desire to avoid one of these responses. Interchurch couples are choosing to ignore their differences and just blend in with the crowd. They both go to communion and participate in the life of the parish but the non-Catholic has no interest in becoming Catholic. It is irrelevant and/or unimportant to them both, which presents another challenge to clergy and laity. Will their joint participation in the Eucharist be a *means* to unity the church talks about and interchurch couples seek? And if this is true, how do we reconcile this situation with denying communion to declared interchurch couples?

I believe it essential to recognize that interchurch families can be wonderful gifts to their parishes. They introduce broader perspectives into the local church, which can actually help strengthen all members' faith. By focusing on their common spirituality while preserving their different church worship styles, traditions, and church cultures, these families model how the larger church should respond. They can be a visible sign to the unity of the universal church.

Welcome and hospitality are keys to inclusiveness that can positively affect all families, but especially interchurch and interfaith families. Every interchurch family's spirituality develops over time as they build their own domestic church. There will be many varieties of interchurch families present in a parish, all building their church of the home. Because an individual's spiritual roots are formed through his or her particular religious tradition, encouraging the sharing of those traditions may result in gifts blessing their partner's church and the family's domestic church. The key is to enfold these families in parish community life whatever their configuration. There are many ways to involve non-Catholics without getting into doctrinal hot water. This crossover helps the membership realize that others can and want to share their time, talent, and treasure for the glory of God even if they are not both Catholic. Ministry fairs or time-talent-treasure sign-ups are excellent ways to reach out to interchurch and interfaith families.

The children of an interchurch family who have grown up in both churches can be an unexpected special blessing to each faith community but can also challenge our sensitivities. Often these youth do not identify with either religious tradition, being equally comfortable in both churches. They easily "double-belong," a term analogous with bilingual or bicultural. This has proven true in our household. All our children are equally comfortable in both churches and with both church families. When they were much younger, a pastor shared his honest concerns. He thought our kids would be "spiritually schizophrenic," and certainly confused and rootless. I quietly lived with that fear for many years and was relieved when his concerns did not come to fruition. How do you feel about double-belonging? What are your specific concerns for children of interchurch families?

I entitled this section "Gift or Challenge?" because interchurch families are both. Even those in the ecumenical movement and the churches they represent struggle with how to balance living out their oneness in Jesus Christ with defending denominational prerogatives and theological distinctions.[6] How do the various responses challenge or resonate with you?

Interfaith Marriages: Special Challenges

Because interfaith marriages often involve both religious and cultural differences, there is an ongoing need for dialogue and understanding. In fact,

I have heard it said that couples living in an interfaith marriage live a life of permanent dialogue, always needing to figure out how to deal with the many issues they face. This generally involves struggle, and the key is to find ways to make the struggle one in which both partners can win, both partners feel respected, both partners' traditions and all that goes with them, valued. This is the self-respect that every human being strives for. It certainly takes patience, dialogue, evolution over time, and a rootedness in the Spirit who knows no spiritual boundaries. Obviously, the Catholic and Jewish faiths share the Old Testament and certain ritual elements that provide a means to commonality, but even when this does not exist, careful attention to both traditions with a look at common elements can provide the mortar for spiritual intimacy. Shared spiritual activity, as mentioned earlier, can be beneficial for interfaith couples. This might be the common element... the mortar for interfaith couples. *Dovetail,* a journal by and for Jewish/Christian families, and the website, *www.dovetailinstitute.org,* are both excellent resources for couples and churches. Both provide a wealth of information and suggestions for joint spiritual activity for couples and families. Included at the end of this essay is a list of resources for interfaith couples that might be helpful in negotiating the challenges. Once again, the local parish or cluster of parishes can provide a venue for interfaith couples to connect.

Pastoral Recommendations

I have already woven many pastoral ideas and suggestions into the fabric of this essay and with each have provided a fuller explanation. I now offer the following recommendations based on my personal and professional experience, literature, and studies:

- Offer hospitality and welcome to interchurch and interfaith couples, with compassion and understanding being central.
- Encourage religious practice of some sort, especially the religious education of the children.
- Seek ways to encourage interchurch families to build the domestic church and provide a variety of suggestions to do so.
- Affirm married interfaith and interchurch couples wherever they are on the journey.

- Check one's own internal attitudes and motives toward interfaith and interchurch couples.

- Recognize that interchurch and interfaith couples can introduce broader perspectives into the local church that can actually help strengthen all members' faith.

- Provide opportunities for interchurch couples to dialogue with other interchurch couples during all stages of the married life cycle.

- Offer a variety of ways for interchurch couples to get involved in parish life.

- Encourage interfaith/interchurch couples to participate in joint spiritual activity through service, outreach, or community action.

Conclusion

> Leaders of the churches have emphasized that growth in the visible unity of the church of Christ is not an optional extra but integral to the life of every Christian. Interchurch families cannot fulfill their vocation to be a sign and means of visible unity within their churches unless they are welcomed, understood, and supported by their extended families, their local congregations and their pastors.[7]

These are the words of some of the pioneers who desire to share their gifts with their church communities as well as the greater church. They are a rich resource that we cannot afford to overlook. Interchurch couples face a plethora of challenges in their own relationship as they seek to build unity in their marriage and families. They are attempting to balance their internal spiritual life with their local congregations, their own desires with the rules of the churches, their own traditions with building a shared spirituality. The church can be a help or a hindrance in response. I challenge all of us to be helpers.

I have heard an interchurch mentoring couple tell a room full of interchurch couples, "Don't lose your religion for the sake of your marriage, but for heaven's sake, don't lose your marriage for your religion." I challenge the church to encourage and support interchurch couples, whatever configuration they are, for the betterment of our church and society.

Interchurch Resources

American Association of Interchurch Families (AAIF). *www.aifusa.org/.*
Association of Interchurch Families. *www.interchurchfamilies.org.*
BRIDGES — *Building Relationship Interaction, Decision-making, Growth and Enrichment Through Spirituality.* Omaha, Neb.: Creighton University, and FOCCUS, Inc., 2002.
Bush, John C., and Patrick R. Cooney, eds. *Catholic/Reformed Dialogue in the U.S.* Interchurch Families — Resources for Ecumenical Hope. Louisville: Westminster John Knox Press, 2002.
Carey, George. *A Tale of Two Churches: Can Protestants and Catholics Get Together.* Downer's Grove, Ill.: InterVarsity Press, 1985.
Center for Marriage and Family. *Ministry to Interchurch Marriages: A National Study.* Omaha, Neb.: Creighton University, 1999.
Committee on Ecumenical and Interreligious Affairs, U.S. Bishops. *A Guide for Catholics Considering Marriage with an Orthodox Christian.* Washington, D.C.: United States Catholic Conference, 1997.
Fournier, Keith A., and William D. Watkins. *A House United: Evangelicals and Catholics Together, A Winning Alliance for the 21st Century.* Colorado Springs: Navpress, 1994.
Gallagher, Rosemary, and Michael Henesy, C.SS.R., *How to Survive Being Married to a Catholic.* Liguori, Mo.: Liguori Publications, 1997.
Kilcourse, George. *Double Belonging: Interchurch Families and Christian Unity.* Mahwah, N.J.: Paulist Press, 1992.
Pontifical Council for Promoting Christian Unity. *Directory for the Application of Principles and Norms on Ecumenism.* Vatican City, March 25, 1993.
Stanko, Sandra L. *United in Heart, Divided in Faith: A Guide for Catholic-Protestant Couples.* Allen, Tex.: SunCreek Books, 2003.
Two Churches, One Marriage. *www.sandiego.edu/interchurch.*
U.S. Bishops. *Follow the Way of Love — A Pastoral Message of the U.S. Catholic Bishops to Families.* Washington, D.C.: USCCB, 1994.

Interfaith Resources

Crohn, Joel. *Mixed Matches: How to Create Successful Interracial, Interethnic, and Interracial Relationships.* New York: Ballantine Books, 1995.

Goodman-Malamuth, Leslie, and Robin Margolis. *Between Two Worlds: Choices for Grown Children of Jewish-Christian Parents.* New York: Pocket Books, 1993.

Guide to Jewish Interfaith Family Life: An Interfaith Family.com Handbook. Woodstock, Vt.: Jewish Lights Publishing, 2001.

Hawxhurst, Joan C. *The Interfaith Family Guidebook — Practical Advice for Jewish and Christian Partners.* Kalamazoo, Mich.: Dovetail Publishing, 1998.

Roberts, Cokie and Steve. *From This Day Forward.* New York: Perennial Books, 2001.

Rosenbaum, Mary Helene, and Stanley Ned Rosenbaum. *Celebrating Our Differences: Living Two Faiths in One Marriage.* Shippensburg, Pa.: Beidel Printing, 1999.

Schaper, Donna E. *Raising Interfaith Children: Spiritual Orphans or Spiritual Heirs?* New York: Crossroad, 1999.

Chapter Fourteen

Interchurch Couples: Potential Challenges and Blessings

Lee Williams

INTERMARRIAGE BETWEEN PROTESTANTS AND CATHOLICS in the United States increased dramatically between the 1920s and the 1980s.[1] Studies indicate that a significant number of marriages today are interchurch, that is, marriages in which each spouse belongs to a different Christian church or denomination. It appears that approximately 40 percent of Catholics are married to Protestants or non-Catholics.[2] Estimates for Protestants marrying Catholics or Protestants of other denominations are even higher.[3]

Interchurch couples are an important group not only because of their numbers, but also because research suggests they are at risk for poorer marital outcomes. Studies have consistently demonstrated a higher incidence of divorce for interchurch couples compared to same-church couples.[4]

Findings have been mixed with regards to whether or not interchurch couples are also at risk for lower marital satisfaction. Some studies[5] have found that couples with different religious affiliations have lower marital satisfaction compared to those with the same religious affiliation, while others have not.[6] Differences in samples may account for some of the inconsistent findings with regards to marital satisfaction. For example, studies that included both interfaith couples (e.g., Jewish-Christian) and interchurch couples were more likely to find differences in marital satisfaction.

Building a Successful Interchurch Marriage

The following section explores the knowledge and skills that interchurch couples need to acquire to build stable and satisfying marriages. This is based primarily on research done by the Center for Marriage and Family (1999) at Creighton University. The research was conducted in two phases. In the first phase, interviews with interchurch couples were conducted. Some of the interviews were done in a focus group setting. The results from these interviews were analyzed qualitatively and provided many insights into the rewards and challenges that face interchurch couples, as well as strategies that many of the couples used to address the challenges.[7] A national survey of interchurch couples was conducted in the second phase and allowed a comparison of interchurch and same-church couples on a wide range of variables (Center for Marriage and Family, 1999). Since the study did not include interfaith couples (e.g., Christian-Jewish, Christian-Muslim, etc.), it is unclear to what extent the findings would apply to them. Although many of the concepts may apply to interfaith couples, there may be important ways in which interfaith couples are different from interchurch couples.

Developing Effective Communication and Problem-Solving Skills

Marriage preparation or marriage education often focuses on teaching couples communication and problem-solving skills so they can manage conflict in a constructive rather than destructive manner. Since religious differences have the potential to create conflict for interchurch couples, it makes intuitive sense that teaching couples communication and conflict resolution skills will be helpful to these couples. Indeed, a couple's ability to communicate was the most important predictor of marital satisfaction among interchurch couples in a national study.[8] Teaching couples effective communication and problem-solving skills can help couples deal with the inevitable conflicts that arise in a relationship, whether of a religious nature or not.

Learning to Manage Religious Differences within a Relationship

In addition to teaching interchurch couples general skills for managing conflict, it may also be important to give them specific guidance in how to manage religious differences. The importance of religious differences was evident in the national survey of interchurch couples, which found that the greater the perceived religious differences between the couple, the greater the likelihood of divorce (Center for Marriage and Family, 1999). Interestingly, this was true for both interchurch couples and same-church couples. Thus religious differences can be important for both interchurch and same-church couples, although interchurch couples are more likely to report religious differences than same-church couples.

Couples who had created successful interchurch relationships suggested several ideas or strategies that couples needed to know to effectively manage religious differences. Interchurch couples emphasized the need for couples to explore each other's personal faith. Couples learned about each other's faith in a number of different ways, such as attending each other's church services, reading materials from their partner's church, or discussing each other's beliefs and practices. It was this exploration of each other's faith that often led to spiritual growth. Unfortunately, some couples may be reluctant to do this exploration, particularly if they have fears or misconceptions about the partner's church or faith.

Another important strategy for managing religious differences is to look for commonalities. Successful interchurch couples often commented on the temptation to focus on differences but stressed the importance of looking for commonalities. Indeed, some couples referred to themselves as an interchurch couple rather than interfaith because they shared the same Christian faith. Others emphasized that they believe in the same God and focus less on differences in church doctrine or beliefs. As one man said, "My God isn't different from hers because I'm Presbyterian. My God, in my view, isn't any different than her God in the Catholic Church." Exploring each other's faith often led to the couple discovering commonalities they did not know existed.

Interchurch couples also warned against pressuring one's partner to change. In interviews with interchurch individuals, many shared how early in their marriage they challenged their partner's beliefs or practices, attempting to point out where they were wrong. This often led to conflict in the couple. In some cases, one partner may try to force the other to change religious affiliation. This can create conflict and resentment. Many couples recognized that their partner's religious beliefs or faith were key to his or her identity and avoided trying to change their partner out of respect for their partner.

Interchurch couples may benefit from other ideas to help them manage religious differences. A view expressed by some interchurch couples was that the division over religious differences that couples sometimes struggle with reflects the division that Christianity experiences with its different denominations and churches. For some couples, this perspective helped them to avoid personalizing the struggle too much. It is also important for interchurch couples to recognize that for many individuals, religious traditions are intimately connected with family traditions. Religious and family rituals may be closely interwoven during religious holidays such as Christmas or Easter. As a result, religious and family identity may be closely connected for many people. Thus challenging peoples' religious beliefs or practices may also challenge their loyalty to their family identity, creating a more intense reaction. Interchurch couples may also need to be encouraged to examine whether the differences they are having conflicts over really reflect a "difference that will make a difference." Conflict over religious differences may also reflect deeper issues in the relationship, such as a power struggle or concerns about commitment.

An area of particular concern in working with couples from different religious backgrounds is that they may have different levels of religiosity. In some cases, individuals may identify with a particular denominational affiliation, but are not actively involved. Although different levels of religiosity can also be found in same-church couples, the research indicates that interchurch couples are more likely to have differences in religiosity than same-church couples (Center for Marriage and Family, 1999). Further work in this area is recommended.

Building a Joint Religious/Spiritual Bond

Another important predictor of divorce among interchurch couples was the extent to which they did religious and spiritual activities together as a couple (Center for Marriage and Family, 1999). The more that a couple did religious and spiritual activities together as a couple, the less likely they were to have divorced. This finding was true for both interchurch and same-church couples. Thus marriage preparation or education should focus on helping couples build a strong religious/spiritual bond.

Some interchurch individuals distinguished between their religiosity (e.g., involvement in church communities) and spirituality (e.g., personal faith or personal relationship with God). Therefore, different strategies might be used to strengthen a couple's religious bond versus their spiritual bond, although one would hope that each would mutually reinforce the other. In terms of strengthening their religious bond, many couples attended each other's churches so that they could worship together. For some couples, participation extended beyond just attending their partner's church services, but also included becoming involved in other activities such as Bible studies, religious education classes, service work, or social events within a church.

In terms of strengthening their spiritual bond, many couples emphasized the need to pray together. Saying grace at meals, reading the Bible together, reading other religious materials, and discussing one's faith were also mentioned as ways to spiritually connect with each other.

Exploring Values regarding Marriage

An individual's values and expectations regarding marriage can be influenced by a number of factors, including families of origin, peers, and the society in which we live. Differences in religious socialization can also lead couples to have different values and expectations regarding marriage in a number of different dimensions, including the very meaning of marriage itself. In the Catholic Church, for example, marriage is considered a sacrament. Many Protestant churches, in contrast, view marriage as a covenant rather than a sacrament. Religious socialization can also impact other values regarding marriage, such as gender roles, what are acceptable forms of family planning, and whether or not divorce and remarriage are morally acceptable. Couples need to carefully examine each person's values and expectations regarding marriage to ensure that they are sufficiently compatible.

Issues regarding Religious Affiliation

Another issue that interchurch couples may need help in exploring is whether or not to change religious affiliation. In the national survey of interchurch couples (Center for Marriage and Family, 1999), a large percentage of couples (43.8 percent) who began as interchurch couples eventually became same-church through one or both partners changing religious affiliation. The most common major reasons given for changing religious affiliation included preferring the new church or denomination, believing the marriage or family would be stronger if both spouses belonged to the same church, desiring to worship together as a couple, and desiring to avoid confusing the children by belonging to different churches.

Although these were compelling reasons for some individuals to change religious affiliation, others had equally compelling reasons not to change affiliation. Strength of denominational identity was the strongest variable in predicting whether or not an individual changed religious affiliation (Center for Marriage and Family, 1999). As expected, individuals with a stronger denominational affiliation at the time of engagement were less likely to have changed religious affiliation. Denominational identity may also be tied up with one's cultural identity. When one man was asked in an interview if he ever thought of changing religious affiliation, he replied no, justifying his answer by saying that he was an "old South Omaha Irish Catholic." Family loyalty may be another factor that prevents others from changing religious affiliation. One man expressed openness to changing religious affiliation in principle, but said he would never do so because he anticipated a strong negative reaction from his family, who was strongly Catholic (and had priests in multiple generations).

Given that such a large percentage of interchurch couples do change religious affiliation (and others entertain the idea), it may be prudent for marriage preparation or education to address the potential advantages and disadvantages surrounding a decision to change religious affiliation. In some instances, individuals who did change religious affiliation found that their families were unsupportive (Center for Marriage and Family, 1999). Thus dealing with family reactions to decisions regarding change of religious affiliation would ideally be included.

The Religious Upbringing of Children

One of the biggest challenges that many interchurch couples report facing is deciding on the religious upbringing of children.[9] Some couples resolve this issue by becoming a same-church couple by one or both partners changing religious affiliation. For interchurch couples that remain active in their respective churches, couples must decide whether to raise the children in one parent's church, or attempt to raise the children in both church traditions. Although less common, some families raise some of the children exclusively in one parent's church, and other children exclusively in the other parent's church (e.g., boys raised in the father's church, girls raised in the mother's church). Some couples favor children being raised exclusively in one church tradition out of a concern that exposing children to different church teachings will be confusing. Other couples, however, believe children will have a deeper and more closely examined faith by being exposed to two different church traditions.

Those doing marriage preparation or education need to encourage interchurch couples to begin a dialogue on the religious upbringing of children as soon as possible. Some couples, however, avoid talking about this issue because it can be a sensitive topic. This is understandable given that the religious upbringing of children can touch on so many core issues. For example, individuals must grapple with how the decision will impact their commitment to their own religious practice. In addition, individuals hope to pass on to their children their core values and religious beliefs. Decisions regarding the religious upbringing of children can also have a significant impact on the couple's relationship with parents or extended family, especially if other family members have a vested interest in the religious upbringing of the children. Thus couples need to fully explore the implications of any decision they make in a number of dimensions.

Offering Acceptance and Support to Interchurch Couples

Although not all couples experienced problems in this area, some couples struggle with a lack of acceptance or support from family members.[10] Thus marriage preparation or education may need to help individuals find strategies for dealing with family issues that can arise for interchurch couples.

In interviews with interchurch couples, several strategies for dealing with lack of acceptance were offered. An important theme was for interchurch couples to not be preoccupied with what others think they should do. Rather, as one woman advised, couples "need to pray about it and need to seek direction and... eventually come down to the decision that they're comfortable with." Couples may also need help to understand what may be behind a lack of acceptance by parents or other family members. Common fears by parents included worrying that the adult child would become less active in church or change religious affiliation by entering an interchurch marriage. In some cases, parents would see this as a personal failure on their part. Others feared that their child would encounter additional difficulties being in an interchurch marriage. Negative preconceptions or attitudes about other denominations could also contribute to a lack of acceptance by family members. Recognizing when and how to gently confront others who are insensitive or unsupportive of the interchurch couple may also be beneficial. Finally, finding support from other interchurch couples either formally (e.g., support group) or informally may be beneficial to many couples.

A Conceptual Map for Working with Interchurch Couples

Based in part on the research, a proposed conceptual map for working with interchurch couples is presented below. Although the focus of this essay is on interchurch couples, this proposed model might also guide those working

The 4 Ds for Interchurch Couples

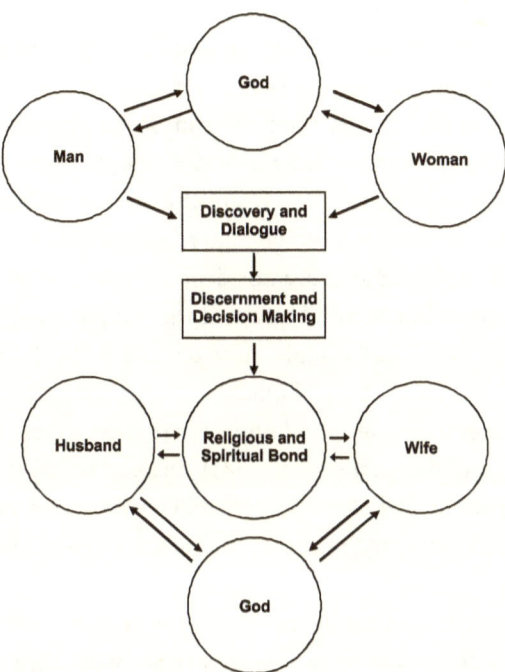

with interfaith couples. In the proposed model, a key developmental task that interchurch couples face is to transition from having two independent religious/spiritual lives to creating a shared religious/spiritual bond. This is a task that all couples must proceed through, but this task can be more difficult for interfaith couples because they generally have greater religious differences. The couple's marriage will hopefully become a catalyst for the couple to form a joint religious/spiritual bond. This bond, in turn, can help sustain and strengthen the couple's marriage. The couple's religious/spiritual bond can become a conduit for God's grace and love. For a couple to create this shared religious/spiritual bond, the couple must engage in several processes, which have been labeled as the 4 Ds.

The first two Ds are discovery and dialogue. Discovery, in part, refers to each individual learning more about his or her partner's religious and spiritual faith. Discovery means examining not only ways in which both partners have religious differences, but also examining what they share in common. With regards to learning more about one's partner, discovery is not possible without dialogue. Yet that dialogue can also bring into focus an individual's own beliefs through comparison and contrast. Thus it is important to emphasize that learning about one's own faith or religious tradition may be part of the discovery process. Dialogue (rather than debate) can create intimacy for couples as they learn more about each other.

The second two Ds are discernment and decision making. Interchurch couples face many important decisions as a couple. For example, should the couple remain interchurch, each faithful to his or her own religious affiliation? Or should one or both change religious affiliation so the couple can worship within the same church or denomination? How will they build a joint religious/spiritual bond? How will the couple manage the religious upbringing of children? Individuals must discern what their needs, beliefs, and desires are on these issues. Collectively, the couple must also discern what is best for their marriage and family. Finally, the couple must ultimately decide how to put into action what they believe to be the best possible course. If successful in all 4 Ds the couple will have formed a strong religious and spiritual bond that can strengthen and nurture the individuals and their marriage.

A free, web-based program developed by the author titled *Two Churches, One Marriage* is consistent with this model for working with interchurch couples. The *Two Churches, One Marriage* program includes the different elements of the model. For example, a unit on managing religious differences emphasizes the need for the couple to explore each partner's religious background, including searching for commonalities. The program contains a unit on communication skills to facilitate the couple's ability to dialogue on issues. Another unit, "The Meaning of Marriage," encourages couples to explore and discuss with each other their values and beliefs regarding marriage. Units on whether or not to change religious affiliation and the religious upbringing of children provide examples of how other interchurch couples have dealt with these topics. These units include exercises to help the couple to begin to discuss and discern how they will handle these decisions in their own relationship. A unit on problem-solving skills is intended to help the couple make decisions in a productive and collaborative manner. Finally, one unit focuses specifically on ways in which the couple can strengthen their religious and spiritual bond (e.g., worship together, pray together).

Challenges and Recommendations for Working with Interchurch Couples

This section outlines some of the key challenges facing the Catholic Church and others who seek to minister to interchurch couples in the future. Recommendations for addressing these challenges are also included:

Celebrate the gifts that interchurch couples possess

Interchurch couples have both unique challenges and unique gifts. Unfortunately, the emphasis has often been on the challenges that these couples can face as a result of their religious differences.[11] What is often overlooked are the benefits or blessings that interchurch couples can experience through their differences. Interchurch couples need to be encouraged to look for the gifts and blessings that come with being in an interchurch union. In interviews, interchurch couples often stated how they benefited from being in an interchurch relationship, particularly with regards to their spiritual life. Couples, for example, often shared how having someone ask them questions about their beliefs or practices led them to more closely examine what they truly believed. Others talked about how being exposed to different perspectives also fostered spiritual growth. One woman, for example, shared how her priest applied the Sunday readings to daily life, while her husband's minister offered a more theological perspective on the same readings. Many individuals also stated that they and their children learned greater tolerance or acceptance of other religious faiths. Religious differences have the potential to enrich not only the couple, but church communities as well. Interchurch couples, for example, can provide an ecumenical witness within the churches in which they reside.[12]

Time the intervention

Interchurch couples are likely to seriously discuss and grapple with their religious differences as they begin to form a strong commitment to each other. For many couples, this may be around the time that they seriously contemplate marriage or getting engaged. Thus a natural entry point in which to offer programs to interchurch couples is in marriage preparation, which is required of those seeking to get married within the Catholic Church. Unfortunately, many engaged couples are reluctant participants in marriage preparation. Often they are too idealistic, or they are preoccupied with planning for their wedding rather than the subsequent marriage. Thus some have questioned whether engagement is the most opportune time to explore issues with couples. As an alternative, some have suggested that couples may be more receptive to exploring issues after they have been married a short time.[13] Some couples that are seriously dating may also be open to exploring how religious differences may impact their relationship should they later consider marriage. Thus it may be important to provide programs that can be accessed by couples at different points in their development and not focus solely on couples who are engaged. One advantage of web-based resources like the *Two Churches, One Marriage* program is that couples can participate in them at any time, regardless of whether they are dating, engaged, or married.

Provide or tailor programs for interchurch marriages

Although interchurch couples have many of the same issues and needs as other couples, they also have special needs. Thus interchurch couples would benefit from supplemental resources or programs that target these needs. Couples who go through marriage preparation could be encouraged to participate in the *Two Churches, One Marriage* program or a similar program. In the Diocese of San Diego, for example, couples who are interchurch or interfaith based on the FOCCUS premarital inventory receive a letter describing the *Two Churches, One Marriage* program in addition to their FOCCUS results. Some dioceses also provide a link to the program on their website.

Offering the *Two Churches, One Marriage* program is just one example of how churches can support interchurch couples. Many dioceses have engaged couples take the FOCCUS inventory, which has a special set of questions for interfaith couples. In addition to having interchurch couples take these questions, dioceses might also consider having these couples take BRIDGES, an inventory that focuses specifically on a couple's spiritual or religious relationship. The materials from both FOCCUS and BRIDGES could provide couples an excellent springboard for discussing how the couples can properly manage their religious differences. For programs that offer mentor couple programs, efforts could be made to match interchurch couples with mentor couples that are also interchurch. Churches (perhaps in cooperation with other churches in the community) might also offer support groups for interchurch couples.

Unfortunately, it appears that efforts to target the special needs of interchurch couples are not commonplace. Among those who reported that religious issues were addressed in their marriage preparation, less than one quarter (24.2 percent) of individuals in interchurch relationships indicated that they were given special instruction or materials because of their different religious backgrounds (Center for Marriage and Family, 1999). Two things probably need to happen before there is a large-scale implementation of programs targeting interchurch couples. First, there will need to be a widespread recognition that interchurch couples deserve special attention. As stated at the outset of this essay, interchurch couples represent a large segment of couples that are getting married and appear to be at higher risk for divorce. Thus ministry to this population would seem to be a priority.

Second, those who minister to interchurch couples (e.g., priests, family life ministers, etc.) must clearly understand the needs, challenges, and blessings that these couples encounter. In the Center for Marriage and Family study (1999), individuals in interchurch marriages were less likely to report that clergy were aware of their needs compared to individuals currently in same-church relationships. Awareness of needs was also strongly correlated with satisfaction with clergy. Thus some education on the needs that interchurch couples have may be needed. Research-based programs such as *Two Churches, One Marriage* may serve a dual purpose of educating couples and those who work with couples.

Call for more research

Unfortunately, those ministering to interchurch couples have had limited research to guide their efforts. The vast majority of research on interchurch couples has focused narrowly on demonstrating whether or not they are at greater risk for divorce and lower marital satisfaction. The study by the Center for Marriage and Family (1999) was one of the first to look at a breadth of issues (e.g., parenting, experience of church, religiosity, other marital variables) regarding interchurch couples. Although this study added significantly to our knowledge of interchurch couples, further research is needed to better understand interchurch couples. In addition, research is needed to identify how the challenges, rewards, and dynamics of interfaith couples are similar or different from interchurch couples.

Another important area of research is to explore the impact of interchurch relationships on children. Examples of questions needing further exploration include: What impact does being raised in an interchurch marriage have on the religious development of children, and how does it compare to children raised by same-church parents? What are the challenges and benefits that these children face? What factors determine whether there are positive or negative outcomes in terms of the religious development of children? How does being raised in an interchurch household impact a child's future decisions regarding mate selection? These are important questions not only for interchurch marriages, but also interfaith marriages.

Very limited research has been done to evaluate existing programs targeting interchurch couples. Two small studies have evaluated the *Two Churches, One Marriage* program. In the first study, 86 percent of marriage educators (n=21) thought the program would be either "very helpful" or "extremely helpful" to interchurch couples. Those who worked "frequently" with interchurch couples rated the program more favorably compared to those who "seldom" or "occasionally" worked with them. In a second study, individuals in interchurch and interfaith relationships (n=48) evaluated the program. Two-thirds (66.7 percent) of the individuals reported that the program was either "very helpful" or "extremely helpful," with the remainder reporting that the program was at least "somewhat helpful." Although promising, additional work is needed to fully evaluate the program. For example, future research might investigate if the *Two Churches, One Marriage* program could be successfully adapted for interfaith couples since there is also limited research evaluating programs for interfaith couples. More research is clearly needed to improve or demonstrate the effectiveness of programs that target interchurch and interfaith couples.

One of the challenges of doing research on interchurch couples is that the topic touches on a number of different domains, requiring a multidisciplinary perspective. For example, both psychological as well as societal factors can influence interchurch relationships. In addition, pastoral and theological considerations are important given the religious nature of the topic. The research conducted by the Center for Marriage and Family (1999) is a good model for conducting future research in this area. The research team was composed of individuals from multiple disciplines (e.g., theology, family ministry, sociology, and marital and family therapy). Clergy from different denominations also served as consultants for the project, as well as the director of Family, Laity, Women, and Youth for the United States Council of Catholic Bishops. Research that includes interdisciplinary collaboration between individuals within the Catholic Church and other organizations (e.g., universities) will be invaluable in advancing our knowledge of interchurch couples. Research of this nature, however, will be difficult to do without external funding.

Create a sense of belonging

One of the challenges facing the Catholic Church in the twenty-first century is to create a sense of belonging for interchurch couples. In the Center for Marriage and Family study (1999), interchurch couples reported a weaker sense of belonging compared to other couples. A little less than a third (32.1 percent) of individuals in interchurch marriages reported a strong sense of belonging to their congregation. In contrast, slightly over half (54.7 percent) of individuals in same-church marriages reported a strong sense of belonging, while half (49.7 percent) of individuals in same-church marriages that were originally interchurch reported a strong sense of belonging.

Creating a sense of belonging for interchurch couples will depend upon outreach. Success may depend upon Catholic churches doing outreach to both interchurch couples and churches of other denominations within the community. Outreach to interchurch couples may take different forms, such as creating special groups or events for them. A church can also demonstrate its commitment to ecumenism through dialogue and events with other churches. One local church has an exchange where clergy from each congregation speak to the other's congregation. Religious or social events can also be used to bring members from different churches together.

Conclusion

Working with interchurch couples offers both opportunities and challenges for the Catholic Church in the twenty-first century. The large number of interchurch couples who are getting married point to an important ministry that deserves attention not only from the Catholic Church, but other denominations as well. Ministering to interchurch couples, however, is not without its challenges. Yet it is also important to recognize the potential blessings that interchurch couples can bring, both to their own relationship as well as the faith communities in which they reside.

Effective ministry to interchurch couples will require the church to invest significant resources in a number of different areas. Fortunately, efforts invested in these areas are likely to create synergisms. Tailoring programs for interchurch couples will communicate that they are valued, which will enhance their sense of belonging within the Catholic Church. Celebrating the gifts that interchurch couples bring will also enhance a sense of belonging. As interchurch couples experience a greater sense of belonging, they may become more involved within the church as laity to help minister to the next generation of interchurch couples. Research can enhance the development programs, making the ministry to interchurch couples more effective. Hopefully the church in the twenty-first century can focus a sufficient amount of its resources to reap these synergies.

Conclusions

Cynthia Dobrzynski

THE AUTHORS OF THESE ESSAYS had the opportunity to interact with one another and with invited participants.[1] The concluding session of the symposium posed several questions to these pastoral ministers and theologians. It allowed them time to imagine and dream of communities that addressed the issues raised in the essays, recognized the challenges, and strove to meet these pastoral needs.

Following are some of the comments:

What does a marriage-willing parish look like?

- Specific monies are annually budgeted toward the support of marriage.
- Marriage preparation is a whole parish responsibility.
- All ministries are supported, not just marriage or sacramental preparation.
- All parish meetings are on the same night so the parish won't pull couples and families apart. This also limits excessive participation by a few people.
- The parish acts as a broker for marriage counseling or at least provides information on marriage friendly therapists.
- Resources on spousal abuse are provided. This is a neglected area in church ministry.
- Prayers of the faithful are inclusive of vocations to marriage. They offer thanksgiving for couples who are witness to the vocation of marriage as well as offering encouragement to those who are struggling.
- The priest includes intentions for birthdays and anniversaries at mass, and they are printed in the parish bulletin.
- Couples function as greeters and give a reflection at the end of the liturgy.
- Couples lay hands on each other and pray for one another.

- Pictures of couples and families' lives are shared.
- Marriage education is across the lifecycle and works within the adult education/faith formation program.

What does marriage as a sacrament have to teach the entire community?

- The essence of the family living room and kitchen should translate to the parish hall and liturgy.
- Family life is sacred.
- Parish secretaries should be trained as ministers, and all faces of the parish need to be welcoming.
- Phone-call ministry or prayer ministries can be a forum to pray for current needs. Any joys or concerns are a source of prayer.
- Weddings are special without spending a lot of money. Don't charge fees for sacraments, but donations are welcome. Get creative. Parish residence requirements violate canon law.
- Parish websites can easily link to marriage support sites.
- People come out for what they need to learn, so offer enrichment for couples of all ages — blended families, early stages, empty nesters.

What characteristics will this marriage-willing parish have?

- Married couples are visible and valuable.
- It is a community with liturgy that speaks of communion and draws married people into deeper awareness of community in their marriage.
- Parishes would have a genuine marriage perspective in parish planning.
- A deep and abiding sense of communion should be evident among all parish members.
- Sacredness of life and personhood is lived out in a variety of vocations. A priority on marriage is not viewed as competitive or exclusionary.
- The parish is a safe place to tell the truth about marriage without pretense.
- Parish leadership is tuned in to the reality of people, including the diversity of family situations.
- Liturgies and homilies relate to people at every lifecycle stage.

As the authors in this volume describe, marriage today is complex, harried, and joy-filled, and it encompasses every possible scenario imaginable. Yet our pastoral pronouncements on marriage often speak in lofty theological terms that at first glance may not seem to have anything to do with the concrete realities of daily married life. Pastoral ministry needs to explicitly make those theological ideals accessible to married couples.

Domestic life for married couples may be filled with the parenting of biological or adopted children, or even grandchildren. If a person today may have multiple careers or employers over the course of a lifetime, and at least some of those changes means geographical relocation, what does that mean for the expectations a person brings to marriage? This generation of young adults is also the first adult generation in which divorce was commonplace. How does this affect the sacramental ideal of permanence in marriage? These and other societal changes complicate the pastoral situation.

In her book *Sacred Dwelling,* Wendy Wright speaks of the need for language that describes the spiritual life in terms of dwelling or habitation. This language of home more accurately reflects the experience of Christian couples and families than does the image of the spiritual life as a journey or pilgrimage. Perhaps marriage ministry needs to incorporate both these languages to adequately describe contemporary life.

In living their vocation of marriage, the couple inhabits a home, perhaps raises children, becomes active in their parish and community, and goes out to the workplace. Yet they also journey together across the lifecycle, living through inevitable stages both together and separately. Significant moments such as baptisms, weddings, and funerals are rites of passage for married couples, families, and the entire community. They are natural moments of connection and opportunities for reflection.

The parish community can serve as a locus for these moments of connection and evangelization. But the mobility of our society means parish connections are only one of many available networks. The situation requires new methods for the revitalization of marriage ministry and deliberate support for marriage. Fortunately, such strategies are developing through initiatives such as the National Pastoral Initiative on Marriage.

Marriage has long been viewed as a visible expression of God's love readily apparent. The grace of the sacrament is meant for the salvation of the married couple in the daily living out of their relationship with God. Whether in the Hispanic model of extended family or the increasingly upwardly mobile children of the previous century's immigrants, interfaith couples or those of Asian heritage, marriage today mirrors the diversity of the church's population. An ongoing marriage ministry needs to take into account this wealth of expression and experience in order to foster human cooperation with divine grace.

As part of the National Pastoral Initiative on Marriage, the United States Bishops Conference published a prayer card for married couples. The prayer is an appropriate conclusion to this volume on sustaining marriage.

Prayer for Married Couples

Almighty and eternal God,
You blessed the union of married couples
So that they might reflect the union of Christ with his church:
Look with kindness on them.
Renew their marriage covenant.
Increase your love in them.
And strengthen their bond of peace so that,
With their children,
They may always rejoice in the gift of your blessing.
We ask this through Christ our Lord.
Amen.

Contributors

Alejandro Aguilera-Titus is the interim executive director of the Secretariat for Hispanic Affairs, USCCB. He has more than twenty-four years of experience in ministry with a strong emphasis on leadership development and formation. Alejandro is a nationally known speaker and writer highly regarded for his practical application of theological thought to pastoral ministry and formation. He holds an M.A. in theology from the University of Portland and a B.A. in communications with a minor in philosophy from the Universidad Iberoamericana. He is co-author of the series Prophets of Hope, St. Mary's Press, and contributing editor of *Liturgia y Canción*, Oregon Catholic Press. He shares an intercultural family with his wife, Mary, and their three children.

Florence Caffrey Bourg is author of *Where Two or Three Are Gathered: Christian Families as Domestic Churches* (University of Notre Dame Press, 2004). Her articles and reviews on theology of marriage and family have appeared in *Horizons, Concilium, INTAMS Review, Theological Studies*, and the *College Theology Society* annual volume. Florence taught at the College of Mount St. Joseph in Cincinnati before returning "home" to New Orleans. She now teaches at the Academy of the Sacred Heart and has been a visiting professor at Loyola University and Springhill College. Florence has been married twenty years and has four children.

Paul Covino is associate chaplain and director of liturgy at the College of the Holy Cross, Worcester, Massachusetts, and adjunct staff member of the Georgetown Center for Liturgy. He is the editor and principal author of the wedding workbook *Celebrating Marriage* (Pastoral Press, 1994) and served on the U.S. bishops' task group for adaptations to the revised *Order for Celebrating Marriage*. He has led many workshops for engaged couples and pastoral ministers and authored numerous articles on the celebration of the wedding liturgy.

Cynthia S. Dobrzynski is the director of mission and values at D'Youville Senior Care in Lowell, Massachusetts. She formerly served as executive director of the National Association of Catholic Family Life Ministers as well as on its board of directors. She is a consultant and educator with many years of experience from the parish to national level. Cindy holds an M.A. in pastoral ministry from Boston College in church leadership and liturgy and worship and a post-master's certificate in the practice of spirituality. She and her husband, David, have been married for thirty years and have three adult daughters.

James Healy has been the director of the Center for Family Ministry of the Diocese of Joliet, Illinois, since 1989. He received his Ph.D. in counseling psychology from the University of Illinois in 1985. He has spoken on marriage topics in over sixty dioceses, and his marriage materials, most notably his *Living Together and Christian Commitment* materials and his *How to Get Married and Stay Engaged,* are used throughout the country. Jim was given the NACFLM ministry award in 2000. He lives in Joliet with his wife, Madonna, and their four children.

Joann Heaney-Hunter serves as an associate professor at St. John's University. She holds a Ph.D. in theology from Fordham University. In addition, she has an M.S. in mental health counseling from Long Island University and is board certified and licensed to practice in the State of New York. She has served as an advisor to the USCCB Committee on Marriage and Family and currently is a theological contributor to the USCCB *For Your Marriage* project. She has co-authored two books on marriage preparation: a Leader's Guide and Couple Guide entitled *Unitas: Preparing for Sacramental Marriage* (Crossroad). Joann is currently writing a book on marriage spirituality for the Crossroad Publishing Co. She resides in New York with her husband of twenty-nine years and has two adult daughters.

Andrew Lyke is the executive director of Arusi Network, Inc., a not-for-profit organization that focuses on the strengthening of marriage in the African American community through education, consultation, coaching, and spiritual retreats. He is also the coordinator of marriage ministry for the Archdiocese of Chicago. With his wife, Terri, he has nationally presented keynote addresses, workshops, retreats, and seminars on marriage and family issues to church, community, and business audiences. They have written articles for local and national publications. Terri and Andrew regularly write for Catholic News Service's *Faith Alive* publication. Their biweekly column,

Family Reflections, was featured in several Catholic diocesan newspapers around the United States from 1994 to 2003.

Bonnie Mack is a part-time program coordinator of marriage preparation and enrichment in the Cincinnati Archdiocese, on staff since 1991. In addition, she coordinates programs for newly married and interchurch couples (Catholic/Protestant) in the archdiocese. She has a B.A. from Baldwin-Wallace College, Berea, Ohio, and taught high school prior to joining the Cincinnati Family Life Office. She and her husband, Tom, have been married since 1969 and have three grown children and five grandchildren.

David M. McCarthy teaches at Mount St. Mary's University in Emmitsburg, Maryland. He is an associate professor of theology and the Fr. James M. Forker Professor of Catholic Social Teaching. He is the editor of *Gathered for the Journey: Moral Theology in Catholic Perspective,* and he is the author of *Sex and Love in the Home: A Theology of the Household and the Good Life.* He lives in Emmitsburg with his wife, Bridget, and their children.

Tim Muldoon is a theologian, professor, and author of three books and a number of popular and scholarly essays in the areas of theology, spirituality, and adoption. His most recent book is *Seeds of Hope: Young Adults and the Catholic Church in the United States* (Paulist Press, 2008), and he is the editor of the 2008 annual volume of the College Theology Society, entitled *Catholic Identity and the Laity* (Orbis Books, 2009). He was the inaugural Director of the Church in the 21st Century Center at Boston College from 2005 to 2007 and now serves as assistant to the vice president for university mission and ministry and teaches in the College of Arts and Sciences Honors Program. His dissertation (Duquesne University, 1998) focused on the understanding of sexuality in the Catholic doctrine on marriage. He and his wife, Suzanne, have been married for sixteen years and have two daughters, both by adoption.

William P. Roberts is professor of theology at the University of Dayton. His principal areas of concentration are Christology, sacramental theology, Christian marriage, and Christian family values and the media. He is the author of eleven books and editor of four. He has also authored over sixty-five articles and book reviews. His most recent book is *Marriage: It's a God Thing,* published by St. Anthony Messenger Press (2007). He and his wife, Challon, have three adult daughters and a granddaughter.

Julie Hanlon Rubio is associate professor of Christian Ethics at St. Louis University. Her articles on marriage and family ethics have appeared in *Theological Studies*, the *Journal of the Society of Christian Ethics*, *Josephinum Journal of Theology*, and *Horizons*. Her first book, *A Christian Theology of Marriage and Family* (Paulist Press, 2003), received a Catholic Press Association award. Recently, she co-edited *Readings in Moral Theology No. 15: Marriage* (Paulist Press, 2009) and authored *Family Ethics: Practices for Christians* (Georgetown University Press, 2010). She lives in St. Louis with her husband and three sons.

Jonathan Y. Tan is assistant professor of religion and culture at Xavier University, Cincinnati, Ohio; editor of *Proceedings of the Catholic Theological Society of America*; assistant editor of the *New Catholic Encyclopedia*, second edition (2003); and author of *Introducing Asian American Theologies* (Orbis Books, 2008). He holds a Ph.D. in religion and culture from the Catholic University of America, Washington, D.C. His many essays have appeared in *Vidyajyoti Journal of Theological Reflection*, *East Asian Pastoral Review*, *Gregorianum*, *Mission Studies*, *Missiology*, and *New Theology Review*.

David M. Thomas has a Ph.D. in systematic and historical theology from the University of Notre Dame. He is the past director of the graduate program in family ministry and adult Christian community development at Regis University in Denver, where he taught for twenty years. Currently he is the co-director of the Bethany Family Institute (UK and USA), associate director of the graduate program in family ministry and faith formation at Dominican University (just outside Chicago), and coordinator of instruction for the deacon formation program for the Diocese of Helena, Montana. Liturgical Press recently published his latest book, *Christian Marriage: The New Challenge*.

Lee Williams is professor in the Marital and Family Therapy Program at the University of San Diego. He is also a licensed marital and family therapist, and an approved supervisor in the American Association for Marriage and Family Therapy. He has published several journal articles and book chapters, primarily in the areas of interchurch couples, marriage preparation, and family therapy training/supervision. He is also a co-author of *Essential Skills in Family Therapy*, a popular text for beginning family therapists.

Notes

Introduction

1. Vatican II, *Dogmatic Constitution on the Church* (*Lumen Gentium*), 11, online.

Chapter 1: David Thomas / Signs of Hope in Marriage Today

1. See their Healthy Marriages website at *www.acf.hhs.gov/healthymarriage/*.

Chapter 2: William P. Roberts / A Spirituality for the Vocation to Marriage

1. For more extended treatments of this topic see my chapter, "Christian Marriage: A Divine Calling," in *Marriage in the Catholic Tradition,* ed. Todd A. Salzman, Thomas M. Kelly, and John J. O'Keefe (New York: Crossroad, 2004), 98–108, and "Marriage as a Unique Vocation" in my book, *Marriage: It's a God Thing* (Cincinnati: St. Anthony Messenger Press, 2007), 75–113.

2. Mary is almost always referred to as the "Virgin" Mary. Would not the title the "Faith-filled" Mary capture better the essence of her spirituality and make clearer her role as model for all members of the church, who, like her, are called to be open to God's Word in whatever state of life they are (see Luke 1:38, 8:19–21, 11:27–28)?

3. The past few decades have seen some exceptions for married Protestant ministers who converted to Catholicism.

4. *Lumen Gentium* (*Dogmatic Constitution on the Church*), 39, 40.

5. *Lumen Gentium,* 41. All translations of Vatican II texts are taken from Austin Flannery, O.P., ed., *Vatican Council II* (Northport, N.Y.: Costello Publishing, 1996).

6. Translations of biblical texts are taken from the New Jerusalem Bible (Garden City, N.Y.: Doubleday, 1985).

7. This is the succinct description of marriage given in *Gaudium et Spes* (*Pastoral Constitution of the Church in the Modern World*), #48.

8. More detailed examples of how the baptismal and marriage promises can be revised are given in *Marriage: It's a God Thing,* 109–13.

9. Reminding us of our water baptism into the death and resurrection of Christ.

10. A more detailed treatment of this topic can be found in chapter 2, "Trinitarian Presence" in *Marriage: It's a God Thing.*

11. For an excellent treatment of the Trinity and the connection between Trinitarian faith and Christian living see Catherine Mowry LaCugna, *God for Us: The Trinity and Christian Life* (New York: HarperCollins, 1991).

12. John L. McKenzie, *Dictionary of the Bible* (Milwaukee: Bruce Publishing Co., 1965), 1. The author points out that Abba is the "Aramaic emphatic form of *'ab*, 'father,' employed as vocative." Jesus' use of the term "was taken up by the early Church."

13. In a footnote to this phrase the New Jerusalem Bible further explains, "God made Christ one with sinful humanity in order to make the human race one with his obedience and saving justice."

14. Benedict XVI, *Jesus of Nazareth* (New York: Doubleday, 2007), 18.

15. Hence, making us temples of the Holy Spirit. "Do you not realize that your body is the temple of the Holy Spirit, who is in you and whom you received from God?" (1 Cor. 6:19; see also 3:16).

16. Robin L. Smith, *Lies at the Altar: The Truth about Great Marriages* (New York: Hyperion, 2006). Smith makes another significant contribution in this book by taking four of the phrases in one of the popular marriage formulas (for better or worse, for richer or poorer, in sickness and in health, till death do us part) and explaining at some length how little most people understand all that is truly implied in these words (chapters 5, 6, 7, 8). I highly recommend a serious study of this book for all who are contemplating marriage, as well as for those who are involved in preparing them.

17. This can prove to be a particularly difficult challenge as children wend their way through the complexity and ambivalence of early and late adolescence, and as they later grow into early adulthood. There can be a thin line between parental guidance and encouragement on the one hand, and, on the other hand, taking control of their lives and making decisions for them.

18. Anthony De Mello, *More One Minute Nonsense* (Chicago: Loyola University Press, 1993), 14.

19. John Van Epp, *How to Avoid Marrying a Jerk: The Foolproof Way to Follow Your Heart Without Losing Your Mind* (New York: McGraw Hill, 2007), 17–29. It is worth noting that the author uses the word "jerk" in a gender-neutral way: "A jerk can be either a man or a woman" (29; see also 17).

20. The author uses the acronym FACES to indicate the five areas that are "crucial for getting to know one's partner." These are "Family background, Attitudes and actions of the conscience, Compatibility potential, Examples of other relationships, and Skills in relationships" (13).

21. Van Epp, 22, *How to Avoid Marrying a Jerk*, 22, emphasis in the original.

22. Ibid., 24.

23. Ibid.

24. Ibid., 29.

Chapter 3: Tim Muldoon /
A Theology for Married People

1. See the 2006 essay "Life without Children," from Barbara Dafoe Whitehead and David Popenoe's "The State of Our Unions," part of the National Marriage Project at Rutgers University (online at *http://marriage.rutgers.edu/Publications/SOOU/TEXTSOOU2006.htm*), which explores the social implications of this development. [Note that all online citations are valid as of September 10, 2007.]

2. See, for example, William V. D'Antonio, James D. Davidson, Dean R. Hoge, and Katherine Meyer, *American Catholics: Gender, Generation, and Commitment* (Walnut Creek, Calif.: Alta Mira Press, 2001), which compares different generations of U.S. Catholics, or Dean R. Hoge et al., *Young Adult Catholics: Religion in the Culture of Choice* (Notre Dame, Ind.: University of Notre Dame Press, 2001), which focuses specifically on young people.

3. A 2004 study by George Barna suggested that Catholics divorce at roughly the same rate as the rest of the U.S. population. The study, while critiqued by some, is one indicator of a more widely evident trend that U.S. Catholics do not vary from the wider U.S. population on many key issues today. (The Barna report is no longer available on its website; however a related *Dallas Morning News* story is reprinted on the *adherents.com* site at *www.adherents.com/largecom/baptist_divorce.html*.)

4. See Edward Schillebeeckx, *Marriage: Human Reality and Saving Mystery* (New York: Sheed & Ward, 1965), chapter 1, "The Formation of Church Marriage," for a careful exploration of the many factors that impacted the church's eventual jurisdiction of marriage. See also Theodore Mackin, *What Is Marriage?* (New York: Paulist Press, 1982), for a thorough exploration of the church's evolving doctrines on marriage.

5. My focus for the purpose of this essay is on practices that are common in the United States, but a similar argument might be advanced that addresses marriage practices in other parts of the world.

6. Indeed, the oldest definitions of marriage that found their way into the church's theology were those taken from Roman jurists like Modestinus and Ulpian; these definitions still find resonance in contemporary Canon Law.

7. I am thinking here especially of the widespread availability of birth control and later the sexual revolution of the 1960s. A case might be made that currents in U.S. society were already confronting Catholic practices regarding sexuality and marriage even earlier, e.g., in the rise of intellectual movements such as Marxism, social Darwinism, and psychoanalysis, but I would argue that such movements challenged both Catholics and other Christian believers, and thus did not put Catholics in a unique position in U.S. society.

8. Here I am departing from the Augustinian trajectory, which posits the primacy of *proles*, in addition to *fides* and *sacramentum* as "ends" of marriage. By the twentieth century, this emphasis on procreation was mitigated somewhat by changing the term "ends" to "goods" (following Dietrich von Hildebrand), suggesting that the church understood marriage not only as a means to procreation, but also as a good *in se* for the spouses themselves. See von Hildebrand's *Marriage: The Mystery of Faithful Love* (Manchester, N.H.: Sophia Institute Press, 1991) as well as *Gaudium et Spes* 48.

9. I agree with Bernard Cooke's assertion that friendship is the basic sacrament, a thesis that he explores in *Sacraments and Sacramentality* (Mystic, Conn.: Twenty-Third Publications, 2004), chapter 7.

10. See *Familiaris Consortio*, no. 66.

11. This is not to say, however, that all ministers are to be single, a point made obvious by the number of married deacons and lay ecclesial ministers in the United States today. On the contemporary theology of ministry in the United States today, see the bishops' document *Co-Workers in the Vineyard of the Lord* (November 2005) at *www.usccb.org/laity/laymin/co-workers.pdf*.

12. In 2003, UNICEF estimated that more than 143 million children were orphans in some ninety-three developing countries alone.

13. I develop this idea of "mystagogy of communion" in my book *Seeds of Hope: Young Adults and the Catholic Church in the United States* (Mahwah, N.J.: Paulist Press, 2008), chapter 4.

Chapter 4: Julie Hanlon Rubio / The Marriage-Friendly Parish

1. John F. Kavanaugh, *Following Christ in a Consumer Society*, rev. ed. (Maryknoll, N.Y.: Orbis Books, 1991).

2. John Paul II, *Sollicitudo Rei Socialis* (Washington, D.C.: United States Catholic Conference, 1987).

3. John Paul II, *Familiaris Consortio* (Washington, D.C.: United States Catholic Conference, 1981).

4. Paul Wilkes, *Excellent Catholic Parishes: The Guide to the Best Places and Practices* (New York: Paulist, 2001), xii.

5. James D. Davidson, *Catholicism in Motion: The Church in American Society* (Liguori, Mo.: Liguori, 2005), 15.

6. James T. Fisher, *Catholics in America* (New York: Oxford University Press, 2000), 121. Of course, not all parishes were dominated by one ethnic group. When parishes first developed in the late 1800s, some were territorial and others were national or ethnic. Still, ethnic and religious cultures were often intertwined and mutually supporting. See Gerald P. Fogarty, "The Parish and Community in American Catholic History," reprinted in Brian C. Mitchell, ed., *Building the American Catholic City* (New York: Garland, 1988): 1–25.

7. John Kosa, "The Emergence of a Catholic Middle Class," in *Catholics/U.S.A.: Perspectives on Social Change*, ed. William T. Liu and Nathaniel J. Pallone (New York: John Wiley & Sons, 1970), 16.

8. George A. Kelly, *The Second Spring of the Church in America* (South Bend, Ind.: St. Augustine's Press, 2001), 7. See also Portier.

9. Davidson, *Catholicism in Motion*, 136.

10. Fogarty, "Parish and Community," 9.

11. Andrew M. Greeley and Mary Greeley Durkin, "The Parish as Organic Community," in *How to Save the Catholic Church*, ed. Mary Greeley Durkin (New York: Viking, 1984), 173.

12. Ibid., 169. See also Philip Murnion, "The Catholic Parish in the Public Square," in *American Catholics and Civic Engagement: A Distinctive Voice*, ed. Margaret O'Brien Steinfels (Lanham, Md.: Sheed & Ward, 2004): 71–91, at 76.

13. Michael Warren, *Faith, Culture, and the Worshipping Community: Shaping the Practice of the Local Church*, rev. ed. (Washington, D.C.: Pastoral Press, 1993), 40.

14. Fogarty, "Parish and Community," 25.

15. Davidson, *Catholicism in Motion*, 12.

16. Ibid. See also Kosa, "Emergence of a Catholic Middle Class," writing in 1962 and predicting that new problems would arise from Catholics' new position in American society, 24.

17. William V. D'Antonio, James D. Davidson, Dean R. Hoge, and Ruth A. Wallace, *Laity: American and Catholic: Transforming the Church* (Kansas City, Mo.: Sheed & Ward, 1996), 10.

18. Fisher, *Catholics in America*, 162.

19. Integration is incomplete. Even in 1994, Catholics were still highly concentrated in the urban Northeast and upper Midwest (ibid., 163). In addition, new immigrants (Mexican, Filipino, Polish, Dominican, and Vietnamese) continue to provide a fresh influx of Catholics who are poorer, less educated, more closely tied to ethnic parishes, and less assimilated to American culture (Davidson, *Catholics in Motion*, 19). Still, the overall upward trend is clear.

20. D'Antonio et al., *Laity: American and Catholic*, 127.

21. Murnion, "Catholic Parish in the Public Square," 72.

22. David C. Leege, "The American Catholic Parish," in *American Catholic Identity: Essays in an Age of Change*, ed. Francis J. Butler (Kansas City, Mo.: Sheed & Ward, 1994), 78.

23. Kelly, *Second Spring*, 7.

24. Murnion, "Catholic Parish in the Public Square," 84. Poor parishes have much more to offer in this area, 85.

25. D'Antonio, *Laity: American and Catholic*, 140.

26. Davidson, *American Catholics in Motion*, 135.

27. Ibid., 68.

28. In 1960, 45 percent of Catholic children attended parish schools. In 1998, only 20 percent did. See Bryan T. Foehle and Mary L. Gautier, *Catholicism USA: A Portrait of the Catholic Church in the United States* (Maryknoll, N.Y.: Orbis Books, 2000), 72.

29. Davidson, *American Catholics in Motion*, 134.

30. Ibid., 182.

31. A recent survey found that parishes offered an average of four organized ministries, though one offered fifty-nine. See Murnion, "Catholic Church in the Public Square," 73.

32. Last spring, my local parish bulletin included an advertisement in the form of a letter from a child begging her parents to buy her a ride bracelet for $25 so that she could ride all day at the parish carnival. This is high price for a day of entertainment, especially for families with more than one child.

33. Greeley and Greeley, "Parish as Organic Community," 173.

34. Murnion, "Catholic Church in the Public Square," 81. Murnion notes that these groups deal with Catholic Social Teaching less by engaging in work for political change and more by encouraging changes in family life and work places, 82.

35. Davidson, *Catholics in Motion*, 138.

36. Warren, *Faith, Culture, and the Worshipping Community*, 118.

37. David McCarthy, "Becoming One Flesh: Marriage, Remarriage, and Sex," in *The Blackwell Companion to Christian Ethics*, ed. Stanley Hauerwas and Samuel Wells (Malden, Mass.: Blackwell, 2004), 276.

38. Warren, *Faith, Culture, and the Worshipping Community*, 66.

Chapter 5: David Matzko McCarthy / Living the Dream

1. Galena Kline Rhoades, Scott M. Stanley, Howard J. Markman, "Pre-engagement Cohabitation and Gender Asymmetry in Marital Commitment," *Journal of Family Psychology* 20, no. 4 (December 2006): 553–60.

2. Kathryn Edin, Maria J. Kefalas, and Joanna M. Reed, "A Peek Inside the Black Box: What Marriage Means for Poor Unmarried Parents," *Journal of Marriage and Family* 66, no. 4 (November 2004): 1007–14.

3. Ibid., 1011.

4. Ibid., 1012.

5. Pamela J. Smock, Wendy D. Manning, and Meredith Porter, "'Everything's There Except Money': How Money Shapes Decisions to Marry among Cohabitors," *Journal of Marriage and Family* 67, no. 3 (August 2005): 680–96.

6. Ibid., 680.

7. Andrew J. Cherlin, "The Deinstitutionalization of American Marriage," *Journal of Marriage and Family* 66, no. 4 (November 2004): 848–61.

8. Ibid., 855.

9. Ibid., 858.

10. Stephanie Coontz, *Marriage, a History: From Obedience to Intimacy or How Love Conquered Marriage* (New York: Viking, 2005).

11. Edward Shorter, *The Making of the Modern Family* (New York: Basic Books, 1977).

12. Anthony Giddens, *The Transformation of Intimacy* (Oxford: Polity Press, 1992).

13. David Crary, "Divorce Rate Drop May Not Mean 'Happily Ever After': U.S. Divorce Rate Falls to Lowest Level since 1970," *The Virginian-Pilot* (May 11, 2007), A5. For the divorce rate, see the Center for Disease Control and Prevention, *National Vital Statistics and Reports* 55, no. 20 (August 28, 2007), www.cdc.gov/nchs/data/nvsr/nvsr55/nvsr55_20.pdf. For the cohabitation rate, see Judith A. Seltzer, "Cohabitation in the United States and Britain: Demography, Kinship, and the Future," *Journal of Marriage and Family* 66, no. 4 (November 2004): 921–28.

14. Ludwig F. Lowenstein, "Causes and Associated Features of Divorce as Seen by Recent Research," *Journal of Divorce and Remarriage* 42, no. 3/4 (2005): 153–71. Coontz argues that the economic independence of women opens the way for the standards of companionate marriage to take priority over traditional gender roles and conceptions of the household (Stephanie Coontz, "The Origins of Modern Divorce," *Family Process* 46, no. 1 [March 2007]: 14). Today, for the middle class, the independence of women has increased the economic benefit of marriage, insofar as households are supported by two incomes. For poor mothers, neither marriage nor independence from marriage tends to improve financial stability. See Barbara Wells and Maxine Baca Zinn, "The Benefits of Marriage Reconsidered," *Journal of Sociology and Social Welfare* 31, no. 4 (December 2004): 59–80.

15. I deal with this problem in chapters 4 and 9 of *Sex and Love in the Home: A Theology of the Household* (London: SCM, 2004).

16. Christopher Lasch, *Haven in a Heartless World* (New York: Basic Books, 1977).

17. Robert Bellah et al., *Habits of the Heart*, updated edition (Berkeley: University of California Press, 1996). See the problem of individualism as it is presented in Seltzer, "Cohabitation in the United States and Britain," 926–28.

18. Bryndl E. Hohmann-Marriott, "Shared Beliefs and the Union Stability of Married and Cohabiting Couples," *Journal of Marriage and Family* 68, no. 4 (November 2006): 1015–28. Hohmann-Marriott indicates that divergent views of household roles are a common reason for the dissolution of cohabitation.

19. See Arlie Hochschild, *The Second Shift* (New York: Viking Penguin, 1989).

20. See David M. McCarthy, *Sex and Love in the Home* (London: SCM, 2001), 17–23.

21. Typically, two different kinds of explanations are offered for the higher rate of domestic violence in cohabitation. One notes a correlation between cohabitation and the isolation of the couple. Couples who live together are more likely to have a relationship apart from communal connections, and isolation of the victim (along with control) is one of the pathologies of domestic violence. A second explanation (which doesn't refute the first) is that cohabitating unions that are marked by violence simply end (as do most cohabiting unions) and do not move on to marriage. See Catherine Kenneyand and Sara McLanahan, "Why Are Cohabitating Relationships More Violent Than Marriage?" *Demography* 43, no. 1 (February 2006): 127–40.

22. See Seltzer, "Cohabitation in the United States and Britain," 924–26. Cherlin uses the term "enforceable trust" in "The Deinstitutionalization of American Marriage," 855.

23. Edin et al., "A Peek inside the Black Box," 1010.

24. Seltzer, "Cohabitation in the United States and Britain," 924.

25. Willard van Orman Quine, *Word and Object* (Cambridge, Mass.: MIT Press, 1960), 3.

26. I am thinking here of G. K. Chesterton's analysis at the beginning of the twentieth century (e.g., *What's Wrong with the World* [New York: Dodd, Mead and Co., 1910]), but his criticisms apply well to the global economy and the kind of democratic politics that connects power to money.

27. See Pius XI, *Quadragesimo anno*, no. 76–98. I am using the edition in David J. O'Brien and Thomas A. Shannon, *Catholic Social Thought: A Documentary History* (Maryknoll, N.Y.: Orbis Books, 1992), 40–79. Pius XI asserts the need for intermediate institutions because social relations have been reduced to a relationship between individual and state — and "the highly developed social life...has been damaged and all but ruined" (no. 78). Subsequently, he attempts to redefine labor associations, which have been reduced to interest groups defined by economic and class interests. He draws attention to the model of the medieval and early modern guilds, which "[bind] men together not according to the position they occupy in the labor market, but according to the diverse functions which they exercise in society" (no. 83).

28. *Gaudium et Spes* in ibid., 164–237.

29. John Paul II, *Letter to Families*, in *Origins*, March 3, 1994.

30. See David Cloutier, "Heaven Is a Place on Earth? Analyzing the Popularity of Pope John Paul II's Theology of the Body," *Sexuality and the U.S. Catholic Church: Crisis and Renewal*, ed. Lisa Sowle Cahill, T. Frank Kennedy, S.J., and John Garvey (New York: Crossroad, 2006), 18–31.

31. Fergus Kerr, in *Twentieth-Century Catholic Theologians* (Oxford: Blackwell, 2007), holds that Catholic theology has increasingly become captive to a nuptial mysticism.

32. The website *For Your Marriage* (*www.foryourmarriage.org*) does a good job noting that sex, for the newly married, is more likely to be a source of stress rather than simply "comfortable and exciting." In a section called "Intimacy and Sexuality," it is clear that a good sexual relationship is dependent on a good interpersonal relationship. But, also on the website, cultural romanticism creeps in. I should emphasize that it is not "front and center." It does "sneak in." We find this "Daily Marriage Tip" for September 1, 2007: " 'In a committed, loving, covenantal relationship sex is sacramental,... a privileged vehicle of grace... open[ing] both persons to becoming life-giving, gracious, and blessing adults.' (Fr. Ronald Rolheiser) How does your sexual relationship make you a better person in the rest of your life?" I understand that we want to invest sex with meaning, but doesn't this statement and question confirm the false cultural view that sex can build a relationship and that it can solve relational problems? Certainly, we should be saying the opposite: if you want a healthy sexual relationship, work on the day-to-day matters of marriage. Sex is "a privileged vehicle for grace." In real life, what does that mean? Liturgically what would it mean? Isn't marriage the sacrament? Isn't the "committed, loving, covenantal relationship" the vehicle for grace?

33. Cloutier, "Heaven Is a Place on Earth?" 30.

34. Ibid., 29, cites a study by Barbara Dafoe Whitehead and David Popenoe of the National Marriage Project, "The State of Our Unions: The Social Health of Our Marriage 2001," *www.virginia.edu/marriageproject/pdfs/print_soulmate.pdf*. Whitehead and Popenoe find that "in a secular society, where sex has lost its connection to marriage and also its sense of mystery, young people may be attracted to the soul-mate ideal because it endows intimate relationships with a higher spiritual, though not explicitly religious, significance. Marriage is also losing its standing as a public institution among these young adults. According to the survey, young adults tend to see marriage as a private matter between two consenting adults" (13).

35. I have before me two lists of programs for young adults (twenty-one years old and older) in the Washington, D.C., area. One is offered by the Archdiocese of Washington and the other by the Mother of God Community. The two sets of programs are remarkably similar, and ten out of twelve programs have something to do with sexuality or gender (the archdiocese includes a lecture on embryonic stem cell research and the Mother of God on relativism). Surely, young people would be interested in a session or two about how to build a strong neighborhood and parish.

36. "Stages of Marriage: Later Years," *For Your Marriage* (Washington, D.C.: USCCB, 2007), *www.foryourmarriage.org*.

37. Nothing related to the wider community is included in the marriage satisfaction survey on *foryourmarriage.org*. See *www.foryourmarriage.org*.

38. "Marriage Quiz of the Month," *www.foryourmarriage.org*.

39. I drew up this list by looking at John XXIII's section on human rights and duties, *Pacem in Terris*, nos. 8–38.

40. To keep the analogy of subsidiarity going, I am echoing Leo XIII on the plight of the worker in *Rerum novarum* no. 2 (O'Brien and Shannon, *Catholic Social Thought: A Documentary History*, 14–39).

41. Bellah, *Habits of the Heart*, xi–xvi.

42. In *The Overworked American* (New York: Basic Books, 1992), Juliet B. Schor argues against the classical and dominant economic theory that (1) modern capitalism has reduced work, and (2) the rise in work hours is due to desires of employees to work more. She shows that the economy has been structured to increase the hours of work and to make a reduction of hours (for many workers) virtually impossible (if they are going to have such things as health care benefits or job security).

43. "Stages of Marriage," *www.foryourmarriage.org*.

44. "Bumps in the Road: Disillusionment," *www.foryourmarriage.org*.

Chapter 6: Florence Caffrey Bourg / Spirituality and the Family Life Cycle

1. *www.usccb.org/laity/marriage/exec.shtm*.

2. See chapter 9 in this volume.

3. When I say "modeled on the celibate lifestyle," I mean practices that presuppose (at least "ideally") conditions such as silence or quiet voices, periods of uninterrupted concentration, sitting still, dedicated "sacred spaces," uncluttered and set apart from ordinary household activities.

4. Session 24, November 1563, *Doctrina de sacramento matrimonii*, canon 10, translation from Norman Tanner, *Decrees of the Ecumenical Councils* (Washington, D.C.: Georgetown University Press, 1990), cited in David G. Hunter, *Marriage, Celibacy, and Heresy in Ancient Christianity: The Jovianist Controversy* (New York: Oxford University Press, 2007), 7. See also Vatican II's *Decree on the Training of Priests* #10 and the *Catechism of the Catholic Church* #1620, which refer to consecrated celibacy as more "excellent" than marriage.

5. See also Hunter, *Marriage, Celibacy, and Heresy in Ancient Christianity*, 3, 82–83. Hunter contends that the idea of ascetic celibacy as holier than Christian marriage, which initially met resistance by Jovinian and a relatively large group of his supporters, eventually prevailed, in part, because it could support the goals of the aristocratic class. "The rhetoric of ascetic superiority proved to be a valuable commodity in the traditional aristocratic search for status and acclaim.... Christian aristocrats of Rome proved to be remarkably adept at adopting aspects of ascetic piety and utilizing these as strategies of aristocratic competition. It was precisely such adaptations that facilitated the conversion of the Roman aristocracy in the last two decades of the fourth century and early years of the fifth century.... Key features of ascetic practice, such as celibacy, could be adopted without entailing any fundamental disruption of the aristocratic way of life. In some cases, asceticism provided a broader array of opportunities to display acts of munificence and new forms of civic pride. In other cases... the selective practice of celibacy allowed greater flexibility in inheritance strategies. Perhaps the most attractive feature of ascetic renunciation, from the point of view of the social elite, is that it provided a ready made 'Christian alternative language of power and society....' That is, the notion that celibacy was superior to marriage was easily absorbed into the traditional aristocratic quest for honor and glory. Ascetic teachers and clergy eagerly colluded in this rhetorical enterprise, promising young virgins, such as Demetrias, that their nobility in this world was merely a prelude to the greater, transcendent

nobility that they would achieve through spiritual marriage. It was a message that late Roman aristocrats were eager to assimilate" (3, 82–83).

6. *Gaudium et Spes*, 43.

7. "Teaching on Marriage Permanence Aids Couples, Say Focus Groups," June 16, 2006, at *www.usccb.org/comm/archives/2006/06-119.shtml*.

8. John Allen Jr., "Coverage of Bishops' Synod on the Eucharist," *National Catholic Reporter*, October 7, 2005, at *www.nationalcatholicreporter.org/word/sb100705.htm*.

9. I've spent fifteen years of my adult life attending mass with restless children (not to mention the years my siblings and I spent restlessly at mass as children). I'm not a specialist in the area, but my impression is that this experience of liturgy hardly enters into our liturgical theology. Is it irreverent during liturgy to clean spilled Cheerios off the floor, to bring a small child to the restroom, or to accompany a wandering toddler in the vestibule? Are these acts an interruption of our devotion to the Lord or a sign of our devotion?

10. See the National Marriage Project's 2006 *State of Our Unions* report titled "Life without Children," at *http://marriage.rutgers.edu/*.

11. Donald A. Miller, *Concepts of Family Life in Modern Catholic Theology* (San Francisco: Catholic Scholars Press, 1996), 212–15.

12. "How to Receive a Sacrament and Mean It," in *The Sacraments: Readings in Contemporary Sacramental Theology*, ed. Michael Taylor, S.J. (New York: Alba House, 1981), 71–80, at 73–74.

Chapter 7: James Healy /
Marriage among the Spiritual but Not Religious

1. See, for example, "Religion and Spirituality: Unfuzzying the Fuzzy," in B. J. Zinnbauer et al., *Journal for the Scientific Study of Religion* 36, no. 4 (1997): 549–64.

2. See the essays by Bonnie Mack and Lee Williams in part 4 of this volume for a fuller exploration of interchurch and interfaith marriages.

3. *Ministry to Interchurch Marriages: A National Study* (Omaha, Neb.: Center for Marriage and Family, Creighton University, 1999).

4. I develop these implications more fully in "For the Spiritual but Not Religious Couple" and "For the Spiritual but Not Religious Parent," in preparation.

5. Dean R. Hoge et al., *Young Adult Catholics: Religion in the Culture of Choice* (Notre Dame, Ind.: University of Notre Dame Press, 2001).

6. *Marriage Preparation in the Catholic Church: Getting It Right* (Omaha, Neb.: Center for Marriage and Family, Creighton University, 1995).

7. See Joanne Heaney-Hunter's essay in this volume.

8. *Time, Sex, and Money: The First Five Years of Marriage* (Omaha, Neb.: Center for Marriage and Family, Creighton University, 2000).

9. John Van Epp, *How to Avoid Marrying a Jerk* (New York: McGraw Hill, 2006).

10. See L. D. Johnson, J. G. Bachman, and P. M. O'Malley, *Monitoring the Future: Questionnaire Responses from the Nation's Top High School Seniors* (Ann Arbor, Mich.: Institute for Social Research, 2005).

11. David Popenoe, "Cohabitation, Marriage, and Child Well-being: A Cross-National Perspective" (New Brunswick, N.J.: Rutgers University, National Marriage Project, 2008).
12. Available online at *http://marriage.rutgers.edu/*.

Chapter 8: Joann Heaney-Hunter / Layers of Marriage Preparation and the Family Life Cycle

1. Franklin Toker, "Florence Cathedral: The Design Stage," *Art Bulletin* 60 (June 1978): 214–31.
2. Mary Bergstein, "Marian Politics in Quattrocento Florence: The Renewed Dedication of Santa Maria del Fiore in 1412," *Renaissance Quarterly* 44 (Winter 1991): 680.
3. Franklin Toker, "Amid Rubble and Myth: Excavating beneath Florence's Cathedral," accessed at *www.neh.gov/news/humanities/1999-03/toker.html*.
4. Franklin Toker, "Excavations below the Cathedral of Florence, 1965–1974," *Gesta* 14 1975): 17–36.
5. John Paul II, *Familiaris Consortio*, no. 66.
6. Center for Applied Research in the Apostolate (CARA), *Sacraments Today: Belief and Practice among U.S. Catholics*, at *http://cara.georgetown.edu/sacraments.html*.
7. Ibid.
8. Christian Smith et al., *Soul Searching: The Religious and Spiritual Lives of American Teenagers* (New York: Oxford University Press, 2005), 193–217.
9. William V. D'Antonio, James D. Davidson, Dean R. Hoge, and Mary L. Gautier, *American Catholics Today: New Realities of Their Faith and Their Church* (Lanham, Md.: Rowman & Littlefield, 2007), 37–49.
10. *Pew Forum Religious Landscape Survey* (2008), accessed at *http://religions.pewforum.org/pdf/report2religious-landscape-study-key-findings.pdf*.
11. John Paul II, *Familiaris Consortio*, no. 68.
12. For example, the Gallup organization is becoming more involved in assisting Catholic parishes in determining the level of engagement among members. For further information, see online Gallup, "Faith Practice," accessed at *www.gallup.com/consulting/faith/18265/Creating-Engagement.aspx*.
13. For an excellent treatment of young adult participation in the U.S. Catholic Church, see Tim Muldoon, *Seeds of Hope: Young Adults and the Catholic Church in the United States* (Mahwah, N.J.: Paulist Press, 2008).
14. CARA, *Marriage in the Catholic Church: A Survey of U.S. Catholics*, October 2007, accessed at *www.usccb.org/laity/marriage/marriage_report.pdf*, 70–82.
15. I recognize that this method may not work with singles, and it is necessary to take strong steps to welcome young adult singles into our communities. See Muldoon, *Seeds of Hope*, 127.
16. Patrick J. Brennan, *The Mission Driven Parish* (Maryknoll, N.Y.: Orbis Books, 2007), 112–24.
17. See online *www.usccb.org/dioceses.shtml* for links to all the U.S. diocesan websites.

18. Further work must be done to explore how parent involvement in a child's preparation for other sacraments can reinforce and enhance the tools to facilitate a child's remote preparation for marriage.

19. See, for example, Joann Heaney-Hunter and Louis Primavera, *UNITAS: Preparing for Sacramental Marriage* (New York: Crossroad, 1998), and Brennan, *The Mission Driven Parish*, 25.

20. Four is not a magic number of sessions, nor is it verified as is data regarding optimal numbers of marriage preparation sessions. See Creighton University Center for Marriage and Family, *Marriage Preparation in the Catholic Church: Getting It Right* (Washington D.C.: USCCB, 1995).

21. For example, couples might reflect on Luke 2:1–19 or Matthew 1:18–25 (the birth of Jesus) or Psalm 139.

22. Muldoon points to the importance of church hospitality in the lives of young adults (*Seeds of Hope*, 112–13). In particular, the time of welcoming can be an opportunity to demonstrate acceptance of the diversity of families that bring children for baptism.

23. For a good resource on raising children in faith, see Jim Campbell, *52 Simple Ways to Talk with Your Kids about Faith* (Chicago: Loyola Press, 2007).

24. *Rite of Christian Initiation of Children*, no. 9. Please note: the circumstances of an individual parish may require that baptisms take place primarily outside of Sunday liturgies. Using good pastoral judgment will determine what works best for families and local parish communities.

25. For example, young families can help contribute to a Thanksgiving basket for a poor family or volunteer once a month to greet people before Sunday mass. Think of activities that families can do together.

26. See USCCB, *Daughters and Sons of Light*, goal 4, accessed at *www.usccb.org/laity/ygadult/sdeng-goal4.shtml*.

27. *Familiaris Consortio*, no. 66.

28. Popular pastoral literature supports this perception. See, for example, Frank Quinn, "Confirmation Is Not Graduation," *Modern Liturgy* 18 (September 1991): 10–11.

29. For current information about marriage trends in the United States, see David Popenoe, "The State of Our Unions: The Social Health of Marriage in America, 2007," accessed at *http://marriage.rutgers.edu*.

30. See Thomas East, Ann Marie Eckert, Leif Kehrwald, Brian Singer-Towns, and Cheryl Tholcke, *Total Faith Initiative* (Winona, Minn.: St. Mary's Press, 2004), chapter 1, and David Cloutier, *Love, Reason, and God's Story* (Winona, Minn.: St. Mary's Press, 2008).

31. How we prevent this is a question of continuing debate and results in differing answers. Moreover, the discussion is not limited to the Roman Catholic Church. See, for example, Bert Roebben, "Youth Ministry in and beyond the Church? The Sacrament of Confirmation in the Roman Catholic Church as a Testcase," *Journal of Belief and Values* 20 (1999): 51–59; William Levada, "Reflections on the Age of Confirmation," *Theological Studies* 57 (1996): 302–12; and Joe Goodwin Burnett, "Reconsidering a Bold Proposal: Reflections, Questions, and Concerns Regarding a Theology of Confirmation," *Anglican Theological Review* 88 (Winter 2006): 69–83.

32. See Smith et al., *Soul Searching*, 72–117.

33. Donna Freitas, *Sex and the Soul: Juggling Sexuality, Spirituality, Romance, and Religion on America's College Campuses* (New York: Oxford University Press, 2008).

34. Colleen Carroll, *The New Faithful: Why Young Adults Are Embracing Catholic Orthodoxy* (Chicago: Loyola Press, 2004), 4–5, 98–103. See also Muldoon, *Seeds of Hope*, 135–37.

35. USCCB, *Renewing the Vision: A Framework for Catholic Youth Ministry*, accessed at *www.usccb.org/laity/youth/rtvcontents.shtml*. Its goals are: (1) to empower young people to live as disciples of Jesus Christ in our world today, (2) to draw young people to responsible participation in the life, mission, and work of the Catholic faith community, and (3) to foster the total personal and spiritual growth of each young person. USCCB, *Sons and Daughters of Light: A Pastoral Plan for Ministry with Young Adults*, accessed at *www.usccb.org/laity/ygadult/toc.shtml*. Its goals are: (1) connecting young adults with Jesus Christ, (2) connecting young adults with the church, (3) connecting young adults with the mission of the church in the world, (4) connecting young adults with a peer community. These tasks facilitate growth of the whole person and connect young men and women with their spirituality, their faith community, and their world.

36. Benedict XVI, *Deus Caritas Est*, no. 10, accessed at *www.vatican.va*.

37. See Luke Timothy Johnson, "A Disembodied 'Theology of the Body': John Paul on Love, Sex and Pleasure," *Commonweal* 128 (January 26, 2001). Articles that help to clarify the addresses are Mary Shivanandan, "John Paul II's Theology of the Body," in *Living Light* 37 (Spring 2001), accessed at *www.usccb.org/education/catechetics/livlghtspr2001.shtml#Shivanandan* and the introductory material in Michael Waldstein, ed., *Man and Woman He Created Them* (Boston: Pauline Media, 2006), 1–124.

38. John Paul II, *Theology of the Body*, nos. 118–33. There also are a number of programs designed specifically for teens. For example, see Jason Evert, Crystalina Evert, and Brian Butler, *The Theology of the Body for Teens* (Westchester, Pa.: Ascension Press, 2006). This series includes teen and leader workbooks, and a DVD series.

39. *Theology of the Body*, nos. 118, 119, 121, 123, 127, 131, 132.

40. Ibid., nos. 25, 34, 35, 93.

41. Ibid., nos. 10, 17, 59, 73, 87, 111, 114.

42. Ibid., no. 100.

43. Ibid., nos. 9, 10, 12, 67, 69, 71, 77.

44. Ibid., nos. 95, 100, 103, 104, 105.

45. NCCB, *Follow the Way of Love* (Washington, D.C.: USCC Publications, 1993), 8. See also John Paul II, *Familiaris Consortio*, no. 42.

46. Mother Teresa, *1979 Nobel Lecture*, accessed at *http://nobelprize.org/nobel_prizes/peace/laureates/1979/teresa-lecture.html*.

47. Jeremiah 1:7–10: "Ah, Lord GOD!," I said, "I know not how to speak; I am too young." But the LORD answered me, "Say not, 'I am too young.' To whomever I send you, you shall go; whatever I command you, you shall speak. Have no fear before them, because I am with you to deliver you, says the LORD." Then the LORD extended his hand and touched my mouth, saying, "See, I place my words in your mouth! This day I set you over nations and over kingdoms, to root up and to tear down, to destroy and to demolish, to build and to plant."

48. Luke 1:46–48. And Mary said: "My soul proclaims the greatness of the Lord; my spirit rejoices in God my savior. For he has looked upon his handmaid's lowliness; behold, from now on will all ages call me blessed."

49. USCCB, *Renewing the Vision: A Framework for Catholic Youth Ministry*, Goal 2, accessed at *www.usccb.org/laity/youth/rtvcontents.shtml*.

Chapter 9: Paul Covino / Learning from the Liturgy

1. *Catechism of the Catholic Church* (hereafter CCC) §1234.
2. My graduate school mentor Mark Searle reviewed the texts of marriage rites from various eras in Christian history and noted that they "show, more than the writings of the theologians, and more than those who romanticize the erotic, a balanced and forward-looking vision of how the mystery of marriage can be understood and lived." See "Marriage Rites as Documents of Faith: Notes for a Theology of Marriage" in Mark Searle and Kenneth W. Stevenson, *Documents of the Marriage Liturgy* (Collegeville Minn.: Liturgical Press, 1992), 262.
3. #1–7 in the *Rite of Marriage*, hereafter RM; #1–11 in the Latin edition of the *Order for Celebrating Marriage*, hereafter OCM.
4. OCM, #17.
5. *Constitution on the Sacred Liturgy*, #9–10.
6. *Gaudium et Spes*, #48.
7. Jack Ziegler, *Marital Blitz* (New York: Warner Books, 1987), 23.
8. RM, #17–18.
9. Ibid., #1–2; OCM, #5–9, 11.
10. OCM, #9.
11. RM, #2; OCM, #2, 6–7.
12. OCM, #6.
13. Ibid., #7.
14. RM, #4; OCM #2–3, 8, 10.
15. OCM, #3.
16. Ibid., #8, 10.
17. RM, #3–4; OCM, #4, 8–11.
18. OCM, #10.
19. Ibid., #4.
20. Ibid., #8.
21. Ibid., #9.
22. Ibid., #11.
23. Ibid., #1, 4–6.
24. Ibid., #4.
25. "It is better to be married than to burn with passion" (1 Cor. 7:9).
26. OCM, #4.
27. Ibid., #5.
28. Ibid., #7–9.
29. Ibid., #7.
30. Ibid., #11.
31. Ibid.
32. RM, #20.

33. *Sacrosanctum Concilium*, #26.
34. Ibid., #26–27; CC § 1140.
35. Austin Flemming, *Parish Weddings* (Chicago: Liturgy Training Publications, 1987).
36. *Book of Blessings*, #195–214.
37. #28.
38. "The Amen Corner," *Worship* 61, no. 1 (January 1987): 79.
39. OCM, chapter 4.
40. See, for example, Joann Heaney-Hunter and Louis Primavera, *Unitas: Preparing for Sacramental Marriage* (New York: Crossroad, 1998).

Chapter 10: Alejandro Aguilera-Titus / Marriage and Family Ministry among Hispanic/Latino Catholics

1. United States Conference of Catholic Bishops, *Renewing the Vision: A Framework for Catholic Youth Ministry* (Washington, D.C.: United States Conference of Catholic Bishops, 1997), 22 (hereafter RVYM).
2. United States Conference of Catholic Bishops, *Many Faces in God's House: A Catholic Vision for the Third Millennium* (Washington, D.C.: United States Conference of Catholic Bishops, 2001), 5.

Chapter 11: Andrew Lyke / Marriage and Family Ministry among African American Catholics

1. Process over content is a concept I learned in a class taught by John Roberto as part of a certificate in Family Ministry program at Loyola University–Institute of Pastoral Studies in Chicago in the early 1990s.
2. Jacob Bronowski, *The Ascent of Man* (Boston: Little, Brown, 1974).
3. Edward T. Hall, *Beyond Culture* (New York: Doubleday, 1976).
4. Eric H. F. Law, *The Wolf Shall Dwell with the Lamb* (St. Louis: Chalice Press, 1993).
5. United States Conference of Catholic Bishops, *Brothers and Sister to Us* (Washington, D.C.: United Sates Conference of Catholic Bishops, 1979).
6. Ibid.
7. Ibid., 11.
8. Cardinal Francis George, OMI, *Dwell in My Love: A Pastoral Letter on Racism* (Chicago: Archdiocese of Chicago, 2001).
9. Research done by the Catholic African World Network. The principal resources used were: *The World Christian Encyclopedia* edited by D. Barrett; *The 2004 Catholic Almanac* edited by Matthew Brunson, D.Min.; the African-American Secretariat of the U.S. Catholic Bishops' Conference; the Internet and global field research.
10. Research gathered from various sociological studies for the African-American Healthy Marriage Initiative, a project of the Administration for Children and Families in the United States Department of Health and Human Services.
11. Cited in Walter Earl Fluker and Catherine Tumber, eds., *A Strange Freedom: The Best of Howard Thurman on Religious Experience and Public Life* (Boston: Beacon Press, 1998), 33.

12. Anthony J. Gittins, *Ministry at the Margins* (Maryknoll, N.Y.: Orbis Books, 2002), 40.
13. Ibid., 121–41.
14. Ibid., 127.
15. *Catechism of the Catholic Church*, chapter 2, article 1.
16. I have used here some remarks that I gave as part of the NACFLM twenty-fifth anniversary conference plenary address: "Then and Now — Retrospective and Prospective."
17. Black Bishops of the United States, *What We Have Seen and Heard* (Washington, D.C.: USCCB, 1984).

Chapter 12: Jonathan Y. Tan / Marriage and Family Ministry among Asian American Catholics

1. The United States Census Bureau adopts a similar approach in its census reports, defining "Asian" as "those having origins in any of the original peoples of the Far East, Southeast Asia, or the Indian subcontinent including, for example, Cambodia, China, India, Japan, Korea, Malaysia, Pakistan, the Philippine Islands, Thailand, and Vietnam" (United States Census Bureau 2003:1). In the past, the United States Census Bureau lumped Asian Americans together with Hawaiians and Pacific Islanders, a category that includes Samoans, Tongans, Tahitians, Fijians, and other ethnicities, despite the fact that Hawaiians and Pacific Islanders have more in common with Native Americans than with Asian Americans in their life experiences, as well as sociocultural and economic-political concerns. It is in Census 2000 that the United States Census Bureau differentiated Asian Americans and Pacific Islanders into separate statistical categories for the first time.

2. Lisa Lowe explains the implications of Asian American heterogeneity as follows: "what is referred to as 'Asian American' is clearly a heterogeneous entity. From the perspective of the majority culture, Asian Americans may very well be constructed as different from, and other than, Euro-Americans. But from the perspectives of Asian Americans, we are perhaps even more different, more diverse among ourselves.... As with other diasporas in the United States, the Asian immigrant collectivity is unstable and changeable, with its cohesion complicated by inter-generationality, by various degrees of identification and relation to a 'homeland,' and by different extent of assimilation to and distinction from 'majority culture' in the United States" ("Heterogeneity, Hybridity, Multiplicity: Marking Asian American Differences," *Diaspora* 1:24–44, at 27).

3. As the U.S. Census Bureau explains: "Some of the Asian groups, such as the Chinese and Japanese, have been in the United States for several generations. Others, such as the Hmong, Vietnamese, Laotians, and Cambodians, are comparatively recent immigrants" (United States Census Bureau 2003:1).

4. In the year 2000, the top five largest immigrant-sending Asian countries were China, Philippines, India, Vietnam, and Korea, with the Indian-born U.S. population showing the biggest increase (United States Census Bureau 2002b:1).

5. See Lee Evelyn, ed., *Working with Asian Americans: A Guide for Clinicians* (New York: Guilford Press, 1997).

6. Statistics show that an average Asian American household has 3.3 members, with the figures higher for specific Asian American communities: Vietnamese

American (4.0 members); Cambodians, Hmong, and Laotians (5.1 members). By comparison, Japanese Americans have the smallest households (2.5 members) (see Vonnie C. McLoyd, Ana Mari Cauce, David Takeuchi, and Leon Wilson, "Marital Processes and Parental Socialization in Families of Color: A Decade Review of Research," *Journal of Marriage and the Family* 62 [2000]: 1070–93, at 1072). In addition, 22 percent of all Asian American families comprise five or more persons, compared with 12 percent of non-Hispanic White families, and 59 percent of all Asian American households have at least three or more members (Sudipta Das, "Life in a Salad Bowl! Marriage, Family Life, and Economic Choices in Asian-American Communities in the United States," *Race, Gender and Class* 13 [2006]: 248–72, at 257–58).

7. Vonnie C. McLoyd, Ana Mari Cauce, David Takeuchi, and Leon Wilson attribute the greater average Asian American household size to the presence of relatives who are not a child or spouse: "Compared with European Americans and African Americans, Asian Americans are more likely to live in households that are comprised exclusively of family members (i.e., family households, as distinguished from households that include individuals who are not related through family ties)" ("Marital Processes and Parental Socialization in Families of Color," 1072).

8. Ibid., 1073.

9. Ibid.

10. See J. Lessinger, *From the Ganges to the Hudson: Indian Immigrants in New York City* (Needham Heights, Mass.: Allyn and Bacon, 1995); K. I. Leonard, *The South Asian Americans* (Westport, Conn.: Greenwood Publishing, 1997); Uma A. Segal, "Cultural Variables in Asian Indian Families," *Families in Society: The Journal of Contemporary Human Services* 72 (1991): 233–41, and Uma A. Segal, "The Asian Indian-American Family," in *Ethnic Families in America: Patterns and Variations,* ed. C. H. Mindel, R. W. Habenstein and R. Wright (Upper Saddle River, N.J.: Prentice Hall, 1998).

11. See Nazli Kibria, *Becoming Asian American: Second-Generation Chinese and Korean American Identities* (Baltimore: Johns Hopkins University Press, 2002); B. L. Sung, "Bicultural Conflicts in Chinese Immigrant Children," *Journal of Comparative Family Studies* 26 (1985): 255–69; Amy Lin Tan, *Chinese American Children and Families: A Guide for Educators and Service Providers* (Olney, Md.: Association for Childhood Education International, 2004); and May Paomay Tung, *Chinese Americans and Their Immigrant Parents: Conflict, Identity, and Values* (New York: Haworth Clinical Practice Press, 2000).

12. See Won Moo Hurh, *The Korean Americans* (Westport, Conn.: Greenwood Press, 1998); Young Lee Hertig, *Cultural Tug of War: The Korean Immigrant Family and Church in Transition* (Nashville: Abingdon, 2001); Kibria, *Becoming Asian American;* and Pyong Gap Min, *Changes and Conflicts: Korean Immigrant Families in New York* (Boston: Allyn and Bacon, 1998).

13. See Nazli Kibria, *Family Tightrope: The Changing Life of Vietnamese-Americans* (Princeton, N.J.: Princeton University Press, 1993); Thanh Van Tran, "The Vietnamese American Family," in *Ethnic Studies in America: Patterns and Variations,* ed. Charles H. Mindel, Robert W. Habenstein, and Roosevelt Wright (New York: Elsevier, 1997), 254–83; and Tuyet-Lan Pho and Anne Mulvey, "Southeast Asian Women in Lowell," *Frontiers* 24 (2003): 101–29.

14. Sudipta Das summarizes the following contributing factors that are distinctive to Asian American families:

"Chinese group participants believed in acquiescing to one's destiny, and thus acceptance of difficult family situations. Paternalistic values, community reputation, social status and family commitments pressurize women to stay with their husbands and children.... For the Korean group, Buddhism and Confucianism, which are the dominant faiths in Korea, emphasize 'the cycle of life,' in which men rule and are privileged to act as they please. A Korean woman would try to blame herself as the cause of family violence and solve it or bear the consequences in silence without bringing any shame to the family.... Members of the South Asian group felt that in their patriarchal society, daughters were 'given away' as property when they married. Arranged marriages do not promote family violence, but the view of women as property does. Additionally, the notion of shame prevents South Asian women from reporting domestic violence, and financial dependence on their husbands makes divorce and a single life thereafter immeasurably unattractive and undesirable financially.... The Vietnamese group defined male authority as sacrosanct, as well as male rights and responsibilities to 'teach' his wife and children by force if necessary.... Finally, the Cambodian group like the Korean blamed women as the cause of family violence and the women's ultimate responsibility to bear the consequences as a victim. Cambodian men felt psychologically insecure of losing authority, because of the financial independence of their employed wives and children that contributed to a post-traumatic stress disorder provoking aggressive behavior." Sudipta Das, "Life in a Salad Bowl!" citing M. R. Yoshioka and Q. Dang, *Asian Family Violence Report: A Study of the Cambodian, Chinese, Korean, South Asian, and Vietnamese Communities in Massachusetts* (Boston: Asian Task Force Against Domestic Violence, Inc., 2000).

15. As Nazli Kibria explains: "The traditional Vietnamese family was modeled on Confucian principles. In the ideal model, households were extended, and the family was structured around the patrilineage or the ties of the male descent line. Women were married at a young age and then entered the household of their husband's father. The young bride had minimal status and power until she produced sons. The patriarchal bargain in this setting was one in which women expected significant rewards in their old age from allegiance and deference to the patrilineal family system... because the middle-class status of families depended in large part on the incomes of the men, the threat of economic impoverishment sustained the ideals of the traditional family system and men's authority in the family. Women feared the economic consequences of male desertion, a not uncommon occurrence, especially when men were on military duty for extended periods. The 'bargain' between women and men that emerged in this setting was one in which women deferred to men's authority in exchange for economic protection" (Nazli Kibria, "Power, Patriarchy, and Gender Conflict in the Vietnamese Immigrant Community," *Gender and Society* 4 [1990]: 9–24, at 12, 13).

16. Stephen Young, "The Orthodox Chinese Confucian Social Paradigms versus Vietnamese Individualism," in *Confucianism and the Family*, ed. Walter H. Stole and George A. DeVos (New York: State University of New York Press), 155.

17. Nazli Kibria describes the dilemma that many first-generation Vietnamese American men experienced: "In the United States, many Vietnamese men faced unemployment or had low-paying jobs that did not usually enable them to support

a family. Compounding the men's economic problems has been a widespread sense of powerlessness and alienation from the institutions of the dominant American society" (Kibria, "Power, Patriarchy, and Gender Conflict in the Vietnamese Immigrant Community," 13–14).

18. Pho and Mulvey, "Southeast Asian Women in Lowell," 102–3.
19. Ibid., 109.
20. Ibid., 110.
21. Ibid., 112.
22. Kibria, "Power, Patriarchy, and Gender Conflict in the Vietnamese Immigrant Community," 9–24, at 14–15.
23. The observations of Pho and Mulvey are especially instructive: "Southeast Asian women who are battered, however, faced cultural and linguistic barriers to services other women do not. Police, the criminal justice system, and social service agencies have neither linguistically nor culturally trained staff to cope with the problem. When available, services are usually not culturally appropriate. In many cases, children are expected to serve as cultural and linguistic translators for their parents. Christine Cole, a victim witness advocate in Lowell, noted: 'It's not fair to say to a child, "Get your parents into court so Mom can prosecute Dad." ' Even perpetrators sometimes translate for victims, reinforcing inequity, dependence, and fear. Traditional roles and prohibitions against speaking of private matters publicly add to the devastation of domestic violence. Many Southeast Asian women fear that reporting abuse to authorities will result in the imprisonment or deportation of their partners or that government intervention will be worse than the abuse itself" (Pho and Mulvey, "Southeast Asian Women in Lowell," 114–15).
24. Ibid., 116.
25. Ibid., 116–17.
26. Ibid., 117.
27. Farha Ternikar, "Changing Marriage Trends in the South Asian American Community" (paper presented at the American Sociological Association 2004 Annual Meeting, San Francisco).
28. Nazli Kibria, "The Construction of 'Asian American': Reflections on Intermarriage and Ethnic Identity among Second-Generation Chinese and Korean Americans," in *Ethnic and Racial Studies* 20 (1997): 523–44, at 530.
29. As Sudipta Das explains: "Most first-generation Asian Americans encourage their U.S.-raised or U.S.-born children to seek same-race or ethnic partners. This trend is stronger in some ethnic groups than in others, such as in Asian Indian, Korean, and Vietnamese communities. Even those first-generation Asians who had married out of their race or ethnic group, whether from love or necessity, indulge in exerting pressure on their children to revert to their cultural tradition and choose ethnic wives or husbands" ("Life in a Salad Bowl!" 252–53).
30. The Knanayas (also known as *Thekkumbhagar* or "Southists") trace their unique ethnic and religious heritage to the Jewish Christian refugees from Edessa led by Knai Thomman (Thomas of Cana), who arrived in Cranganore (Kodungalloor) on the Malabar Coast in Kerala, India, in the year 345. The practice of endogamy has ensured the continued survival of their distinctive Jewish-Christian heritage and traditions in the midst of the numerically larger ethnic Indian Saint Thomas Christians who comprise the Syro-Malabar Catholics (also known as *Vadakkumbhagar* or "Northists"). On August 29, 1911, Pope Pius X officially

recognized and sanctioned the unique status and distinctive Jewish-Christian identity of the Knanaya Catholics by erecting a vicariate apostolic (subsequently elevated to the status of eparchy on December 21, 1923, and archeparchy on May 12, 2005) at Kottayam for their pastoral care. See Placid J. Podipara, *The Thomas Christians* (London: Darton, Longman & Todd, 1970); Jacob Kollaparambil, *The Babylonian Origin of the Southists among the St. Thomas Christians* (Rome: Pontificium Institutum Studiorum Orientalium 1992); Jacob Vellian, *Knanite Community, History, and Culture* (Kottayam: Jyoti Book House 2001).

31. Raymond Williams observes that about one-third of the Knanaya community belongs to the Malankara Syriac Oriental Orthodox Church under the oversight of the Jacobite patriarch of Antioch, while two thirds are Syro-Malabar Catholic. According to Williams: "Of the 125,000 Knanaya in the Knanaya Catholic diocese of Kottayam, which was established as a separate jurisdiction in 1911, approximately 9,000 people in 2,000 registered families live in North America, primarily in Chicago (700 families), New York/New Jersey (650 families), and Los Angeles (200 families), which are the only associations that have resident priests (assigned by Bishop Kuriakose Kunnasserry). Other associations are in Houston (160 families), Washington (22 families), Philadelphia (35 families), Tampa (27 families), Miami (35 families), and Detroit (35 families)" (1996:146). The first Knanaya organization in the United States is the Knanaya Association of North America (KANA), which was established in Chicago in 1979. Knanaya Catholics organize themselves under the umbrella of the Knanaya Catholic Congress of North America (KCCNA). The Knanaya archbishop of Kottayam regularly assigns priests to minister to the spiritual and pastoral needs of the Knanaya Catholics in the United States. See Raymond Brady Williams, *Christian Pluralism in the United States: The Immigrant Experience* (Cambridge: Cambridge University Press, 1996), 68, 146.

32. Ibid., 121.
33. Ibid., 120.
34. Ibid., 119.
35. Ibid., 118.
36. Farha Ternikar made these observations in his paper noted above.
37. Pelikan as quoted in Joseph Carey, "Christianity as an Enfolding Circle," *U.S. News & World Report* 106, no. 25 (1989): 57, emphasis added.

Chapter 13: Bonnie P. Mack / *Interchurch Marriages: Challenges and Blessings*

1. Benedict XVI, address at ecumenical meeting, Warsaw, Poland, May 25, 2006.
2. Association of Interchurch Families, "Interchurch Families and Christian Unity," at *www.interchurchfamilies.org/confer/rome2003/documents/roma2003_en.pdf*, pages 1–2 (retrieved July 2007).
3. United States Conference of Catholic Bishops, "A Select Snapshot of Marriage in the U.S." online at *www.usccb.org/laity/marriage/marrsnapshot.shtml*.
4. Archdiocese of Cincinnati, "Marriage Preparation Guidelines throughout the Lifecycle," 11.

5. Gerard Kelly, "Pioneers Not Problems: Interchurch Families," online at *www.terraspiritus.com.au/member/sample_view.cgi?aid=111*.

6. Michael Kinnamon, "Nine Questions/ Challenges for the Ecumenical Movement in 2007," *Ecumenical Trends* (Garrison, N.Y.: Graymoor Ecumenical and Interreligious Institute), 36, no. 6 (June 2007): 14–15.

7. "Interchurch Families and Christian Unity," paper adopted by the Second World Gathering of interchurch families from eleven countries, held in Rome in July 2003.

Chapter 14: Lee Williams / Interchurch Couples: Potential Challenges and Blessings

1. M. Kalmijn, "Shifting Boundaries: Trends in Religious and Educational Homogamy," *American Sociological Review* 56 (1991): 786–800; W. Sander, "Catholicism and Intermarriage in the United States," *Journal of Marriage and the Family* 55 (1993): 1037–41.

2. Center for Marriage and Family, *Marriage Preparation in the Catholic Church: Getting It Right* (Omaha, Neb.: Creighton University, 1995); W. V. D'Antonio, D. R. Hoge, K. Meyer, and J. D. Davidson, "American Catholics," *National Catholic Reporter,* October 29, 1999, 20; D. R. Hoge and K. M. Ferry, *Empirical Research on Interfaith Marriage in America* (Washington, D.C.: United States Catholic Conference, 1981).

3. A. L. McCutcheon, "Denominations and Religious Intermarriage: Trends among White Americans in the Twentieth Century," *Review of Religious Research* 29 (1988): 213–27.

4. H. M. Bahr, "Religious Intermarriage and Divorce in Utah and the Mountain States," *Journal for the Scientific Study of Religion* 20 (1981): 251–61; L. L. Bumpass, T. C. Martin, and J. A. Sweet, "Background and Early Marital Factors," NFSH Working Paper no. 14, Center for Demography and Ecology: University of Wisconsin, Madison, 1989; V. R. Call and T. B. Heaton, "Religious Influence on Marital Stability," *Journal for the Scientific Study of Religion* 36 (1997): 382–92; Center for Marriage and Family, *Ministry to Interchurch Marriages: A National Study* (Omaha, Neb.: Creighton University, 1999); T. B. Heaton, S. L. Albrecht, and T. K. Martin, "The Timing of Divorce," *Journal of Marriage and the Family* 47 (1985): 631–39; T. B. Heaton, "Factors Contributing to Increasing Marital Stability in the United States," *Journal of Family Issues* 23 (2002): 392–409; T. B. Heaton and E. L. Pratt, "The Effects of Religious Homogamy on Marital Satisfaction and Stability," *Journal of Family Issues* 11 (1990): 191–207; E. L. Lehrer and C. U. Chiswick, "Religion as a Determinant of Marital Stability," *Demography* 30 (1993): 385–404.

5. S. K. Chi and S. K. Houseknecht, "Protestant Fundamentalism and Marital Success: A Comparative Approach," *Sociology and Social Research* 69 (1985): 351–74; N. D. Glenn, "Interreligious Marriage in the United States: Patterns and Recent Trends," *Journal of Marriage and the Family* 44 (1982): 555–66; T. B. Heaton, "Religious Homogamy and Marital Satisfaction Reconsidered," *Journal of Marriage and the Family* 46 (1984): 729–33; Heaton and Pratt, "The Effects of Religious Homogamy on Marital Satisfaction and Stability," 191–207.

6. S. T. Ortega, H. P. Whitt, and J. A. William, "Religious Homogamy and Marital Happiness," *Journal of Family Issues* 9 (1988): 224–39; C. L. Sheehan, E. W. Bock, and G. R. Lee, "Religious Heterogamy, Religiosity, and Marital Happiness: The Case of Catholics," *Journal of Marriage and the Family* 52 (1990): 73–79; L. M. Williams and M. G. Lawler, "Religious Heterogamy and Marital Satisfaction: A Comparison of Interchurch and Same-Church Individuals," *Journal of Family Issues* 24 (2003): 1070–92.

7. L. M. Williams and M. G. Lawler, "The Challenges and Rewards of Interchurch Marriages: A Qualitative Study," *Journal of Psychology and Christianity* 19 (2000): 205–18.

8. L. M. Williams and M. G. Lawler, "Religious Heterogamy and Marital Satisfaction: A Comparison of Interchurch and Same-Church Individuals," *Journal of Family Issues* 24 (2003): 1070–92.

9. Williams and Lawler, "The Challenges and Rewards of Interchurch Marriages," 205–18.

10. Lee M. Williams and Michael G. Lawler, "Interchurch Couples and the Issue of Acceptance," *Pastoral Psychology* 47, no. 1 (1998).

11. Michael Lawler, *Ecumenical Marriage and Remarriage: Gifts and Challenges to the Churches* (New London, Conn.: Twenty-Third Publications, 1990).

12. Ibid.,

13. Cf. R. F. Stahmann and W. J. Hiebert, *Premarital and Remarital Counseling: The Professional's Handbook* (San Francisco: Jossey-Bass, 1997).

Conclusions: Cynthia Dobrzynski

1. The author wishes to thank Leif Kehrwald of the Center for Ministry Development for co-leading the final session that synthesized the conclusions of the researchers.

Index

Administration for Children and Families (U.S. Department of Health and Human Services), 148–49
Ad uxorem (Tertullian), 111
African American Expression, 137
African American Healthy Marriage Initiative (AAHMI), 148–49
African Americans
   Catholic family life ministers, as strangers to community of, 148–49
   Catholic marriage ministry finding its place with, 150–51
   erosion of families, 144–45, 150–51
   prophetic role of, 148
   spirituality of, 149–50
   statistics relating to, 144
Alcott, Bronson, 76
American Association of Interchurch Families (AAIF), 170
American democratic liberalism, practices resulting from, 24
Americanized family (Asian American), 154–55
anxiety gap, 84
arranged marriages, challenges of, in Asian American community, 161–62
Arusi, 138–39
Ascent of Man (Bronowski), 139
ascetic celibacy, 215–16n5
Ashford, John, 138
Ashford, Pam, 138
Asian Americans, 152–53
   dialogue with, 167–68
   empathizing with, 166
   families, types and characteristics of, 153–56
   marriage among, 156–58
   marriage and family life of, pastoral response to, 164–68
   outreach to, 164–65
   paternalism in families, 224n14
   patriarchal order of first-generation marriages, challenged, 158–60
   patriarchal worldview of many groups, 157
   retaining aspects of their native culture, 155–56
   selection and training of pastoral leaders for, 165
   traditioning for, 166–67
   women, outreach to, 160–61

Asian and Pacific Presence: Harmony in Faith (U.S. bishops), 153
assimilation, cultural, 126, 128
Association of Interchurch Families (AIF), 170
Augustine, 25, 27

Balsam, Charles, 83
Baltimore Catechism (illustrated, 1962), 58
baptism. *See also* baptism preparation
   as basis for sacramental nature of marriage, 112
   as beginning of sharing in Christ's death and resurrection, 16
   call to sacramental marriage rooted in, 16
   empowerment resulting from, 11
   gifts for, service or charitable donation in lieu of, 67
   as learning experience for the parents, 66–67
   preparation for, with interchurch families, 175
baptismal promises, renewal of, revising, 12
baptism preparation
   implementing RCIA-style process for, 94–96
   importance of, 82, 83
   inadequacy of programs for, 83–84
   leading to increased involvement in the parish community, 96
   linking with parent spirituality, 92–96
   as marriage enrichment, 91–93
Bellah, Robert, 49
Benedict XVI, 14, 99, 169
"Best Is Yet to Come," 138
Beyond Culture (Hall), 140
Bible study groups, 42
bicultural family (Asian Americans), 154
Book of Blessings, 116, 119
BRIDGES spiritual inventory for couples, 194
Bronowski, Jacob, 139
busyness
   emptiness in, 34–35
   reflecting on, 43

Caplan, Gerald, 87
Caring for Marriage, 87–88
Carter, Dorothy, 138
Carter, Maurice, 138

Catechism of the Catholic Church, 20–21, 108, 116
Catholic Action, 39
Catholic Charities, 54
Catholic Church
  accepting commercialization of marriage, 63–64
  developing precise legal structure related to marriage, 23
  gradual response of, to Roman marriage law, 24
  hopefulness of, regarding marriage, 7
  as immigrants' advocate in the United States, 126
  overtures from, times of openness to, 83
  providing support for Hispanic marriages, 129–30
  relationship of, with the African American community, 148
  self-reported involvement in, 80, 81–82
  suggestions for pastoral response of, to Asian American families, 164–68
  theology of, resonating with African American history and culture, 147
Catholic family life ministers, as strangers to African American community, 148–49
Catholicism, role of, for infrequent church-goers, 82
Catholic leaders, challenge facing, related to marriage, 23
Catholics
  attrition among, 91
  challenges for, in sustaining and celebrating marriage, 46–47
  considering life through lens of Christian faith, 21
  marginalized in America, before Vatican II, 36–37
  similarity of, to rest of U.S. society, 22
  upward mobility of, 38–39
  U.S., changing attitudes toward religion, 90–91
"Catholic Wedding Guide," 63
celibacy
  idealization of, 58
  as means of living out one's baptismal commitment, 12
  official bias in favor of, 10–11
Cherlin, Andrew, 47, 48
Chicago, Archdiocese of, Family Ministries Office, 149
children
  changing lives of the parents, 17
  encouraging religious practice for, 173
  in interchurch families, 189–90
  as outstanding gift of marriage, 111–12
  preparing, for marriage, 18
  religious upbringing of, for interchurch couples, 189–90
Christian Family Movement, 44

Christian Life Communities, 42, 44
Christian lifestyles, ranking of, 58–62
Christian perfection, 28–29
Chupungco, Anscar, 110
Code of Canon Law, 20, 29–30, 111
Coffin, Bill, 148–49
cohabitation, 24, 47
  differing conclusions about, 85
  divorce and, 47, 48
  domestic violence and, 213n21
  inadvisability of, 84–85
  not fulfilling need for commitment, 84
  not improving transition from companionship to marriage, 50
  resulting in fewer marriages, 48
common lifestyle, shared, by celibates and parishioners, 62
communication, related to marital satisfaction, 185
communion
  God drawing people into, 28–29
  marriage as sacrament of, 26–27
  mystagogy of, 31
  as primary fruit of marriage, 30
  work of, for families, 35
community
  developing, among parishioners, 43–44
  responsibility of, for creating lifetime faith partnerships, 90
community networks, using, in pastoral approach to marriage, 53
companionate love, appeal to, 51
companionate marriage, 48
  failure of, 49
  standards of, taking priority, 212n14
  uneasy relationship of, with demands of the home, 49–50
companionship, as fundamental reason for marriage, 26
Confirmation, spiritual and religious development stunted after, 97–98
Coontz, Stephanie, 48–49, 55
cooperation, mimicking market competition, 54
Council of Trent, decree on marriage, 60
couples
  busyness of, 34
  cooperating with the creator by procreation and education of children, 111
  engaging in service together, 64–65
  entering marriage mutually, 115–16
  facing themselves and their relationship, 17
  freedom of, to marry, 6
  joining in religious and spiritual activities, 187–88
  living marriage in the Father's name, 13–14
  living marriage in the name of the Holy Spirit, 15–16

couples (*continued*)
  living marriage in the name of the son, 14–15
  mature, experiencing shift in vocation, 74
  offering resources for, 31
  placing spousal relationship before others, 16–18
  prayer for, 202
  praying together, 118
  responsibility of, for creating a good marriage, 7–8
  shifting interpersonal weight of marriage to social side of life, 56
covenants, 8
Covino, Paul, 57
creation, God's will for humans reflected in, 11
cultural conflict family (Asian Americans), 154
culture
  black and white, differences between, 139–41
  high context and low context, 140

Davidson, James, 38
Day, Dorothy, 39, 86
De Mello, Anthony, 17
Deus Caritas Est (Benedict XVI), 99
disillusionment, as stage of marriage, 56
divorce
  among African American couples, 144
  among Asian American couples, 155
  among couples who have cohabited, 47, 48
  lower rates of, for couples sharing joint religious activities, 170
  rate of, among Catholics, 209n3
  reasons for, 48
  risk of, factors affecting, 86
Dogmatic Constitution on the Church, 111
domestic church, 173, 174, 179
  building daily, in the home, 95
  cultivating authentic love in, 2
domestic violence
  in Asian American communities, 158–61
  among cohabitors, 50
Dovetail, 180
Dumas, Helen, 138
Dumas, Martin, 138
Duris, Larry, 138
"Dwell in My Love" (George), 143–44

ecclesial integration, 126, 128, 131, 133
ecumenical marriage, 79–80
Emerson, Ralph Waldo, 13, 76
empty nesters, 18, 73–74
Encuentro & Mission: A Renewed Pastoral Framework for Hispanic Ministry, 127, 129–30
Encuentro 2000, 130

enculturation, for African Americans, 137
endogamy, 158, 162–64
engaged couples, supporting, through prayer, 116
entrance procession, instructions for, 115–16
Eucharist
  attendance at, as gauge of being a good Catholic, 82
  dividing interchurch families, 176–77
exogamy, 158
extended family structure, 150, 155

FACES, 208n20
faith, shaped by family of origin, 100–101
faith communities, building lifetime partnership with, 90
faith formation
  nurturing future generations, 90
  process of, 89–90
faithfulness, 18
faith journey, 78–79
faith-sharing groups, 44, 71
faith traditions, young adults' participation in, 91
faith transmission, as lifetime process, 90
Familiaris Consortio (John Paul II), 35, 60, 91, 97, 111, 173
families
  assault on, in the United States, 144–45
  Catholic, in pre–Vatican II America, 37–38
  centrality of, to understanding social relations, 51
  difficulty of, in surviving time rationing, 54
  as domestic church, 37–38
  fourfold mission of, 35
  as key subsidiary institution, 51
  support of, through faith formation, 90
family holiness, 101
family life cycle, teachable moments in, 65–66
family of origin, teaching about life and faith, 100–101
Family Perspective in Church and Society (U.S. bishops), 116
family relations
  created anew, with every marriage, 49
  reduced to individualism, 49
First Communion
  for interchurch families, 176
  turning into catechetical opportunity, 69–70
  variety of practices surrounding, 67–70
First Five Years of Marriage (Creighton study), 83
Fisher, James, 38–39
Fleming, Austin, 116
FOCCUS premarital inventory, 194
Follow the Way of Love (U.S. bishops), 100
forgiveness, 15

For Your Marriage (U.S. bishops' website), 53, 56, 64
Four Womanly Virtues, 159, 160
functional associations, 53

Gaudium et Spes, 51
gay marriage, 25
General Directory for Catechesis, 128
George, Francis, 143–44
Getting It Right (Creighton study), 82–83, 170
Gittins, Anthony, 147
God
  brought into middle of marriage, 9
  love of, related to love of neighbor, 9
Gospel, inculturation of, 128–29
grace, 15–16, 28, 32, 75, 114, 118–19, 201–2
Granovetter, Mark, 83
Greeley, Andrew, 41–42
Greeley, Mary, 41–42
Gregory, Wilton, 138

Hall, Edward T., 140
Healthy Marriage Initiative (HMI), 85, 148–49
Heller, Christopher, 83–84
Hispanic/Latino Catholics, U.S.
  challenge of cultural identity, 125–26
  facing difficulties in getting married, 124
  marriage and families, strength of, 122–23, 129–30
  ministry for couples and families, pastoral recommendations for, 130–35
  parish communities of, culturally diverse, 125–26
  sharing language, culture, and faith, 123–24
  youth ministry for, 127–28
Hispanic Presence: Challenge and Commitment (U.S. bishops), 122, 126–27
Hoge, Dean, 81
holiness
  association of, with institutional religion, 60, 61–62
  family's call to, 101
  perceptions of, by students, 58–60
Holy Name Society, 44
homogamy, 158
hospitality, 147
  with interchurch couples and families, 171, 175, 179
  offering, during wedding, 115
host, role of, 147
household economy, disappearance of, affecting marriage, 49
household networks, as subsidiary form of association, 53

households
  building faith in, as proximate preparation for marriage, 100–102
  natural economy of, 54
Hovda, Bob, 117
How to Avoid Marrying a Jerk (Van Epp), 84
human dynamics, universal, 19

immediate marriage preparation, 28
  for interchurch couples, 170–73
immigration, effect of, on Hispanic families, 122–23, 24
Immigration and Nationality Act of 1965, 152–53
inculturation
  of the Gospel, 128–29, 131
  liturgical, 110
Indian Americans, endogamy among, 162–64
individualism, as primary language of social interaction, 49
inertia, avoiding, 17–18
infant baptism, facilitating parent preparation for, through an RCIA model, 93–96
Infant Baptism Basics (Heller), 83–84
interchurch couples, 79–80
  additional research on, areas for, 195–97
  building a successful marriage, 184–88
  challenges and recommendations for working with, 193–97
  conceptual map for working with, 190–92
  creating a sense of belonging for, 197
  decisions for, regarding religious affiliation, 188–89
  handling children's religious upbringing, 189–90
  marital satisfaction of, 184
  needs of, clergy's awareness regarding, 195
  offering acceptance and support to, 190
  preparation for, 170–78
  at risk for poorer outcomes, 184
  support for, 80–81
  unique blessings of, 193
interchurch families
  preparation for, 170–78
  presenting gifts and challenges to their parishes, 178–79
interchurch marriage
  defined, 169–70
  focused on commonalities, 174
  pastoral recommendations for, 180–81
interchurch mentors, 172
interfaith couples, conceptual map for working with, 190–92
interfaith marriage, 79
  defined, 170
  special challenges of, 179–80
interpersonal love, centrality of, to understanding marriage, 8–9
interpersonal relationship, idealization of, 51

interracial family (Asian American), 155
interviews, as method for reflecting on faith and moral priorities, 71–72
intimacy, 15, 26

Jesus
  acceptance of, as Savior, 14
  as sign of God's forgiveness, 14–15
John Paul II, 91
  addressing assembling of black Catholics, 146
  on the commitment to live simply, 41
  on consecrated virginity or celibacy, 60
  developing modern Catholic vision for marriage and family, 35
  on the family as the civilization of love, 52
  impact on, of personalist philosophy, 25–26
  on need for different aspects of formation for marriage, 28
  Theology of the Body, 99–100
  on three stages of marriage preparation, 90

Kavanaugh, John, 34
Kelly, Gerard, 178
Knanaya Catholic Youth League of North America (KCYLN), 164
Knanayas
  church affiliation of, 226n31
  endogamy among, 162–64
  heritage of, 225–26n30
Kurtz, Joseph, 61, 71

lay people, speaking unscripted during worship, 71
Legatus, 42
Leo XIII, 52
lex orandi, lex credendi, 108
Lies at the Altar (Smith), 17
life, growing through dying, 18
liturgical inculturation, 110
liturgy
  bringing ordinary life into, 75
  as form of primary theology, 108
  interplay of, with theology, 107
  providing opportunities for faith formation, 70–71
  for the wedding, as opportunity for evangelization, 31
local economies, as common activities directed to common goods, 54
love
  appeal to, to counterbalance materialism and individualism, 51
  romantic conceptions of, eroding marriage, 48
Lovingood, Gretchen, 137
Lovingood, Ken, 137
Lyke, Jim, 138

marital difficulties, understanding of, 27
marital life cycle, teachable moments in, 65–66
marital support and education, gap in, 7
marriage
  anxiety gap about, 84
  approach to, both ancient and developing, 32
  as cornerstone of Asian American families and communities, 156
  as joining of two families, for Asian Americans, 156–57
  balancing of, with single life, 32
  becoming life-filled, 18
  becoming a matter for individuals, 53
  bishops' pastoral letter on, 118, 119
  bride and groom as ministers of the sacrament, 117
  calling people to live out their baptismal commitment, 11–12
  Catholic discourse slanted toward early years of, 74
  Catholic understanding of, 25
  celebrating, every time a sacrament is celebrated, 32
  celebrating within Sunday Eucharist, 117
  celebration of, 31
  challenges inherent in, 8
  Christ-centered, sustaining, 42–43
  church's hopefulness regarding, 7
  commercialization of, 62–64
  companionate, 48, 49
  conferring adulthood on Asian Americans, 156
  covenantal nature of, 8
  creating a new family from existing families, 116
  creating a positive experience at time of, 83
  deinstitutionalization of, 47, 48–50
  difficulty of, in surviving time rationing, 54
  disconnection of, from having children and living together, 38
  divinely ordered, 112
  as end point, 55
  ends of, 209n8
  eroding from within, because of making passion and intimacy as ideals, 48
  established by covenant, 111
  formation of, 30–31. *See also* marriage preparation
  fruits of, related to relationship to the church and the world, 30
  generating intergenerational conflict in Asian American families, 156–58
  goods of, 209n8
  grace of, 201–2
  holiness of, students' perception of, 59
  hope for, impeded by contemporary parish life, 38

marriage (continued)
  idealization of, 52
  inability to achieve longevity in, fear of, 84
  incidence of, related to income and job security, 47
  increasing deliberateness about, 6
  institution of, broken in the African American community, 145
  levels of prevention for, 87–88
  living, as a Christian calling, 43
  ministry toward, as part of social justice ministry, 1
  oldest definitions of, used in church's theology, 209n6
  part of the order of creation, 112
  pastoral imperative for, 1
  personal virtues needed for, 18
  positive indicators for, 6
  prerequisites for, related to quality of relationship and stability of assets, 47
  presupposing a solidly grounded relationship, 18–19
  primary and secondary purposes for, 74
  promoting, through social justice work, 55
  promotion of, 32
  purposes of, 112
  raised to level of a sacrament, 21
  rate of, dropping, 84
  reflecting God's intimate communion with Christ, 14
  regarded as secular matter, 24–25
  as religious vocation, 26
  as response to the Trinitarian God, 16
  rite of, encouraging theological reflection on, 118
  romanticizing of, 62–64
  as sacrament, lessons provided by, 200
  sacrament of, unfolding over time, 112–13
  sacramental nature of, rooted in baptism, 112
  as sacrament of communion, 26
  sentimentalization and sexualization of, 55
  shifting nature of, to sign of achievement, 46–48
  as social body in itself, 51–52
  stages of, 55–56
  support for, available during liturgy and other parish activities, 57
  sustaining of, 31
  as symbol of prestige, 47–48
  as symbol of unity and love between Christ and church, 111
  theology of, 20–21, 23, 28–30
  trinitarian approach to, 12–16
  tying, to social networks, 52–55
  as type of religious vow, 28
  values and expectations of, exploring, 188
  viewing, through a theological lens, 26–28
  as vocation, 10–12
  weakening, as social institution, 22

Marriage, a History (Coontz), 48
marriage ceremonies, including renewal of baptismal vows, 12
marriage education, 185
Marriage Encounter, 7, 44, 109, 137–38
marriage enrichment, increasing opportunities for, 7
marriage and family ministry, developing, for Hispanics, 133–35
marriage formulas, analysis of, 208n16
marriage maintenance, taking collection for, 66
marriage ministry and theology, focused on the wedding, 108
marriage preparation, 185. *See also* immediate marriage preparation; proximate marriage preparation; remote marriage preparation
  helpfulness of, 82–83
  importance of, 82
  times for, aside from just prior to wedding, 92
  timing of, 193–94
marriage vows, revising, 12
married life
  as form of primary theology, 108
  encouraging respect for, 99
married people, theology for, 21–22, 26
McCarthy, David, 43, 62
McQuaid, Tom, 138
Miller, Donald, 74
Ministry to Interchurch Marriage (Creighton study), 79–80
Ministry at the Margins (Gittins), 147
mixed marriage, defined, 169, 170
monastic life, development of, 28
moral discernment, instruction in, 72
morality, tiered interpretation of, 61
morality courses, 72
moral minimalism, 61
Mother Teresa, 101
Mulvey, Anne, 159–60
Mutual Invitation process, for group facilitation, 141–42

National Association of Black Catholic Administrators (NABCA), 146
national parishes, 126–27
National Pastoral Initiative on Marriage (U.S. Bishops' Conference), 1, 201
neighbor, love of, related to love of God, 9
newlyweds
  engaging in service experiences, 64–65
  follow-up with, after marriage, 172
nonmarital religious vows, 29
nuptial blessing, 111

Offices for Black Catholic Ministries (OBM), 145–46
On the Good of Marriage (Augustine), 25

Opus Dei, 42
"Order for the Blessing of an Engaged Couple," 119
Order for Celebrating Marriage, 108, 110–11
　on celebrating marriage within the Eucharist, 117
　doctrinal principles in, 111–12
　preparation for, in the U.S., 118, 119
　principles in, relating to marriage as sacrament, 112–13
organized religion, viewed as threat to spirituality, 77

parenthood
　biological and adoptive, complementary notions of, 30
　as sharing in God's creative life-giving, 14
　as teachable moment in marital/family life cycle, 66
parish communities
　proximate preparation for marriage in, 102–4
　supporting young people, methods for, 102–4
parishes
　activities, unrelated to families, 38, 41
　activities of, that push Adult Catholics, 42
　in America, pre–Vatican II, 36–38
　building, on religion, 38
　choice of, factors affecting, 39–40
　contemporary, positive view of, 41–42
　contradicting call to live more simply, 41
　creating deliberate support for married life, 57
　development of, 210n6
　efforts in, for social justice, 39–40
　emphasizing spiritual formation and service, 65–66
　life in, changing shape of, 38–42
　life of, suggestions for reshaping, 42–45
　little direct involvement in, by families, 40
　marriage-willing, characteristics of, 199–200
　not supportive of marriage, 35
　overinvesting in activities not directly related to families, 41
　parental involvement in, increasing, 96
　as place of refuge, 35
　size of, 39
　upward mobility of, 39
Parish Weddings (Fleming), 116–17
partnership of the whole of life, 30
paschal mystery
　families entering into, 101
　lifelong marital cycle and, 16–19
Pastoral Constitution on the Church in the Modern World (Second Vatican Council), 111
Pedersen, Mary Jo, 83
Pelikan, Jaroslav, 166–67

Perry, Harold, 144
personalism, nuptial, 52
personalist philosophy, 25–26
Pew Forum Religious Landscape Survey, 91
Pho Tuyet-Lan, 159–60
Pius XI, 53
play, sacramental possibilities of, 42
prayer, opportunity for, placing at center of parish life, 44
prayer groups, 42
prayer for married couples, 202
Pre-Cana, 136–37
preferential option for poor families, 86
priests, married, 61
primary theology, 108
Prosper of Aquitaine, 108
proximate marriage preparation, 18, 28, 97
　baptism preparation as, 92–96
　evangelization of teens and young adults as, 97–100
　in the household of faith, 100–102
　for interchurch families, 177–78
　in the parish community, 102–4

Quadragesimo anno (Pius XI), 53
Quine, Willard, 51

racism, in the twenty-first century, 142–44
Rackover, Elizabeth, 64
Rahner, Karl, 74–75
reconciliation
　emphasis on, for interchurch couples, 175–76
　sacramental theology of, 29
Redd, Martin, 138
Redd, Pat, 138
Relationship Attachment Model (RAM), 19
relationship education, for teens and young adults, 98
relationships
　human, mirroring relations within the Trinity, 28
　prior understanding of, necessary for marriage, 27–28
religion
　acknowledging commonalities in, 174
　relation of, to spirituality, 77–81
　separating tradition and Catholic culture from, difficulty of, 171–72
religious affiliation, for interchurch couples, 188–89
religious culture, sensitivity to, 171–72
religious development, stunted after Confirmation, 97–98
religious differences, learning to manage, 185–87
religious education, relating, to community life, 44–45
religious language, sensitivity to, 171–72

religious life
  development of, 28
  as means of living out one's baptismal commitment, 12
religious socialization, 188
religious/spiritual bond, forming, as a couple, 187–88
remote marriage preparation, 18, 28
  for interchurch families, 173–77
Renewing the Vision: A Framework for Catholic Youth Ministry, 98, 131
reverence, associating silence with, 69
Richardson, Beverly, 138
Richardson, Leonard, 138
Rite of Christian Initiation of Adults (RCIA), 94–95, 109
Rite of Marriage, 108, 110–12
  allowing provision for interpretation, 110
  as continuing resource for married couples, 114
  nonverbal ritual elements of, 115–18
  scriptural themes in, 113
  theological motifs in, 113–14
rite in print, compared to rite in action, 110, 114–15
Roman Empire, fall of, church's response to, 23–26
romanticism, 6
Romantic movement, 76
Rubio, Julie, 62

sacramental economy, moving marriage to the center of, 28–29
sacramental marriage, call to, rooted in baptism, 16
sacramental preparation, 92
sacraments, understanding, as celebrations of the Church, 116
Sacred Dwelling (Wright), 201
sacred/secular life, division of, 58–62
Schillebeeckx, Edward, 9
Schor, Juliet B., 215n42
secondary theology, 108
Second Vatican Council, 2
selection factor, related to cohabitation, 85
self, dying to, 16–17
service, opportunity for, placing at center of parish life, 44
sex
  mistaking, for love, 18–19
  as source of stress, 214n32
sexual abuse crisis, 7
sexual behavior, among teens and young adults, 98
sexuality
  as dimension of a sacramental marriage, 25–26
  encouraging respect for, 99
show-and-tell, students bringing a visible sign of God's invisible grace, 72–73

silence, associating with reverence, 69
single life, as invitation from God into communion, 27
small faith communities, 42
Smith, Robin, 17
social justice
  approach to, impeding hope for marriages, 38, 39–40
  related to spiritual life, 44
social networks, using, in pastoral approach to marriage, 53
social services and activities, in the pre–Vatican II American church, 37
Sodality, 44
solitude, 26, 27
Sons and Daughters of the Light, 98
soul mates, 214n34
"spiritual but not religious," 76–77, 91
spiritual development, stunted after Confirmation, 97–98
spirituality
  relation of, to religion, 77–81
  triple meaning of, 10
spouses, living out their baptismal commitment, 112
State of Our Unions (Popenoe and Whitehead), 85
status quo, risk of maintaining, 71
St. Ignatius parish (Boston College), 66, 70
stranger, role of, 147
Strength of Weak Ties, 82–83
subsidiary institutions, 51, 54
systemic racism, 143–44

teenagers
  evangelization of, as proximate preparation for marriage, 97–100
  gifts of, appreciating and learning from, 101–2, 104
Ternikar, Farha, 162
theology
  interplay of, with liturgy, 107
  primary, 108
  secondary, 108
  usefulness of, 21
theology of the body, 52, 99–100
Theology of the Body (John Paul II), 99–100
theology of marriage, 20–21, 23, 28–30
theology for married people, 21–22, 26
Thoreau, Henry David, 76
Three Obediences, 159, 160
Thurman, Howard, 145
traditional family, for Asian Americans, 153
traditioning, 166–67
Transcendentalist movement, 76
trinitarian spirituality, 12–16
Trinity, explaining, 15–16
Two Churches, One Marriage, 192, 194, 195, 196

United States, divided by family structure, 85–86
unselfishness, 18
upward mobility, impeding hope for marriages, 38–39

Van Epp, John, 19, 84
Vietnamese Americans
  factors causing problems in marriages of, 159
  patriarchal gender roles for, 159–61
  women assuming new socioeconomic power, 159–60
Vietnamese families, traditional, patriarchy in, 224n15
Vision for Youth Ministry, 127
vocations
  people failing in, 29
  ranking of, 58–62, 69
volunteer work, couples engaging in, 53
vows, proclamation of, 117

Warren, Michael, 42–43, 44
wedding industry, 63–64
wedding liturgy
  as capstone of marriage preparation, 109, 118
  encouraging theological reflection on, 118
  incorporating into marriage ministry, 109
  as opportunity for evangelization about Christian marriage, 119–20
  representing primary and secondary theologies, 108

weddings
  nonverbal ritual elements of, 115–18
  as opportunity for evangelization, 110
  as parish celebrations, 116–17
  parishioners participating in, 116–17
  vulnerable to commercial exploitation, 63–64
Welcome Your Child (Pedersen), 83
welcoming, of interchurch couples and families, 171, 172–73, 175, 179
What Do You Ask of God's Church (Balsam), 83
What We Have Seen and Heard (African American Catholic bishops), 149–50
wife abuse, in Asian American communities, 158–61
Williams, Raymond, 163–64
Worldwide Marriage Encounter (WWME), 137
Wright, Wendy, 201

Young, Stephen, 159
Young Adult Catholics: Religion in the Culture of Choice (Hoge et al.), 81
young adults
  evangelization of, as proximate preparation for marriage, 97–100
  gifts of, appreciating and learning from, 101–2, 104
young people, support of, in the parish community, 102–4

Ziegler, Jack, 110

Also in the Series

Robert P. Imbelli, ed.
HANDING ON THE FAITH
The Church's Mission and Challenge
Catholic Press Award Winner!

- What is the substance of Catholic faith and hope?
- What are the best means for conveying the faith, particularly in North America?

In *Handing on the Faith* Robert P. Imbelli, a renowned theologian and teacher, introduces the work of leading Catholic theologians, writers, and scholars to discuss the challenges of handing on the faith and the opportunity it creates for Catholics to rethink the essential core of their identity.

This volume includes original contributions by figures such as Robert P. Imbelli, Mary Johnson, William D. Dinges, Paul J. Griffiths, Luke Timothy Johnson, Robert Barron, Robert Louis Wilken, Michael J. Himes, Christopher and Deborah Ruddy, Terrence W. Tilley, Thomas Groome, Bishop Blase Cupich, and John C. Cavadini.

0-8245-2409-8, paperback

Also in the Series

Lisa Sowle Cahill, John Garvey,
and T. Frank Kennedy, Editors

**SEXUALITY AND
THE U.S. CATHOLIC CHURCH**
Crisis and Renewal

Catholic Press Award Winner!

No issue in the contemporary church evokes more controversy than sexuality. In the wake of the clerical abuse scandals, the Catholic Church has come under intense scrutiny, criticized for being either too repressive or too lenient in its approach to human sexuality. In *Sexuality and the U.S. Catholic Church,* Lisa Sowle Cahill, John Garvey, and T. Frank Kennedy, S.J., introduce the work of leading Catholic theologians, writers, and scholars to help ground the conversation in the tradition, identify modern-day challenges, and point to resources for the future.

978-0-8245-2408-1, paperback

Of Related Interest

Joann Heaney-Hunter and Louis Primavera
UNITAS
Preparing for Sacramental Marriage

Based on the Rite of Christian Initiation for Adults, this marriage formation program is designed to help couples appreciate the importance of sacramental marriage in their lives and in the life of the wider church community.

Unitas Leader's Guide
978-0-8245-1755-7, paperback

Unitas Couples Workbook
978-0-8245-1756-4, paperback

Unitas Videotapes (set of 3)
978-0-8245-1757-1

Support your local bookstore or order directly from the publisher at
www.crossroadpublishing.com
To request a catalog or inquire about quantity orders, contact
sales@crossroadpublishing.com